Grantsmanship

A master grantwriter and a veteran funder reveal the keys to winning grants

FOR THE GENIUS IN ALL OF US™

Goodwin Deacon
Ken Ristine

Grantsmanship for the GENIUS™

One of the **For the GENIUS**® books

Published by
For the GENIUS Press, an imprint of CharityChannel LLC
424 Church Street, Suite 2000
Nashville, TN 37219 USA

ForTheGENIUS.com

Copyright © 2016 by CharityChannel LLC

All rights reserved. No part of this book shall be reproduced, stored in a retrieval system, or transmitted by any means, electronic, mechanical, photocopying, recording, or otherwise, without written permission from the publisher.

Limit of Liability/Disclaimer of Warranty: This publication contains the opinions and ideas of its author. It is intended to provide helpful and informative material on the subject matter covered. It is sold with the understanding that the author and publisher are not engaged in rendering professional services in the book. If the reader requires personal assistance or advice, a competent professional should be consulted. The author and publisher specifically disclaim any responsibility for any liability, loss, or risk, personal or otherwise, that is incurred as a consequence, directly or indirectly, of the use and application of any of the contents of this book. Although every precaution has been taken in the preparation of this book, the publisher and author assume no responsibility for errors or omissions. No liability is assumed for damages resulting from the use of information contained herein.

For the GENIUS®, For the GENIUS logo, and book design are trademarks of For the GENIUS Press, an imprint of CharityChannel LLC.

Library of Congress Control Number: 2015949672
ISBN Print Book: 978-1-941050-34-7 | ISBN eBook: 978-1-941050-35-4

Printed in the United States of America
10 9 8 7 6 5 4 3 2

This and most For the GENIUS Press books are available at special quantity discounts for bulk purchases for sales promotions, premiums, fundraising, or educational use. For information, contact CharityChannel, 424 Church Street, Suite 2000, Nashville, TN 37219 USA. +1 949-589-5938.

Publisher's Acknowledgments

This book was produced by a team dedicated to excellence; please send your feedback to Editors@ForTheGENIUS.com.

Members of the team who produced this book include:

Editors

Acquisitions: Linda Lysakowski

Comprehensive Editing: Susan Schaefer

Copy Editing: Stephen Nill

Production

Layout: Jill McLain

Illustrations: Theodore Deacon

Design: Deborah Perdue

Administrative

For the GENIUS Press: Stephen Nill, CEO, CharityChannel LLC

Marketing and Public Relations: John Millen

About the Authors

Goodwin Deacon

Goodwin Deacon earned a PhD in English from the University of Wisconsin-Madison and began her career as an English professor at the Universities of Utah and Idaho. In 1980 she moved to Seattle and began a second career as a grantwriter, working for Seattle Opera, Seattle University, Children's Hospital Foundation, and later Edmonds Community College. At the same time, she continued teaching humanities at Antioch University Seattle, including writing classes.

In 1992 she became a consultant, offering grantwriting and prospect research services through her business, Deacon Consulting. She has worked with a wide variety of nonprofit organizations in the Puget Sound region in the fields of the arts, education, healthcare, social services, and the environment.

In 1990, Goodwin founded the Puget Sound Grantwriters Association, a networking and training organization that helps grantwriters improve their skills, meet funders, and form a community with each other. She has also taught grantwriting at Discover U., the University of Washington Fundraising Management Program, and Antioch University Seattle. She is a frequent speaker on panels and at conferences, and offers workshops on grantwriting and research. Goodwin continues to serve on the board of the Puget Sound Grantwriters Association.

Ken Ristine

Ken Ristine has worked in the nonprofit sector since 1977, though his experience working with people and understanding financial systems began with several jobs he held during college. He began honing his writing skills as a ghostwriter for a ghostwriter.

After college, he worked as a research analyst for a nonprofit alcoholism program on labor/management agreements that were precursors of employee assistance programs. He moved on to United Way, first with fundraising and later in the community affairs division.

In 1984, he became the planning, allocations, and community affairs director for another United Way. Five years later, he joined the staff of a private family foundation where he is now the senior program officer. Throughout his career in nonprofits, he's consulted with dozens of nonprofits on program design and implementation, fundraising, proposal development, nonprofit tax issues, and organizational development. Ken is a frequent speaker at conferences and classes on nonprofit work.

Dedication

To my husband, Theo, for cheering me on with this project and bringing me coffee in bed every morning.

—Goodwin

To Jan, for her support of this book and so much more.

—Ken

Authors' Acknowledgments

I'm grateful to my husband, Theodore Deacon, for creating the illustrations, charts, and diagrams for this book. Many thanks to Sylvie McGee for her advice about researching federal grants, and to Barbara Miller for letting us use quotes from her jargon files.

I'd like to acknowledge the many nonprofit staff and boards I've worked with over the past several decades, and especially the hardworking board members of the Puget Sound Grantwriters Association (PSGA) from whom I've learned so much. Thanks to the members of the PSGA listserve for answering my questions and giving me several excellent quotations for this book. The students in my classes have helped me better understand the challenges faced by beginning grantwriters, and have given me many ideas that I've used in my own work.

I would also like to thank Stephen Nill of For the GENIUS Press, who encouraged us to write this book and is giving us the chance to share our knowledge with a wider audience.

—Goodwin

I want to acknowledge the volunteers and staff who are the backbone of the many nonprofits I've worked with over the years. I've learned something at every speaking engagement or conference where I've presented. It's been said there are no dumb questions; I would add there are no questions that a presenter can't learn from.

Sharing knowledge means balancing all that you know with what your audience is prepared to learn. Every presentation I make teaches me something about that balance. There are thousands more words that could have gone into this book. But as I wrote, and rewrote, I tried to keep in mind those countless volunteers and staff people. As a result, I hope that this book includes what people in the nonprofit sector want to learn and what they are ready to learn. If we've hit that balance, then this book will bring value to new grantwriters as well as those with years of experience.

Finally, we want to acknowledge Susan Schaefer, our manuscript comprehensive editor. Presenting to classes and at conferences is one thing. Pulling together years of materials into a manuscript is quite another. Susan's expertise as a professional and a reader provided us invaluable insight.

—Ken

Contents

Foreword xix

Introduction 1

Part 1—Quick-Start Letter 7

    Chapter 1—Planning the Letter 9

    Chapter 2—Let's Write! 17

Part 2—Laying the Groundwork 29

    Chapter 3—What Are Grants and What Can They Do? 31

    Chapter 4—What Kinds of Funders Are There? 41

    Chapter 5—Why Do Funders Make Grants? 55

    Chapter 6—Types of Grants: What Makes a Fundable Project? 65

    Chapter 7—Grants and Your Organization's Budget 75

Part 3—Getting Ready 87

    Chapter 8—Getting Your Organization Ready to Write Grants 89

    Chapter 9—Researching Funding Sources 101

    Chapter 10—Increasing Your Chances of Success 113

    Chapter 11—Approaching Funders 121

Part 4—Writing: The First Stage 133

    Chapter 12—Preparing to Write 135

    Chapter 13—Getting Your Message Across 143

Contents

    Chapter 14—Letters of Inquiry, Part 1 153

    Chapter 15—Letters of Inquiry, Part 2 165

Part 5—Writing a Full Proposal.................................. 175

    Chapter 16—Cover Letters, Cover Sheets, Proposal Outlines, and Summaries 177

    Chapter 17—Logic Models.. 189

    Chapter 18—Needs Statements................................. 199

    Chapter 19—Goals and Objectives 211

    Chapter 20—Project Plans.. 225

    Chapter 21—Evaluation Plans................................... 235

    Chapter 22—Project Budgets 249

    Chapter 23—Organizational Information...................... 261

    Chapter 24—Sustainability 271

Part 6—What Comes Next? 281

    Chapter 25—Meeting with Funders: Site Visits................. 283

    Chapter 26—Acknowledgment and Stewardship................. 291

Appendix A—Model LOI... 299

Appendix B—Sample Grant Proposal for SCUM 303

Appendix C—Code of Ethics of Grant Professionals Association 311

Appendix D—Chicago Area Common Grant Application 313

Index.. 321

Summary of Chapters

Part 1—Quick-Start Letter..........7

This section will show you how to write a short letter to a funder requesting a grant. This way you can get off the ground running, and then get into more detail later on.

Chapter 1
Planning the Letter..........9

Most funders screen requests through letters or online applications. The Quick-Start Letter will help you create a draft that will help you with either approach.

Chapter 2
Let's Write!..........17

It's important to catch a funder's attention, but you also have to be concise. Having the right information on hand can help you do both.

Part 2—Laying the Groundwork..........29

Learning about the world of grants will help you become a better grantwriter. It's especially important to understand funders' motivations for giving.

Chapter 3
What Are Grants and What Can They Do?..........31

Most people have heard of grants, yet few understand all the intricacies of getting them. This chapter will outline some of the basics that will help you understand the other topics in this book.

Chapter 4
What Kinds of Funders Are There?..........41

From private foundations and corporate giving programs to government agencies, there is a wide variety of sources for grants. Each type of funder has its own approach that you need to understand.

Chapter 5

Why Do Funders Make Grants? 55

Funders don't make grants just because they have money. When you understand a funder's motivation, you can form a relationship that may result in a first grant and others in the future.

Chapter 6

Types of Grants: What Makes a Fundable Project? 65

There are three main types of grants: capital, program, and organizational. If you understand why a funder requests each type, you can craft a better proposal.

Chapter 7

Grants and Your Organization's Budget 75

The amount of money distributed in all grants, including large foundations, composes only a small portion of nonprofit revenues. Successful organizations understand how grants fit into the overall revenue picture.

Part 3—Getting Ready 87

To be successful, you need to make sure there's a good match between your organization and the funders you approach. It's also important to develop a relationship with grantmakers.

Chapter 8

Getting Your Organization Ready to Write Grants...................89

Nonprofits need to have several elements in place before they're ready to write successful grants. We'll go over the infrastructure you need and how to get your first dollars.

•• Summary of Chapters **XV**

Chapter 9
Researching Funding Sources............................ 101
It's worth using paid subscription databases to narrow down the most promising foundation prospects, including private, public, and corporate foundations. Corporations that give directly rather than through foundations require different resources. We'll also discuss how to research government grants.

Chapter 10
Increasing Your Chances of Success...................... 113
Proposals need to be tailored to the interests and requirements of each funder; sending out the same letter to dozens of funders rarely works. It's important to work with your bosses and coworkers to gather important information about the work of your organization and to help them understand what you do.

Chapter 11
Approaching Funders 121
A solid grants program involves meeting funders before you submit a proposal. There are ways to develop a relationship with them that will increase your chances of success.

Part 4—Writing: The First Stage...................... 133
Here we talk about screening tests and gathering the material you'll need to write. We have some writing tips for you, and then we discuss how to write a compelling letter of inquiry.

Chapter 12
Preparing to Write 135
Before you can begin writing the proposal, you may need to pass a screening test. Be sure you're aware of final submission requirements. Determine what information you'll need to gather from other people, and get them started on these tasks in plenty of time.

Summary of Chapters

Chapter 13
Getting Your Message Across.................................. 143
Skilled grantwriters are aware of their audience and write with a minimum of jargon. Format your proposals so as to make them easily readable.

Chapter 14
Letters of Inquiry, Part 1 153
Letters are the preferred initial contact for a great number of funders. They are also a tool that can help you when completing an online screening form or online application.

Chapter 15
Letters of Inquiry, Part 2 165
Budgets can seem scary, but they're really quite manageable if you take them one step at a time. We discuss how much to ask for, and what comes after the letter of inquiry.

Part 5—Writing a Full Proposal........................ 175
This section goes into detail about each section of a standard grant proposal. We'll help you understand what funders are looking for.

Chapter 16
Cover Letters, Cover Sheets, Proposal Outlines, and Summaries...... 177
Cover letters give you the opportunity to introduce your proposal to funders in your own format. Many funders ask applicants to complete fill-in-the-blank cover sheets as well. A proposal outline will give you an overview of the narrative. Summaries or abstracts are the first section of the proposal narrative—they're crucial for making a good first impression.

Chapter 17
Logic Models... 189
Logic models are charts that some funders ask grantseekers to complete to map out their projects. They are also a way that you can evaluate your own project planning.

Chapter 18
Needs Statements..199
Compelling grant requests address important community needs. Your needs statement can address both a community situation and a funder's reasons for making grants.

Chapter 19
Goals and Objectives......................................211
Goals and objectives are ways of connecting your work to your mission. Writing them the right way is critical to your grant success.

Chapter 20
Project Plans..225
This is where you describe the details of how you plan to carry out your project: the who, how, where, and when. You'll lay out your strategy for reaching your goals.

Chapter 21
Evaluation Plans..235
Just as goals and objectives state your criteria for success, your evaluation plans state how you will measure that success. They are the mirror image of your goals and objectives. It's important to state how you plan to evaluate both the work you will have done and the impact of that work.

Chapter 22
Project Budgets...249
A budget plan tells funders what resources you need to carry out your project. It also provides a way for you to describe how you'll gather those resources.

Chapter 23
Organizational Information..............................261
Your nonprofit's background explains who the applicant is and establishes its credibility as an organization capable of carrying

out the grant project. Most grants require several standard attachments—gather them early in the grantwriting process and keep them updated.

Chapter 24
Sustainability 271
Grants are often one-time investments in grantees. Knowing that your organization can sustain itself tells a funder that its investment will have an impact for years to come.

Part 6—What Comes Next? 281
After you submit your proposal, a funder may ask for a site visit. When you finally get an answer to your request, there is important follow-up to do, especially if you receive a grant, but even if you don't.

Chapter 25
Meeting with Funders: Site Visits 283
Many funders meet face-to-face with potential grantees as a part of their review process, usually at your site of operations. Understanding what a funder wants to accomplish with these meetings can help you get the most out of them.

Chapter 26
Acknowledgment and Stewardship 291
How you manage your grant can be a key to receiving your next one. Acknowledging a grant and taking care to report on your use of the money can help you build your relationships with funders.

Foreword

Combine the experience and vision of two authors—a grantwriter and a funder—and you have **Grantsmanship for the GENIUS.** This partnership paints the whole picture of the world of grants from both perspectives.

Goodwin Deacon and Ken Ristine have woven into its fabric a 360-degree view of grantsmanship. In their view, and mine, it's not enough to write a grant proposal; you must understand how the funder will perceive it. Who better than a funder could possibly provide the full story? Whether you are new to the field or well advanced, you will gain a perspective quickly putting you miles ahead of the game.

Besides being veterans in the grantsmanship field, the authors are experienced teachers of the subject. Tapping their years of classroom experience, mentoring to their professional peers, and consulting to innumerable nonprofit organizations, the authors have mastered the fun, conversational style common to all *For the GENIUS* books. In other words, they know how to explain even murky concepts so they are easily grasped.

Becoming a skilled and accomplished grant professional takes years of experience. But let's be honest—in the real world, we don't *have* years to gain competency. We have to get started *quickly*, and we have to get started *on the right foot*. Even so, as we grow in experience we also need an authoritative guide to help us broaden and deepen our skills and to fill in the inevitable gaps. Therein lies another remarkable contribution of **Grantsmanship for the GENIUS,** no doubt borne of their collective years of experience teaching the subject: The authors have organized this book to give you both a quick start *and* a full treatment of the subject. You'll start quickly yet progress rapidly and deeply in your expertise of grantsmanship. As a result, I recommend this book for both beginners looking for a quick start and experienced grant professionals who have gaps in their knowledge or want a refresher.

Just to underscore the depths to which the authors take us, they cover such concepts as logic models and theory of change, often difficult for grantwriters to understand—especially those new to the field. The book explains such concepts in simple language and makes even formal terms less intimidating.

The innovative "Quick-Start Letter" in **Part 1** will help you create a rough draft of a letter of inquiry. The authors don't make you wade through long explanations before having you roll up your sleeves! They show you what to do and how to go about doing it. They even provide a model Letter of Inquiry in **Appendix A**.

After the quick start, in **Part 2** the authors lay the groundwork by thoroughly covering the fundamentals. They want to make sure you have a solid understanding of where grants fit in the overall scheme of things, what kinds of funders are out there, why these funders make grants, what types of grants they make, and more.

In **Part 3** they discuss organizational readiness to write grants, how to research grants, how to increase your chance of success, and how to approach funders.

In **Part 4** they get you ready to write to get your message across. In **Chapters 14** and **15** they provide a thorough discussion of letters of inquiry—the perfect complement to the Quick-Start Letter they provided in **Part 1**.

In **Part 5** they lead you through the process of writing a full proposal. They lay out each aspect clearly and in the kind of detail you need to succeed.

In **Part 6** they talk about what happens after the proposal is submitted, focusing on site visits, acknowledgment, and stewardship.

If you are sensing that I consider **Grantsmanship for the GENIUS** to be a huge step forward for the field of grantsmanship, you are right. I hope you will join me in recommending this book far and wide.

Danny W. Blitch II, GPC
Organizing Editor and Coauthor of *Prepare for the GPC Exam: Earn Your Grant Professional Certified Credential*

Introduction

When a reporter asked Willie Sutton why he robbed banks, the notorious outlaw allegedly replied, "Because that's where the money is!"

In a similar vein, social critic Dwight MacDonald famously described the Ford Foundation as "a large body of money, completely surrounded by people who want some."

When we've asked new grantwriters why they wrote to Funder X for a grant, they sometimes say, "Because they give grants to nonprofits, and we're a nonprofit." Grantwriters' long-term success depends on how fast they get past the idea that all funders are the same and that they make grants for tax deductions, enhancing their public image, or any of the other ancillary benefits that might come from making charitable grants.

Funders—foundations, corporate donors, and government agencies—are organizations with missions of their own. Funders are like Rumpelstiltskin in reverse: Instead of spinning straw into gold, they spin gold into something practical and useful, like straw.

Their agents—the spinning wheel, if you like—are nonprofit organizations that know how to turn funding into community benefits. When a nonprofit approaches a funder for a grant, it essentially says, "We know what you want to do for the community, because we've read it in your guidelines. We share your interest and concern. Our organization wants to benefit the community in a similar way and knows how to do it. With your support, we can improve people's lives."

When new grantwriters (or their bosses) first see a long list of funders, they sometimes think, "Terrific! Look how many places there are giving money away to nonprofit organizations! If we just write a letter explaining who we are and why we need the money, surely one of these people will give us a grant." Using an Excel spreadsheet and the mail-merge feature, you can send your letter to scores of funders with the click of a mouse.

This method, which is usually called the shotgun approach, may get your organization a grant or two—or not. More likely, funders will consider it spam and delete it, or toss it in the round file.

Introduction

Most people who pick up this book are looking for a better approach. Yes, you likely feel pressure to find dollars quickly. Yet you also want your grantseeking to support a long-term vision to grow your organization. That means forming partnerships based on the work of your organization and the interests of the funder.

There are many reasons why the shotgun approach fails to create solid and lasting relationships. At the root of all of those reasons is the fact that funders make grants based upon what they want to accomplish for their communities. Your best approach for creating a long-term program supported by grant funding is to create partnerships with funders based upon their interests and your organization's mission and activities.

We expect that most readers of this book will be fairly new to grantwriting, or looking for a refresher. Maybe you've written a few grants, or perhaps you're planning your first proposal. Or you might have been writing grants for a while, and you want to see how your approach compares to someone else's. You might be a staff member or a volunteer. The key is that you want to know more and you sense there is something special that you need to know.

And in a way, that's true. Over the years, both of us have been asked many times, "What do I need to know to begin writing grants?" Because we're both natural-born teachers, our first impulse is to respond with far more information than you need or can absorb. Instead, in the first chapter of this book, we will share a few key concepts at the heart of grantwriting, rather than overwhelm you with information.

The primary concept is this: You've got to get beyond choosing funders based upon the idea that "They give grants to nonprofits, and we're a nonprofit."

Essential to a successful grantwriting effort is the understanding that funders make grants to help carry out their own charitable missions. This book is about figuring out what a funder cares about and how you can put that knowledge into action.

How This Book Is Organized

We've organized this book into six sections.

Part 1 is about the Quick-Start Letter. We know our readers already have ideas in mind for grant requests. The Quick-Start Letter helps you create a rough draft of a letter of inquiry, or LOI, the kind of letter you might send to a funder as an initial approach for a grant. This exercise helps you better understand the topics in the following chapters.

Part 2 is about laying the groundwork. We go over key topics that grantwriters need to understand as they begin working on grants.

Part 3 covers gathering your organizational information, finding funders, and determining how your work fits with funders' goals.

Part 4 discusses how to prepare for the writing phase, including some tips on qualities of good writing and bad habits to avoid. It then goes into detail on how to write an LOI.

Part 5 explains how to write a full proposal. It discusses each section of a standard grant proposal, goes over the technical aspects, and provides tips about project development.

Part 6 covers what happens next. We discuss site visits, how to acknowledge a grant, what to do if you don't get the grant, and the importance of filing timely grant reports.

Sidebars

Throughout the book, we use sidebars to make a key point or provide an example. Due to our work we've had the chance to see many examples of the concepts we point out in the book. These illustrations clarify the principles we discuss.

We want to be clear that all of the information in each sidebar is true to the best of our knowledge. But we also believe that we also owe confidentiality to many of the organizations we've worked with or observed. So we've changed the names and abbreviated the anecdotes.

If some readers believe that they recognize the organization that a sidebar refers to, they may be partially right. None of the situations we cite are unique, and it would not be unusual for readers to feel that an example seems familiar. That's why we've chosen these examples. And we can assure you that while we change names and slightly alter details of our examples, they all represent situations that actually occurred.

> **One Word or Two?**
>
> Throughout this book, we have chosen to spell a number of key terms as one word rather than two. These include grantwriter, grantwriting, grantseeker, and grantmaker. Spelling each of these terms as two words is equally acceptable, but we're following the usage of the Puget Sound Grantwriters Association, an organization founded by Goodwin.
>
> *Observation*

The main types of sidebars you'll see in this book are titled Inspiration, ideas and examples highlighting good approaches; Perspiration, which provide practical tips for your work; Pure Genius!, great examples of putting ideas into action; and Uninspired, unfortunate situations that we've come across over the years.

Also, there are some more functional sidebars such as Definitions, key terms that need explaining; Examples, which point out a best practice that is routine yet still worth citing; and Observations, concepts that are best noted with an overview rather than a specific example.

Finally, there are cautions that we highlight with either Important! or Watch Out! These include examples of serious stumbling blocks we've seen over the years. Often they are obstacles or errors that many organizations run into due to their enthusiasm and desire to do the right thing.

We hope you find this book a reference you'll use again and again. We know that your success as a grantwriter will be the result of organizational commitment. This book can help when you have to explain grants and funders to others in your organization, whether staff or volunteers. We've written this book for the reader, and for the people to whom readers have to explain these ideas.

Part 1

Quick-Start Letter

Grantwriting changes daily with increasing technology. Yet letters are still an important tool for the initial contact on a grant request. Whether your organization has received a grant from the funder before or this is your first request, each and every grant begins with an initial contact. The Quick-Start Letter helps you open your eyes to ideas about grants and grantwriting at the core of the rest of this book.

Chapter 1

Planning the Letter

In This Chapter...

- Why a letter?
- What do funders want to know?
- What information will you need before you write?
- What will the final letter look like?

You've picked up this book because you want to write a grant or write better grants. You might be a staff member, a volunteer, or a board member of a nonprofit. No matter why you're reading this book, we assure you that we've taught sessions attended by hundreds of people in similar situations.

In this opening chapter, we're going to walk you through the steps of writing a basic, short request to a funder in the form of a letter. These letters are often called LOIs, letters of inquiry. They are the preferred method for the initial approach to many funders. And, for those funders that request other methods for an initial contact, such as an online screening, having a draft LOI at your side can help you do a better job using those formats too.

We want to immerse you in creating an LOI. We're calling our approach the Quick-Start Letter. Think of it like the shortcut instructions you sometimes get with new software. If you have an idea that you're in a hurry to send to a funder, this letter will give you a good beginning.

We hope you'll go ahead and write such a letter, whether you're in a hurry or not. After you've drafted one, you'll have a better understanding of the requirements and challenges of writing grant proposals. As you read the rest of the book, our advice will make more sense because you will have already had hands-on experience with grantwriting.

The Quick-Start Letter is one way to expand your understanding of project design, program development, and grantwriting. Too often grantwriters learn about a project only when they're handed the assignment to raise funds for it. But good projects begin with ideas taken from the day-to-day experience of the organization's work. Those ideas become the core of a project's design. Sharing those ideas is also important to showing that an organization is capable of implementing the project and defining what success will look like.

That background is important, but too often ignored. It's very common for grantwriters to write from the point of view that the day they begin looking for grants is the beginning of the project. As a result, much of the good thinking that went into the project's design gets lost. Yet the core ideas of your project are what will help you make a connection with funders.

The Quick-Start Letter

There is a saying that the key to success in fundraising is "making the right ask to the right person at the right time." The same goes for grantwriting.

With thousands of funders making grants, it can be difficult to sort out what the right ask, the right person, and the right time mean for each one. Also, the variety of forms funders use complicates the process. As a result, we can't walk you through a typical application process because there is no typical process.

In general, the larger the funder is, the more complicated its application process. Yet whether a funder makes grants based solely upon a letter or through an online process, there is basic information that all funders ask for. That's why we begin this book with the Quick-Start Letter.

We developed the Quick-Start Letter as a guide for how all LOIs should be organized. It's based on looking at the common grant applications (CGAs) developed by twenty-four of the Regional Associations of Grantmakers (RAGs) around the country. Even though the formats of those CGAs vary, they all ask for the same basic information. It's also information that funders not using a CGA want for their applications.

CGAs have two basic features in common:

- General information that provides a snapshot of your organization today
- Program description that applies to your specific request

The general information includes organization name, address, current leadership, and other information that applies to the organization as a whole. The program description focuses on your specific request. Program descriptions usually ask you to describe your organization's history, mission, and current programs. But because it's a part of your request, you share that information with an eye to the purpose of your request.

You'll find that much of the work we recommend you do, beginning with the Quick-Start Letter, is aimed at anticipating questions funders will ask.

Why a Letter?

A good letter conveys facts in a way that is memorable and compelling. It allows you to provide information while telling your organization's story. That is why such a large percentage of funders ask grantseekers to write a letter as the initial contact for a grant request.

But a letter can also be a tool. More and more funders are using an Internet interface to submit grant proposals. Some of these systems ask you to upload a PDF

What Is a RAG?

There are about thirty-four Regional Associations of Grantmakers (RAGs) around the country. They vary from very large, multistate organizations to local associations. For example, the Southeastern Council of Foundations includes 330 foundations and corporate giving programs in eleven southeastern states. At the other end of the spectrum is the Arizona Grantmakers Forum that focuses on funders in that state alone.

All these groups share a general goal of providing resources to educate and inform the funders they work with.

Definition

copy of a letter. Others ask you to complete a screening tool or the funder's application form. If you have a draft letter by your side when you complete such forms, you can do a better job. If you haven't drafted a letter, you risk falling into the trap of filling in each box on the form as a separate item. The result is that your submission will feel disjointed and may even contradict itself in spots.

The draft letter helps you complete those forms in a way that flows from question to question, just as if the funder were reading your letter.

Telling Your Organization's Story

What do we mean by "story"? Over the past twenty years, storytelling has gained greater respect as a way in which we gain knowledge, retain it, and share it with others. Storytelling came long before the written word and the printing press. And there has also been a growing acceptance of using fiction-writing tools to tell nonfiction stories. Truman Capote's *In Cold Blood* and Alex Haley's *Roots* are two examples of this technique in books. Now this approach is often used to personalize feature writing.

A grantwriting aphorism you may hear is "If you've seen one foundation, you've seen one foundation." That applies to any type of funder, not just foundations. No two funders are alike. While all funders make grants, their values—the reasons they make grants—and the processes they use are unique to each.

As a result, you need a tool that can help you deal with the wide variety of application processes you'll face. The Quick-Start Letter is that tool. It will aid you in doing your best with any application process, whether an initial letter, an online screening questionnaire, or an application form.

How to Tell Your Story

Integrating fiction tools in your nonfiction writing is a skill you can learn. A good example is the feature article on page one of the *Wall Street Journal*. William Blundell's book *The Art and Craft of Feature Writing: Based on the Wall Street Journal Guide* was created from Mr. Blundell's notes for teaching writers at the *Journal* how to write those articles.

Grantwriting isn't a writing contest. But since you always face space limitations, you have to make every word count. And learning these skills is more about understanding how to craft your work rather than being a matter of talent.

Inspiration

Beginning to Write

Before you begin to write, there are pieces of information that you should have at hand. This information falls into two categories, both of which are reflected in the structure of every CGA we looked at. First is basic information about the nonprofit applying for the grant. The second is information about the project at the heart of the grant application. Here is a list of items:

- Name of the specific organization that will apply for the grant. Usually, that organization needs to have 501(c)(3) status from the Internal Revenue Service or be sponsored by such an organization.

- A summary of the organization's history, mission, and its current work.

- The purpose of your project; that is, what it will accomplish. Rather than saying, "Our organization needs a grant to…" think of a programmatic goal such as "distribute more food to low-income families in our community."

- A description of the need or opportunity you want to address.

- Background about how the organization learned about the opportunity or problem.

- A list of the resources needed to carry out your project.

What Do You Want to Accomplish?

Grantwriters sometimes get off track because they hear funders say, "Tell us what you want to do."

What funders mean is, "Tell us what you want to accomplish."

We don't know of any funder with a goal of building buildings. We know of thousands of funders that make grants for building projects. Buildings are only tools, just like any other line item on a grant budget. A building can help you serve more people or communities.

Telling a funder what you want to do means sharing a compelling need and a plan for addressing that need. After you've done that, you can talk about the tools you need to pursue your plan, such as a new building.

IMPORTANT!

- A plan for obtaining the resources you need.
- A specific amount you want to request from the funder.
- Contact information for the person who can respond to the funder's questions and/or help with next steps in the process.

Organizing Your Letter

The elements outlined above are the key points in funders' checklists. The way we organized the list may feel artificial at first. But this order weaves facts into the story so that they are memorable and compelling. Remember, you're writing for the reader, not for yourself.

When funders begin reviewing grant requests, several thoughts come to mind:

- What is this organization and what does it do?
- Whom does it help?
- Does this nonprofit serve a geographic area where we make grants?
- How large is this organization (e.g., budget, programs, and number of clients)?

Also, funders may wonder, "What does this organization want from us?" While you may be eager to put that in the letter right away, the goal of your first few paragraphs is to answer these questions in a way that builds a connection between your project and the funder's interests. When you do that, you change the question in the funders' minds from "What do they want from us?" to "How can we help them?"

Grantwriting seems like a puzzle to many people. And like a jigsaw puzzle, it's a little easier if you can see the picture on the box. That's why many grantwriters have asked

Are You a 501(c)(3)?

While we address a wide range of funders in this book, keep in mind that most limit their grants to organizations that are IRS-designated 501(c)(3) public charities. If your organization isn't already a 501(c)(3) public charity, you either have to get that status or find an organization with that status that will assist you as a fiscal sponsor.

We include more background on public charity status in **Chapter 3**.

IMPORTANT!

us over the years if funders will provide a copy of a successful application. While you can get copies of federal grants that were funded, which are part of the public record, private funders generally don't provide copies of grants they've funded.

But even if you can see a successful application, simply reading it won't tell you why it was successful. In **Appendix A** we provide a model LOI. This letter is consistent with the structure and content outlined in the book. But in addition to being a good letter, it includes annotations that tell you about each feature of the letter, and how and why it's written as it is.

Before moving to the next chapter, read the model letter and annotations. They will help you better understand the points we make in the next chapter, "Let's Write!"

To Summarize...

- The Quick-Start Letter is a tool for improving your responses to any grants process.

- Using a story style makes the facts easier to remember and helps funders see how your project relates to their grantmaking.

- All funders ask similar questions. They just use different formats and may pose those questions in different ways.

- The goal of your initial contact is to connect with a funder's mission and interests.

Chapter 2

Let's Write!

In This Chapter...

- How should you start your Quick-Start Letter?
- How do you catch funders' attention?
- What should you put in and leave out of your request?
- What's the best way to end the letter?

How do you begin any letter? Usually with some reference to something that you and the person you're writing to have in common. A letter to your mother, a best friend, or even a cover letter with your résumé will seek to make some connection. The same goes for letters to funders.

If your organization has received grants from the funder before, you can reference them. A letter that begins "We want to thank the James Foundation for its past support of our work…" reminds the funder about past grants. Or in the case of funder staff changes, it may let a new staff person know that your organization is a past grantee.

Whatever introductory statement you make, keep it short. You want to get to the point of your letter: the change you want to make in your community. You don't need to heap praise upon the funder for its work in hopes of making a connection. What's important is that you are asking the funder to help you to accomplish something that you, and hopefully the funder, believe is important.

Focusing the Letter on Your Project

Begin your letter with an opening that tells the reader what the letter is about. In the model LOI in **Appendix A**, the key phrase is, "to help... increase the amount of food available to low-income families...." While the letter eventually asks for a grant of $10,000, it doesn't start with, "We're writing to ask for a grant of $10,000 to..."

The first approach helps the reader focus on what you want to accomplish, while the second focuses on asking for money. Getting your reader to focus on what you want to accomplish is the best way to connect with a funder's mission and concerns for its community. If you start by asking for money, it can cause the funder to feel that you're writing only because it gives away money.

Occasionally you'll come across funders that ask you to state a dollar amount early in your letter. In that case begin with a sentence about what you want to accomplish and follow with a sentence such as, "We're writing to request a grant of $10,000 to help us..." That approach still focuses on what you and the funder want to accomplish while also giving that funder a dollar amount early in the letter.

Introducing Your Organization

Say a funder reads your opening and thinks, "That might be a good idea." The funder's next thought will be, "Who is this group and what does it do?"

Even if you've received grants from this funder in the past, you need to introduce your organization. Every grant request needs to stand on its own, and this specific one might stress aspects of your organization that are different from past grants. Your introduction should touch on the organization's history, mission, and current operations.

A letter might say, "North Haven Child Care was founded in 1990 by several local families concerned about the lack of affordable child care in our community." Sharing the roots of your organization can provide a bridge to your organization's current mission and say something about its values.

You follow that sentence with a short mission statement, something we like to call a *walking-around mission statement*. In this case, the next line might be, "North Haven Child Care provides affordable child care for working families in our community, especially those headed by single mothers."

A short description of your organization's programs and budget size helps a funder understand if the letter is from a single-program organization with a $100,000 annual budget or a multiprogram organization with a $3 million annual budget. There's often room for both—you just have to set the stage.

The next few sentences may be something like, "We have two programs: before- and after-school care for children in grades K–4 and full-time child care for toddlers and infants. We serve just over eighty children a year on an annual budget of $950,000."

Now you might add a few more facts about the program that is the focus of this letter. For example, a request to expand the before- and after-school care might add another sentence such as, "The before and after-school program works with thirty-five students at our nearby elementary school. The school provides space, and we provide the program."

> ### Walking-Around Mission Statement
>
> Your walking-around mission statement is based on your formal mission statement, but it's simpler and more memorable. It's like the answer you'd give someone at a party who asks, "What does your organization do?"
>
> You'd never repeat your organization's formal mission statement at a party. But you certainly could tell someone about what your nonprofit does. It's okay to be conversational; just avoid slang and exaggeration.
>
> **Definition**

What's the Need?

The introduction should lead to the need or opportunity that your project addresses. A powerful way to make that transition is with a line such as, "In the course of our work, we've seen that..."

This transition is critical. Many organizations jump right into describing their projects, sometimes in great detail. But since projects are supposed to be solutions, it is critical that funders understand the opportunities or problems that the solution is meant to address.

> ### A Solution in Search of a Problem
>
> When a grant request jumps right into describing a project without outlining the need, it can sound like a solution in search of a problem. Funders often read such requests and wonder what a project is trying to accomplish. That is why the project narrative in CGA forms almost always asks for a description of the need before a description of the project.
>
> Your description of the need should reinforce your planned project. If you skip over it, you'll confuse funders and undermine your project's credibility.
>
> **Uninspired**

As you write your letter, think back to the early discussions that led to the project. Those discussions provide background that begins to tell the story of your project. A building project might begin with a discussion about needing more room to serve an increasing number of people asking for assistance. A program expansion might begin with the staff noticing that a significant number of clients are coming from a particular area quite a distance from your current site. Or the impetus for your project might simply be that your organization consistently has a waiting list for people who need its services.

A child care organization might say, "In the course of our running the before- and after-school care at the local elementary school, we've had requests to offer the program at other nearby schools. For example, in the past year, we've had several families in our program who have had to move. When they found that there was no before- and after-school program in their local elementary, they came to us and asked us to start a program in their new school."

From this beginning, you can go on to outline other work you may have done to demonstrate that there were enough families interested at these new schools to make new programs worth opening. The advantage of this approach is that it tells a funder that the need emerged from grassroots concerns.

You hope that a grantmaker will read your description of the need and begin thinking, "This sounds like an issue we should address." When a funder reaches this conclusion, your project may seem rather obvious and simple. That's the goal of your letter.

Many grantwriters believe that a proposal failed because it didn't make the project sound important enough. But a successful grant request is compelling

Chapter 2—Let's Write!

> ### Make Sure You Understand the Need
>
> Too often grantwriters are handed a project and asked to go find the money to carry it out. As a result, there is a tendency to treat the point at which you're assigned the project as the beginning of your narrative.
>
> What gets lost in that exchange is all of the organization's knowledge that went into determining the need, designing the project, and assessing your organization's capacity to carry out the project. If you're not involved in the project design and just get handed an assignment to "go raise the money," you have to work to get that information.
>
> Including background information builds a rapport with the funder and its goals. If you fail to provide this, your request may sound like an idea cooked up in a conference room during a brainstorming session on "What can we do to raise more money?"
>
> It's always a good idea to show a funder that a project originated with an idea sparked by your organization's day-to-day work.
>
> **Observation**

because the needs it addresses are important, not because the solution seems earth-shattering.

Your Project: The Solution to the Problem

There are two essential elements to a project narrative:

- Conveying a sense that you looked at or are aware of more than one way to address the need you've outlined

- A description of your project

You want to convey a sense of deliberation when you introduce your project. A project is the solution to the problem you've outlined. Yet you don't want to sound like you chose that solution at random.

That doesn't mean you have to have a long, drawn out deliberative process for each project. You can use a well-crafted line such as, "We looked at several ways to address this need for before- and after-school care at other nearby schools. We settled on our approach based upon the limitations imposed by state regulations, our partnership with the school district, and the cost of providing service." This transition paves the way for you to discuss the project's details.

It can be tempting to jump right into describing the project. But a simple transition sentence or two builds credibility for the approach you've chosen. The next few paragraphs should outline the project in enough detail to show that it will address the needs you highlighted and produce the accomplishment you described in the opening lines of the letter.

At this point in your letter, you hope the grantmaker recognizes that your issue is central to its priorities, that your organization seems to be a good one to help, and that your approach makes a lot of sense. If your letter has led a reader to those thoughts, you have a foot in the door with the funder.

The Budget—Expenses

Funders that like the letter so far will begin to have three thoughts:

- What will it cost to do this?
- Where does the organization expect to get those resources?
- What does it want us to do?

The expense portion of your budget answers that first question. Your letter will summarize the budget. Funders generally don't expect that a letter or an online screening will provide a lot of detail about a budget, but a summary is essential.

The expense portion of your budget answers the question about how much your project will cost. A line-item budget helps you determine the total cost. You generally cite only the total budget figure in a letter or a summary in an online screening questionnaire. But you can only provide that total amount when you have a complete budget on hand.

The expense portion of the budget is the easiest. Once you decide what you need

Don't Write on Spec!

Funders using letters or online screenings for an initial contact by grantseekers sometimes see requests that appear to be speculative. Since a letter or an online screening seems easy to complete, some grantseekers submit proposals based only on rough notes. It is easy to assume that, if a funder shows interest, you will build out the details in a full application.

The danger is that if a grantmaker is interested and follows up with questions, you may not have answers. Also, since a funder expects you to have a rough outline of a budget, you risk having to dramatically revise those figures when you create a detailed project plan. That can undermine your credibility with the funder for that request and others in the future.

WATCH OUT!

to do and what it will take to carry that out, all you have to do is price those activities and materials.

The Income Section

The income portion of your budget takes more work. At times, your plan for gathering resources will feel like guesswork. Income estimates address the funder's concern about how you plan to garner the resources you need for the project. Describing that plan needs a bit more detail than the expense portion of your budget at this point.

Your income plan is built upon the basic characteristics of the nonprofit economy. Charitable organizations generally have five categories of income they can pursue:

- Earned income (fees for services, tickets, memberships that buy rights to services, etc.)
- Government grants
- Individual giving (annual campaigns, special events, federated campaigns, etc.)
- Private grants (foundations and corporate giving programs)
- Other income (endowment earnings, organization reserves, and debt)

For example, the fundraising plan for a $100,000 project might be outlined like this: "We plan to raise the funding for this project through $25,000 from individual giving and $75,000 from private grants. To date, we've raised just over $20,000, most of it from our board and other key individual donors."

Timelines

A budget needs a timeline. Saying, "We will spend $20,000 on counseling services" really doesn't say much without a time frame. Spending $20,000 for counseling services over the next three years says one thing, whereas $20,000 a month is a much bigger commitment to counseling. Operating budgets, new program start-ups, and program expansion budgets are usually keyed to a timeframe such as a fiscal year.

A capital campaign budget will usually be hooked to key steps in the project such as:

- Acquiring the needed land
- Planning, design, and permits
- Site work
- Construction
- Equipment and furnishings

The project may also be connected to specific events such as groundbreaking, construction finish, occupancy, and finally, opening.

Conclusion and Signature

At the close of your letter, you can express your hopes to explore the project further and clearly state contact information for that purpose. Having the right person cited as a contact is critical so that staff can contact you with questions or discuss next steps.

Finally, your letter must be signed by a key person, such as the organization's executive director or board chair. Funders want to know that the nonprofit stands behind everything stated in the letter. Only the executive director and the board truly have the responsibility for making the commitment to accept a grant and spend it as intended.

A grantwriter, or even a chief development officer, has little or no influence over the program side of an organization. Likewise, a program director has little or no control over the accumulation and allocation of resources. A letter signed by anyone below the top level can represent only a partial commitment of the organization.

Editing Your Draft

Now that you have a draft, put it away for a few days before you start modifying it for a specific funder. You need to get away from your letter so you can read it with fresh eyes. If you start editing too soon, you can easily read things into it that aren't there. Before you send your letter to the funder, have someone else read it.

Finally, as you edit, keep in mind why you are writing to that particular funder. You want to keep the focus on the information that will help the grantmaker see how your request helps it meet its own goals. In the end, good grantwriting is about making the connection between your organization and what a funder wants to accomplish with its grants.

LOIs

> ### Use Letterhead!
>
> The final version that you send to a funder must be on organizational letterhead. You'd be surprised at how many letters to funders end up on plain paper with no contact information. It doesn't have to be preprinted letterhead. A standard letterhead set up as a header in your Word program is fine.
>
> Also, address the letter as personally as possible. Often, websites will tell you who should receive your submission. If that information isn't available, address your request to the funder's director. Your organization loses credibility if you send a letter addressed, "Dear Funding Committee:" to a funder that clearly tells you to send letters to "Ms. Jane Doe, Executive Director."
>
> **IMPORTANT!**

Even if you've just begun working with grants you've probably heard of LOIs. LOI can stand for Letter of Interest, Letter of Inquiry, or Letter of Intent.

Such letters are a common method for making the initial approach to many funders. In our research for this book a look at a random sample of funders making $2 million to $5 million in grants per year show showed that 40 percent of them ask for a letter as an initial contact. Others don't specify the format, while the remaining ones use some mix of online forms, full proposals, or application forms.

With technology, this is changing. More and more funders use online formats. Some allow you to upload a PDF copy of a letter, while others ask you to complete an online summary or screening. That's why we will talk about letters in multiple roles. While often the format for making an initial contact on a request, letters are also a tool that can help you do a better job with those other initial forms of contact with a funder.

To Summarize...

- Describe your organization and its mission in everyday terms if your mission statement is overly formal.

- Describe your organization's work in a way that supports your request.

- The executive director or key board member must sign all requests. This tells the funder that your request is a priority for the organization.

- Pay attention to detail, even if it means getting someone else to proofread your work.

programs
year
form
interest
invitation
support
research
rfp
noza
information
collaboration
means
database
requests
financial
question
need
proposal
government
guidelines
organizations
donations
private
mission
results
board
online
members
work
who
grantmakers
lists
family
ideas
501C3
vision
grants
help
key
relationship
applications
sponsor
fit
terms
pay
assets
success
sources
find
apply
focus
vision
page
state
address
federal
want
fund
submit
fiscal
events
give
email
website
letter
time
development
best
start
ways
statements

Part 2

Laying the Groundwork

Now that you've tried your hand at the Quick-Start Letter, it's time to go back and fill in the foundations of grantwriting. Understanding the funding landscape will make you a better grantwriter. In this section, we'll define what grants are, and discuss their sources and types. Most important, we'll talk about why funders make grants. If you understand funders' motivations for giving, you'll be able to do a better job of persuading them that their organizations and yours can work together to benefit the community.

Chapter 3

What Are Grants and What Can They Do?

In This Chapter...

- What is a 501(c)(3) organization?
- What's the difference between a public charity and a private foundation?
- What are grants, and what can they do?
- What are some limitations on grants?

In the first two chapters we breezed by a lot of important information, such as what a nonprofit is, who is eligible to receive grants, and what grants really are. Now that you've taken a shot at writing an LOI with the Quick-Start Letter, you're ready to go into more depth about the grantseeking process and how to prepare for writing successful grants.

Here we'll discuss the fact that most organizations eligible to receive grants have 501(c)(3) public charity status from the IRS. We'll talk about the difference between private foundations and public charities. (There are other kinds of 501(c) organizations, but donations to them are not tax deductible.) Other entities are eligible for grants because they are considered part of government, such as public universities, or because they are affiliated with a religion.

You will also see that funders make grants for a specific purpose and expect results that can be measured or at least demonstrated. They can help your organization and the people you serve in a wide variety of ways. It's also possible to get unrestricted grants for operating expenses, but usually funders give these to nonprofits with whom they already have a close relationship.

What Do We Mean by the Terms Nonprofit, Funder, and 501(c)(3)?

In this book, we use the terms "nonprofit" and "funder." We have also referenced 501(c)(3) recognition. Before we go further, let's clarify both our informal usage and the technical side of those meanings.

Most organizations that *seek and receive grant money* are recognized by the IRS as exempt from federal income taxes under Section 501(c)(3) of the Internal Revenue Code. They are also recognized by the IRS as public charities rather than private foundations. In this book, when we use the term "nonprofit" this is the kind of organization we mean.

Many of the entities that *make grants* are also 501(c)(3)s, but are typically recognized by the IRS as private foundations rather than public charities—though some are,

Public Charity or Private Foundation?

Generally, private foundations make grants to public charities. While they can make grants to other private foundations, there are risks to the funder in doing so—and most funders simply decline to do so.

To be a public charity, an organization has to either meet a "public support test" or be one of the kinds of organizations that automatically qualify for public charity status. The public support test requires that you receive financial support from a wide variety of sources. So you can't plan on starting a charitable organization and expect to keep running it year after year through grants from only two or three sources of funding.

Even if you could find such dedicated funding partners, your status would soon change to that of a private foundation because of your limited donor base, per IRS regulations, and then you would not be eligible for most grants.

IMPORTANT!

indeed, public charities. In this book, we refer to them, as well as corporate giving programs and government grantmakers, as "funders."

How Do You Get 501(c)(3) Recognition?

Chances are, you aren't going to be starting a nonprofit organization. You'll probably either be employed as a grantwriter by an existing one, or, if you're working as an independent grantwriter, your clients will already be recognized as 501(c)(3) public charities.

So we won't dwell on how to create a nonprofit. Just so you know, though, starting a new nonprofit organization requires two essential actions. First, you have to decide what kind of organization you want to operate and then form it under state law as a tax-exempt entity. Usually, you do this through your state's secretary of state office. It's a relatively simple process.

The second key step is applying to the IRS for recognition as a 501(c)(3) entity that's classified as a public charity. This process is much more complex, and you may want to consult an attorney with expertise in the field of tax-exempt organization law. Applying for and getting 501(c)(3) recognition and public charity classification from the IRS, which starts with the submission of IRS Form 1023, can take up to six months or longer, and cost several hundred dollars.

Charitable Purpose

According to the IRS website, "The exempt purposes set forth in Internal Revenue Code Section 501(c)(3) are charitable, religious, educational, scientific, literary, testing for public safety, fostering national or international amateur sports competition, and the prevention of cruelty to children or animals." The IRS applies these terms in ways that also allow for such groups as arts and environmental organizations.

Your 1023 application must comply with the charitable purposes allowed under the Internal Revenue Code. Your organization must operate solely for its stated charitable purpose. The IRS is strict about enforcing the rules for 501(c)(3)s; for instance, such tax-exempt organizations are not allowed to engage in political campaigning or lobbying to any "substantial" extent. (To find out what's meant by "substantial lobbying," you may need to consult an attorney.)

There are many other forms of tax-exempt entities recognized under the Internal Revenue Code 501(c). In fact, there are twenty-nine categories ranging from Rotary Clubs to cemetery associations. Organizations that are not 501(c)(3)s are generally not eligible for grants, and contributions to them are usually not tax deductible. However, payments or donations to such organizations may be deductible as business expenses.

You may have heard of a Rotary Club raising money for a charitable project and claiming that contributions are tax deductible. That is probably true. The fine print will tell you that contributions go to the Rotary Club Foundation, not the Rotary Club. The difference is that the foundation is a separate 501(c)(3) organization affiliated with the Rotary Club that carries out charitable projects. The regular Downtown Rotary Club organization is a 501(c)(4)—it's tax exempt, but donations to it are not tax deductible.

Donations to political organizations are not tax deductible. But organizations that attempt to influence legislation, such as Greenpeace, often have separate branches set up as 501(c)(3)s that can accept tax-deductible donations, like the Greenpeace Fund. These groups may conduct educational campaigns to increase public awareness of their cause, but are not allowed to do direct lobbying of elected officials.

Other types of organizations eligible to receive grants are those that are considered a branch of government. These include public schools, community colleges, and public universities, along with parks departments and similar government entities. Religious organizations are also eligible for some grants; these can include not only houses of worship, but also schools, hospitals, and social service groups run by religious entities. Some large Catholic universities, for instance, do not have their own 501(c)(3)s but instead rely on their affiliation with the Roman Catholic Church for their tax-exempt status.

Grants to Individuals

Individuals are eligible for certain types of grants under specific circumstances. For instance, there are many grants for educational purposes, often called scholarships or fellowships. Talented people such as artists, composers, and writers can receive grants to create a piece of art or music, or to write a book. Many of these grants are given to winners of competitions.

Although this book is aimed at people who are writing grants for nonprofit organizations, individuals seeking grants for themselves will be able to apply much of its advice to their own proposals. If you're applying for a fellowship to write a book or study abroad, the application form will probably ask you to state why you want to do this project, define your goals, say what you expect to accomplish, describe your plan of work, and state how you will evaluate the success of your project. These are all elements of grant proposals for nonprofits as well.

Finally, on the paperwork side, understand that you may have to file other papers or permits in your state or local area to operate. The treatment of nonprofit organizations, including charitable nonprofits, varies from state to state. Also, charitable status with the IRS does not automatically exempt your organization from sales taxes, property taxes, or business license regulations.

Example

The Dangers of Relying on Just a Few Donors

The Big Bend Princess Foundation was created to raise money for scholarships. These were awarded to young women selected by local groups such as Kiwanis and Rotary Clubs for the Big Bend Princess Pageant. In its early days the foundation struggled to raise the money from groups and individual donors.

Over the years the Big Bend Festival grew. As a way of getting its name in front of the event's large audience, the Sweet Soda Company made a grant for scholarships to the Big Bend Princess Foundation. Eventually other fundraising declined and continuing support by the Sweet Soda Company composed the vast majority of the foundation's annual support.

When the Sweet Soda Company decided to cut back its grants, the Big Bend Princess Foundation approached local foundations for grants to replace the loss. But it soon learned that the IRS had reclassified the Big Bend Princess Foundation from a public charity to a private foundation. Why? Since one major donor provided the bulk of its support for several years, the foundation had lost its public charity status.

This can happen even if an organization has half a dozen key donors who provide most of the support. That's why organizations have to develop a base of support in order to be viable grant recipients year after year.

So What about Grants?

Everyone's heard of grants, but what are they really? Here's a definition to start with:

A grant is a sum of money given by one party (a funder) to a recipient for a specific purpose and with an expectation of certain results.

The fact that recipients are often 501(c)(3) public charities is a result of the IRS regulations on funders such as private foundations, community foundations, and corporate giving programs. Further, many government grant programs often favor 501(c)(3) public charities in their application processes. But grants are also made to a wide variety of other recipients, as noted earlier in this chapter.

A Specific Purpose, Expecting Results

Why did we say "for a specific purpose, with an expectation of certain results" in the basic definition of a grant?

In the Quick-Start Letter, we asked you to think about describing the purpose of your grant in terms of what it would accomplish for your community. We stressed this approach as opposed to jumping right in and asking the funder to purchase a cooler/freezer or to simply make a grant of $10,000.

Compare this with how most of us deal with our own charitable giving. We receive dozens of solicitations every year from charitable organizations, via email, phone, snail mail, and many other avenues. The organizations tell us about their programs and ask for our support. If we have some disposable income and believe in the cause, we may send a gift—$25, $50, or even more. All we expect in return is a thank-you note, a receipt for our tax-deductible donation, and further mailings keeping us up to date on the organization's activities (and asking for more support). We don't expect an organization to tell us exactly what it did with our specific donation, though it may tell us that $25 can feed an impoverished child's family for a month or $100 can buy them a goat.

Funders, on the other hand, expect more. When you write a grant proposal, you have to explain what you want to accomplish, why, who needs your services, what you expect to achieve, how much the whole project will cost, and specifically how you will use the donor's money.

When you receive funding, you will have to account for the expenditures in detail and send a report at the end of the grant period on exactly how the whole project turned out. In many cases, the donor expects you to state specific expected results or outcomes, and report at the end on the extent to which you did or did not achieve them.

What Can Grants Do for Your Organization?

Grants can be a key part of your organization's budget and can assist in accomplishing a host of goals. For instance:

- Grants can help you start a new program, or expand an old one.
- They can help you try out a new idea to benefit your clients.
- They can help you mount an artistic production or exhibit.

> **Observation**
>
> ### Isn't There an Easier Way?
>
> "All this sounds so complicated! I just want to help people—can't I just go and do that?"
>
> You certainly don't need to set up a nonprofit 501(c)(3) public charity to help people if you can fund your work in other ways, either through your own resources, or by selling services, or through money people will give you without regard to taking a charitable deduction on taxes. That leaves aside, of course, any state or local regulations.
>
> If you feel you have a cause that can attract grants and you want to apply for them but don't want to set up your own nonprofit, there is another option: working with another organization that is already a 501(c)(3) public charity. In many communities, there are multipurpose organizations that serve as incubators for small efforts just getting started. Over time these efforts may become programs of the larger entity or grow to be their own, independent organizations.
>
> You may still have to do fundraising for your work, but the larger organization can take care of much of the technical detail. This kind of relationship is called "fiscal sponsorship," which we'll explain in **Chapter 8**.

- They can help you hire someone to train your staff in how to use new technology.

- They can help you build a new facility or renovate an old one.

Note that each example tends to have a distinct beginning and end.

What *Don't* Grants Do?

That leads us to what grants don't tend to do well or at least easily. It's harder to get grants for the general operations of your organization. They're usually not going to be given to you to be put in your general account to cover rent and utilities, or to pay salaries for general and unspecified purposes. Those are "operating expenses" that your organization needs to pay for through earned income and unrestricted donations.

This is not to say that it's impossible to get operating grants—they do exist. But usually there's already an established relationship between the funder and the grantee. For instance, a foundation may have funded a specific project and been pleased with the results, so staff invites the organization to apply for a general operating grant. Or someone on the board of the funding organization may be familiar with the work of the nonprofit and wants to support its mission.

Family foundations and smaller foundations do make unrestricted grants—but usually these are very similar to direct gifts from individuals. The foundation may donate to the same organizations year after year, often without soliciting a lengthy grant proposal. There is usually a close relationship between the

---

Watch Out for Scams!

What about that guy on TV with the question marks all over his suit who says you can get a grant for anything you need? Or those ads saying the government and other funders give away millions each year to people who just know how to ask?

Sadly, the grant field is full of scams like these. Sometimes the operators will invite you to send for a free booklet that will give you a whole list of grants you can apply for. You'll probably find out you don't qualify for any of them. The operators may even offer to fill out the applications for you, for a substantial fee up front. These schemes rarely, if ever, produce actual grants for individuals. If you're eligible for some kind of assistance from the government or a nonprofit organization, you don't have to pay anyone to help you get it.

WATCH OUT!

donors and the organization. While these gifts are technically grants because they're made by foundations, in many ways they're more similar to personal donations. If the funder does require a letter, it may be more general than a formal grant proposal, updating the foundation on the nonprofit's activities and requesting support for the coming year. Reports on the use of funds are also less formal, describing the organization's successes and challenges in the year past, but not necessarily accounting for the specific use of the foundation's funds.

Grantwriters can be confused by funder guidelines or database entries that list "general operations" among the types of grants made by the funder. In most cases, this is not an invitation for organizations unknown to the funder to write a proposal requesting unrestricted monies. "General operations" is included in the list of grant types because funders want to retain the flexibility to make this kind of grant to organizations they know. But usually an initial request needs to be more specific.

To Summarize...

- To become a 501(c)(3) organization, you must apply to the IRS and fit its definition of "charitable purpose."

- It's important to understand the difference between a private foundation and a public charity.

- When funders make grants, they usually expect specific results.

- Grants can help your organization in many ways, but they usually don't provide unrestricted operating funds unless the funder already knows you well.

Chapter 4

What Kinds of Funders Are There?

In This Chapter...
- What are private foundations?
- How are community foundations different?
- Why do corporations make grants?
- What's involved in getting federal grants?

Grants come primarily from three types of funders: foundations, corporations, and government. Each of these types has different sources of funding, different structures, and different reasons for giving. It's important to understand where funders' money comes from and why they're motivated to give. As a grantwriter, you'll want to understand how each type of funder works, and whether it's a good match for your organization and the kind of project for which you're seeking support.

Foundations include a wide range of organizations. There are private foundations and public foundations, family, community, and private operating foundations. Recognizing the differences among these types will help you understand how best to approach them.

Corporations give in several different ways, and can be excellent partners for your nonprofit if you're a good match for their goals. But their reasons for giving, and their values, may differ from those of foundations, so they're looking for different qualities in grant proposals.

Federal grants are difficult to get but can provide funding for years if you succeed in winning an award. Proposals for federal grants are complex, so you may want to consult with an expert who specializes in this field if you plan to apply. Nonprofits that receive federal awards must adhere to meticulous rules for reporting their achievements and expenditures, so make sure your organization is able to comply before you submit an application.

Foundations

In general, foundations are private entities unconnected with the government. Often foundations are nonprofit corporations, but they may also be established as charitable trusts. In either case, they have charitable status with the IRS under Section 501(c)(3). All of their efforts must be in support of the foundation's charitable purpose consistent with those outlined in IRS regulations.

> **Charitable Trusts**
>
> Most private foundations are nonprofit corporations, just like the public charities that seek grants from them. But some private foundations are organized as trusts. The reasons that some benefactors choose to use a trust rather than incorporating a nonprofit corporation don't affect your grantwriting. The Murdock Charitable Trust, for instance, is for all intents and purposes a private foundation.
>
> **Definition**

Private Foundations vs. Public Charities

In the last chapter, we discussed the difference between private foundations, which have a limited number of donors, and public charities, which must meet a public support test. Not every group that calls itself a foundation is a private foundation. Many using that label are in fact public charities. There are significant differences between the two types:

- Private foundations are required by law to spend a certain amount (usually 5 percent) of their assets each year on activities related to their charitable purpose. The bulk of this amount, called "qualified distributions," constitutes their grants to nonprofit organizations. Foundations that are public charities have different rules and set their own distribution rate.

- Private foundations are classified as such because they have a limited number of donors. They have special rules regarding the people and groups that they can do business with. For example, there are limitations on the kinds of business they can do with family members of benefactors and members of their boards of directors.

- Private foundations must file a 990-PF tax form with the IRS, listing their sources of income and the grants they make. Public charities file a Form 990 that does not require them to reveal individual donors publicly. This is probably the most important difference, from a grantseeker's point of view.

Private foundations come in two main varieties: operating and grantmaking. Operating foundations fund and carry out their own work. The few grants they make are usually in direct support of their own programs. Grantmaking foundations make grants, usually to 501(c)(3) public charities, to carry out work in the community that supports the foundation's charitable mission and goals.

Types of Private Grantmaking Foundations

Private grantmaking foundations can be independent or family foundations. Both types have assets that come from the gifts of one or more benefactors, usually an individual or a family.

The difference between independent and family foundations is the composition

> **Casey Family Programs**
>
> The Casey Family Programs are classified as a private operating foundation. Its mission is "to provide and improve—and ultimately prevent the need for—foster care." Casey "provides foster care and other direct services to 1,100 children and families." It also offers consulting and research services to help improve child welfare systems, and it gives nonpartisan information and education to government policy makers. While most of the foundation's funds go to the programs it runs itself, the foundation does make a few grants to other organizations that share its mission.
>
> **Example**

of the board. A family foundation will be governed primarily by family members. An independent foundation will have independent directors, for the most part. For example, when the Ford Foundation was established by Henry Ford's son Edsel Ford, it was governed primarily by family members. By the '50s the foundation was governed by non-family members, making it an independent foundation. Legally there is no difference between the two, and usually you wouldn't see much of a difference in how either type of foundation makes grants. The operations and grants of independent and family foundations are funded by the foundation's assets and earnings from investments. They don't actively solicit contributions, though they may receive donations or bequests from people closely associated with the foundation.

Public Foundations

There is another category of funders whose members are incorporated as 501(c)(3) public charities. They may call themselves foundations, but they differ from private foundations in that they raise funds from multiple donors, and they make grants. Two of the oldest examples of such organizations are community foundations and United Ways. Public charities don't have the same requirements for distributing funds as private foundations.

Community foundations are donor-based organizations. They often administer "donor-advised funds" that can be used to make grants. The individual donors still maintain complete control over gifts made from these funds, but they may seek advice from the staff of the community foundation in deciding where and how to give. This means that grants coming from a public foundation may actually be an extension of an individual's or family's giving.

In the past few decades, many organizations have developed to gather

> ### Get to Know Your Community Foundation
>
> Getting to know the staff at a community foundation can help you connect with those donors. At some community foundations, staff will share nonprofits' grant applications with the holders of donor-advised funds when they fit the interests of those individuals.
>
> Also, community foundation staffs keep up with the interests of other organizations in the area such as local private foundations. They can sometimes advise you when your request might fit those other funders' priorities.
>
> **Inspiration**

donations that they use for their grantmaking programs. These might be considered a type of community foundation. They just define their communities by a common cause or interest instead of geography: for example, an environmental foundation or a foundation serving the LGBTQ community. These foundations are tightly organized around their missions, and their grants go to projects that are clearly aligned with those interests. These funders can be good sources of support when you have a program that fits their mission and goals.

Corporations

Corporations can make tax-deductible gifts of up to 10 percent of their net income per year. Most give no more than 2 percent, but many do make charitable donations and grants. However, corporate giving as a whole comes to only about 5 percent of U.S. private giving. In approaching corporations, it's important to understand their reasons for donating.

Who owns a corporation? If it is public—traded on a public stock exchange like the NYSE—it is owned by its shareholders. The executives are obligated to make company decisions in the best interests of those shareholders, which usually means trying to maximize the share price. Private corporations are different; the owners may have no one to answer to but themselves. Still, their business interests usually come first.

When corporations make grants, they ask the question, "How will this benefit our company?" This isn't just a preference, but a duty that comes from case law resulting from shareholder lawsuits seeking to prevent a publicly held corporation from making charitable grants that are not in the best interest of the company. Some of a corporation's reasons for giving:

- It will make our community a better place for our employees to live and work. (This one is often listed in the guidelines for corporate giving.)
- It will bring us positive publicity.
- It will win goodwill for us in the community. ("Goodwill" is an actual line item sometimes listed in corporate financial statements as an asset.)
- It will associate our brand with a good cause.
- It will bring us more customers.

- It can build employee morale and allegiance.

- The after-tax cost of giving is less than the face value of the gift due to tax deductions for charitable giving.

When you write a proposal to a corporate donor, you need to let the donor know right up front how funding your organization's project will help the corporation—i.e., what's in it for them. This is not a cynical view of corporate behavior, nor is it branding big business as the "bad guys." It's just a realistic assessment of corporate motivations for giving.

Corporations give through several different avenues.

Corporate Foundations

Some companies set up private foundations to handle their giving. These entities are separate from the corporations, with their own boards. They may publish grant guidelines on a company website or on a separate foundation website. They must file 990-PF forms with the IRS, and these are available for viewing online, just like those of a private foundation.

> **Inspiration**
>
> ### Do Any of Your Volunteers Work for Corporations That Make Grants?
>
> Corporate grant guidelines often ask if any of the company's employees volunteer for the nonprofit that is applying for a grant. If you can answer "yes" to this question, you have a much better chance of receiving an award. The logic behind this practice is that corporations want to encourage their employees to volunteer, and supporting the organizations where they volunteer is a good way to do this. So make sure you know where your volunteers work, and find out if their companies make grants. If they do, ask your volunteer to make a call to the community relations manager when you're planning to submit a proposal. This can greatly strengthen your case.

Corporate foundations usually have small asset bases. Their grant dollars come each year through a gift from the sponsoring company. The amount of the contribution usually depends on how well the corporation is doing financially that year. A company's foundation allows it to make significant charitable gifts when it makes sense from a business and tax-timing standpoint.

Direct Giving

Many corporations give directly from their corporate revenues, either in addition to or instead of a foundation. The 3M Company, for example, gives both ways. Smaller businesses are less likely to have a foundation.

Companies that give directly usually have an office of community relations, social responsibility, corporate citizenship, or something similar. They may have guidelines for submitting grants, but these may be looser than those of corporate foundations.

Unlike foundations (corporate or private), corporate direct giving programs do not file 990-PFs and do not have to disclose information about their grants to the public. They may discuss their giving in their annual reports and on their websites, and they may list some of the nonprofit organizations they have supported. But they usually don't publicize the amounts of their gifts, so finding out the size and recipients of their grants takes a lot more sleuthing than it does with foundations, corporate or otherwise. We'll talk about how to do that in the next chapter.

Employee Giving Programs

Many corporations encourage their employees to make charitable contributions through a workplace United Way campaign, but some have their own in-house employee giving programs. The Boeing Company has its Employees Community Fund, which is funded by voluntary payroll deductions and managed by the employees themselves. The fund managers, a rotating group, are given time away from their regular jobs to direct the fund. It has guidelines and application

---

Corporate Employees Make Great Volunteers!

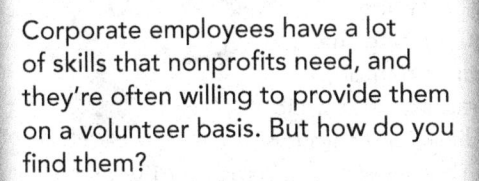

Corporate employees have a lot of skills that nonprofits need, and they're often willing to provide them on a volunteer basis. But how do you find them?

You may want to ask local companies how you can recruit their employees as volunteers for your organization. They may have electronic bulletin boards where you can post volunteer opportunities. If you can persuade corporate employees to volunteer for your nonprofit, you'll be getting some valuable help and, at the same time, strengthening your relationship with the company, which may lead to cash grants in the future. Corporate employees can also make excellent board members.

Inspiration

forms just like any other foundation. Boeing employees conduct site visits and allocate grant awards.

Other Kinds of Corporate Support

Corporate giving is usually a fairly small part of companies' budgets since they may have trouble justifying direct philanthropy to their board and shareholders. But corporations often support nonprofits more generously in ways that are more closely related to their own marketing. They're willing to spend a lot more money if the expense can be justified as a form of advertising. These kinds of support are not grants, but grantwriters need to be aware of them.

> **WATCH OUT!**
>
> ## Is It Okay to Take Money from Controversial Sources?
>
> Sometimes corporations that need to burnish their image (or atone for past transgressions) may offer you funding that you'll want to think twice about. Should an environmental organization accept money from an energy company after a big oil spill? Should a homeless shelter accept funding from a liquor distributor? Many people say, "Of course not! That would be a betrayal of your principles!" Sometimes this is the right call, but other times it's more complicated.
>
> For an alternative view, read George Bernard Shaw's play *Major Barbara*, or watch the wonderful 1941 movie. Shaw believed there was no such thing as "dirty money" because all money was tainted by greed and selfishness. In his preface to the play, Shaw asserts that an officer of the Salvation Army told him "they would take money from the devil himself and be only too glad to get it out of his hands and into God's."
>
> It's true that dollars don't come with résumés describing their history. But still, when you accept funding from a controversial source, you need to consider whether it will reflect badly on your organization and alienate other donors. Not every nonprofit can be as cavalier about its funders as the Salvation Army of Shaw's time.
>
> These contrasting views highlight the need for an organization to have a gift acceptance policy. Such a policy helps board members, staff, and volunteers understand how to handle offers of gifts that may be controversial.

Sponsorships

Sponsorships are forms of underwriting for a special fundraising event such as a golf tournament, race, or auction. Corporations get to put their names out in front of your donors, who are their potential customers.

Cause Marketing

A corporation may agree to give a contribution to your organization for every item it sells in a given timeframe. "Come in today, and for every mattress sold, we'll make a donation to Toys for Tots!" In exchange, the nonprofit allows the corporation to use its name in advertising this agreement.

In-kind Giving

This refers to the direct donation of goods and services to a nonprofit. For instance, Microsoft has an extensive software donation program. Some companies will donate their employees' or managers' time and expertise to a nonprofit—you might be able to find someone to help you develop your website or formulate a business plan. When you're planning a project for which you intend to seek grant funding, think about whether some of what you need could be provided through in-kind giving. Maybe you need furniture, equipment, and software for your new employment resource center. If some of this can be donated directly, you won't need to raise as much through cash grants.

Government Grants

Government grants range from multiyear, multi-million-dollar funding provided by the federal government to relatively small contributions from municipalities. The size of the grant is often, though not always, proportionate to the amount of time and effort that must go into applying for it. Large government grants also require meticulous accounting once they are awarded.

Federal Grants

The topic of federal grants is far too large to be explained in detail in a book of this scope, and if you're new to grantwriting, you'll want to seek a detailed resource. If you're thinking about applying for federal funding, we recommend you start with a book dedicated to this topic, such as *Writing to Win Federal*

Grants: A Must-Have for Your Fundraising Toolbox by Cheryl Kester and Karen Cassidy (CharityChannel Press, 2015).

The federal government awards billions of dollars in grants each year. Grants are made by twenty-six government departments including the Departments of Education, Labor, Homeland Security, Health and Human Services, and many more. Together they offer more than a thousand grant programs. When you hear that the government is "putting more money" into some issue or cause, such as early childhood education, some of that money is probably being allocated in the form of grants to public and private agencies and organizations, many of them nonprofits.

Grants funded by federal monies can come through many avenues. In addition to direct federal support, grants can come through state and local governments. One example is Community Development Block Grants (CDBG). The federal government allocates funding to localities such as cities and counties, basing the amount on a formula that includes population and economic status.

Although many CDBG dollars are spent by local governments on public projects, localities can also spend a portion of those dollars on human services. The decision-making process begins at the local level. While projects and the grant applications must meet federal guidelines, building a relationship with the local authority parallels our recommendations for working with funders throughout this book.

Grants that come directly from the federal government are usually posted on the *grants.gov* website. This website allows you to research which grants (called "grant opportunities" or "funding opportunities") are available from the federal government and provides links to grant announcements. It tells you everything you need to know to find and apply for a grant. Almost all federal proposals are submitted through the *grants.gov* portal.

Register Early!

Before you can apply for a federal grant, your organization needs to register with *grants.gov*. The process is not too difficult, but it can take up to four weeks to complete. So if you're even thinking about applying, make sure your organization has a DUNS number (a unique identification number provided by Dun & Bradstreet) and is registered on the grants.gov website. You can find instructions here: http://www.grants.gov/web/grants/applicants/organization-registration.html.

IMPORTANT!

Federal grant awards are much larger than most private grants. They may be worth millions of dollars and cover three years or more. Many large institutions, especially universities, community colleges, and medical research facilities, receive hundreds of millions of dollars in federal grants each year.

Naturally, the competition for these grants is very stiff. Federal grant applications are lengthy and complex, and even excellent proposals may miss the cut-off for receiving an award by only a point or two. This can be very discouraging if the applicant has spent weeks or months preparing the request. On the other hand, if you win a grant it can keep a program funded for years.

Federal grants come with strict accounting requirements that may overwhelm the ability of smaller organizations to track the use of funds. Every penny must be accounted for and reported. Organizations without well-staffed and sophisticated accounting departments may find federal grant awards to be more trouble than they are worth.

If you think your organization can write a competitive federal grant proposal and this is your first time doing so, you may want to hire a grant consultant experienced in this field. An expert consultant can guide you through the

> **Submit Early!**
>
> All federal grants have deadlines for submission, and they are absolutely inflexible. If the guidelines say the proposal is due at 5 p.m. on Friday, January 16, they mean it. The federal agency doesn't care if you broke your leg on the way to work that morning—5 p.m. Friday is 5 p.m. Friday, no matter what.
>
> With online submissions through *grants.gov*, it's especially important to submit your proposal several hours early, at least. (Several days ahead of the deadline is better.) Because so many people wait until literally the last minute, the servers may get clogged, and your grant may not go through on time. If you hit send at 4:59:02, and hundreds of other applicants do the same thing within the same minute, your proposal may not arrive until 5:00:01. And even one second can be late enough to disqualify that 150-page proposal you spent weeks writing. Don't let this happen to you!
>
> **IMPORTANT!**

process, save you time, and greatly increase your chances of success (though nothing is guaranteed, of course).

State, County, and Municipal Grants

Grants are also available from levels of government closer to home, and usually the application process is less intimidating than the one for federal grants. The granting agency may offer workshops for proposal writers that you can attend in person. (The federal agencies offer these workshops too, usually online.) You can also talk to someone in the agency office who will be glad to answer your questions. The application format is likely to be shorter and less difficult than for federal grants. But local government agencies also demand careful accountability from grant recipients—you'll need to submit reports showing how you spent every penny.

Sometimes local government applications may seem excessively complex, considering the amount of funding offered. For instance, grants to arts organizations with a maximum size of $2,000 or $3,000 can take hours of work—because the guidelines ask for budgets going back several years (in a required format) and for detailed records on performances and attendance. Part of the reason may be that the agency you're applying to (in this case, the arts commission) uses these statistics to make its case for funding to legislators or the city council. The funder needs your help to obtain the funds it awards in grants.

Fair but Strict

One advantage of government grants at all levels is that the award system must be fair and transparent. The granting agency must establish clear rules and procedures and apply them impartially to all eligible applicants. The agencies must explain how they will evaluate proposals—often there is a scoring system, with a certain number

> **Check Those Details!**
>
> A nonprofit that relied upon a significant amount of direct federal funding found out that its application for renewing that funding wasn't even going to be reviewed. The reason? The funding agency contended that the application failed to meet the requirement for uniform one-inch margins on all sides of the document's pages. Even Congressional intervention couldn't get the application back into the hopper.
>
> **Uninspired**

of points applied to each section of the grant. Also, they must allow you to see copies of proposals that have been successful in past years. Sometimes these are made available online; other times, especially for local government, you can go into the agency's office and read them there. All of this provides an element of fairness and accessibility that is not always present with private grantmakers.

Federal funding processes are much stricter than their private funding peers about issues such as formatting, attachments, and correctly completed forms. The reason is that, if they allow an exception to one rule, then other applications that don't follow the rules would have to be allowed as well. The agency could be accused of favoritism if it overlooked the rules for one applicant but not for all.

To Summarize...

- It's important to understand the characteristics of each of the different categories of funders.
- Foundations come in several forms, each of which has its own peculiarities.
- When corporations make grants, they want to know how the donation will benefit their employees and/or shareholders.
- Federal grant proposals require a huge investment of time and expertise, but federal awards can be in the millions of dollars and fund a program for years.

Chapter 5

Why Do Funders Make Grants?

In This Chapter...

- How can you learn to think like a funder?
- Why is there sometimes a disconnect between funders and grantseekers?
- How can you learn about funders' motivations for giving?
- What you can do to show alignment with their mission?

If you think of a funder primarily as a pot of money waiting to be grabbed by whichever grantseekers write the most convincing pleas, your grantwriting probably won't be very successful. Funders have their own missions and their own motivations for giving. You'll be a better grantwriter if you try to figure out what those are and address them.

Funders care about your clients, not your organization, and that's a good thing. They see nonprofits as a means to an end. They respond well to grantseekers who approach them as partners, saying in essence, "Let's see how we can work together to improve and benefit our communities." You want to let them know that you understand and share their goals and that your organization is a well-qualified, trustworthy agent that can help them turn their vision into reality.

Unfortunately, this is not always how nonprofit executives see the grantseeking process. They look at their budgets and see grants as one of several income streams that can help them reach their revenue target for the year. The question they're asking is not, "How can we help funders achieve their goals?" but "How can grants help us achieve ours?" The grantwriter is often in the uncomfortable position of acting as a diplomat, having to explain each side's motivations to the other. We can't make this problem go away, but we can clarify the issues by bringing them out in the open.

Looking closely at funders' mission statements can help you understand their reasons for giving. This will provide a key for how you can attune your proposals to their desired achievements.

But first, let's do a thought experiment to see what it might be like if *you* were the funder. You don't have to imagine that you're wealthy—maybe you just know someone who is, and who has faith in you. You may be able to understand funders' questions better if you think about why they were written.

Thinking Like a Funder

Let's say you get a call one day from your good friend Elizabeth who's been very successful in business. She wants to meet for lunch. Over a nice glass of chardonnay, she says, "I think you know that my company has really taken off over the last few years, and I've made more money than I ever dreamed possible.

"I have the chance to do a lot more for the charities I've supported over the years as well as others I'm interested in but haven't been able to help before. My accountant suggests that I set up a foundation."

"Why is that?" you ask.

"There are times when I can give larger amounts, but those might not always be the right times to make big gifts to the charities. Also, if I ever sell the company, I might want to make a very large gift that can be distributed over time."

Chapter 5—Why Do Funders Make Grants?

"That makes sense," you say. "You've always been very generous to charities. So how can I help?"

"We've known each other a long time, and I've always trusted your judgment," says Elizabeth. "I think you could help me figure out how to make sure my money really does some good in the community and doesn't get wasted. I'd like to ask you to be on the board of my foundation."

"I'm flattered," you say. "What would it involve?"

"Well, first we need to figure out what areas the foundation will fund. I care about education, the environment, the arts, and of course, basic health and human services. But I think the harder part will be setting up the grant guidelines. What kinds of questions should we ask applicants, so we can find out which ones are the most trustworthy and competent, and what projects are most likely to result in lasting benefits?"

"It sounds like a big responsibility," you reply, "but I'm honored that you have so much trust in me. I'd love to be a part of this."

So now imagine you're at a meeting of the newly formed foundation board, and you're trying to develop the grant guidelines. What questions do you want to ask applicants? Before you read further, write down a few. Remember, you're trying to find out which nonprofits will be the best stewards of your friend's hard-earned money, and which projects will best succeed in helping the community.

When Goodwin does this exercise in her classes, students suggest questions like some of these:

- How long has your organization been around? What have you accomplished?
- Who is on your board?
- What kinds of people do you serve? How many?
- What is your organization's overall budget?
- Where does your organization get its revenue?
- Why is this project important?
- Who will benefit from it?

- What do you expect to accomplish?
- What will it cost?
- How long will it take?
- Is anybody else funding this?
- How will you keep the project going after the grant runs out?

These questions look a lot like traditional grant guidelines, and that's no surprise. Guidelines are a funder's attempt to put its good intentions into words, and to elicit from applicants the information it needs to make good funding decisions. You can see why funders need good data to help them decide where to make grants.

You can learn a lot simply by doing this thought experiment—putting the funder's hat on your own head. When you read guidelines, ask yourself, "Why does the funder want to know that? What is the funder really trying to find out from us?" Funders don't ask questions just to make your life difficult—they're trying to get the information they need to make wise decisions about how to allocate their resources in ways that best fulfill their own missions.

> ### Nobody Wants to Hear How Desperate You Are for Money
>
> You'll notice one kind of question missing from our list: "How badly do you need the money?" Funders don't want to hear that you're desperate for funding or that you'll have to close your doors if you don't get this grant. They may decide, "Well, if the Society for Good Intentions is about to collapse without this grant, maybe another nonprofit would be better at dealing with the issues addressed by this group."
>
> Funders want to assist successful organizations, not needy ones. You're not the guy at the end of the freeway ramp carrying a sign saying, "Will work for food." You're the person helping that guy get off the street and find a job.
>
> **Uninspired**

It's about Your Clients, Not Your Organization

Some years ago, we had a speaker named Peter Berliner at a meeting of the Puget Sound Grantwriters Association. He was a program officer for the Paul G. Allen Family Foundations, a major funder in the Pacific Northwest. During the Q&A session after his presentation, a young woman raised her hand and started to say, "Would you support an organization that..." At this point, Peter interrupted her and said, "I'm sorry, but I need to make something clear. We don't support organizations; *we make change happen.*"

That comment made a big impression on those of us in the audience. We realized what Peter meant was that funders don't support nonprofits for their own sake—funders want to create positive changes in the community.

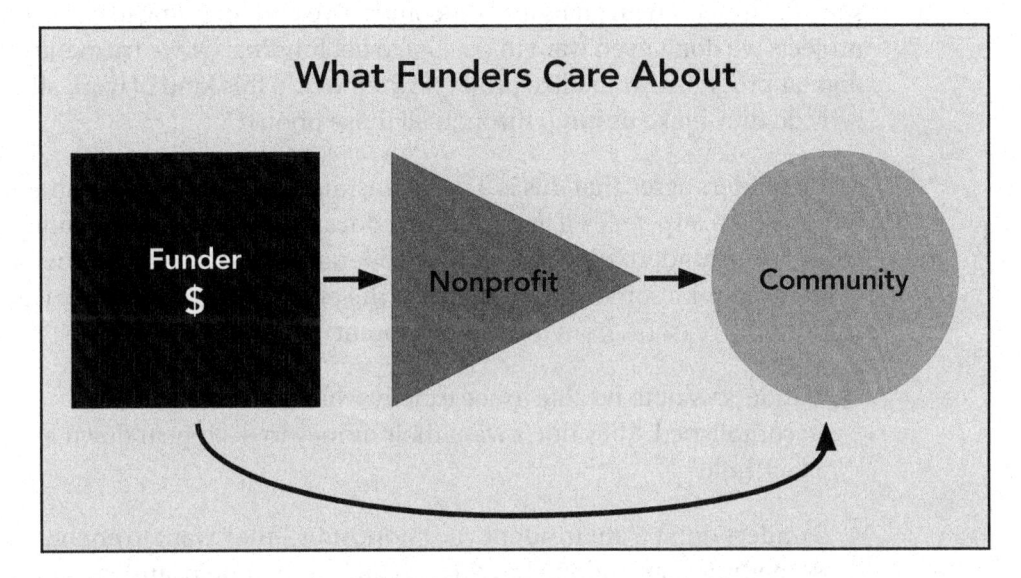

What Funders Care About

Funder $ → Nonprofit → Community

Funders have their own missions and their own agendas. They have things they want to accomplish, and in a sense, they "hire" nonprofits to carry out their plans. The nonprofits that carry out the work are agents that transform dollars into richer, fuller lives.

Grants are not about organizations—they're about the clients. When you write grant proposals, remember that funders aren't interested in your organization for its own sake—funders are interested in your clients and in how your programs are going to make the community a better place to live. Keep your eye on the people who are the end users of funders' money.

The Great Disconnect

There's only one problem with this line of thinking. While funders are looking for projects that will produce measurable results to benefit the community, nonprofits often come to the grantseeking process with a different agenda: They need funds to support their programs, and they look at grants as one of several funding streams. Sure, sometimes they have a project, but more often than not, they're looking for a way to fund their ongoing operations.

You often hear complaints about this disconnect at meetings of grantwriters: "Why can't the funders understand that we need operating funds—support for the good work we do day in and day out? Why are they always asking for specific projects with goals and outcomes? We end up trying to come up with projects we don't even want to do, just to get funding. Or we try to make our regular programs sound like projects when we do this kind of work all the time. Why do they make us jump through all these hoops?"

Many funders agree that this is a problem, and realize that project grants can be burdensome, especially if grant funding doesn't cover indirect (administrative) costs. Some funders advocate for more operating grants. But still, the majority of grants require some kind of results at the end of the grant period. Here are some of the reasons, from the funders' point of view:

- Funders want to be able to see exactly what their dollars have accomplished. They don't want their money to disappear down a black hole.

- Funders don't want to adopt your nonprofit—they want to enable you to do something you couldn't have done without their help, and then they want to move on to help another organization.

- Funders don't want you to become dependent on them. This is why the "seed money" metaphor is so popular. They want to help incubate a new idea or an expanded program, but then they want you to find other ways to keep it going.

Sometimes funders do recognize the need for operating grants and allow that kind of proposal. But even then, they will probably want to know what the organization's goals are for the year, and how a grant will help you achieve those goals.

In the end, there really is a complicated dance between funders and grantseekers. While both sides want to benefit the community, funders want visible results, while organizations want ongoing support. Successful grantseekers are aware of the funders' point of view and write proposals with that in mind.

Keep a file on each funder. Research news articles and blogs, note funder names from donor lists at other nonprofits, note incidental conversations at donor events, and keep notes from various funder databases. Over time, that file will fill up, and you'll understand each funder more and more.

How Do You Determine Each Funder's Motivation?

Funders have specific motivations for giving, and it's important to understand what they are. When you visit a funder's website, it's easy to skip over the introductory information and head directly to "How to Apply." But your chances of success will greatly improve if you carefully examine what funders are saying about who they are, how they came to exist, and what they want to accomplish with their grantmaking.

Begin by reading the background information on the website. Examine the mission statement, if there is one. Sometimes there's no clear mission statement as such, but you can get a sense of how the funder sees its purpose by reading the introductory material, often provided under "About Us." Read the history of the funder, if it's provided, and learn about the founding donors. Who were/are they, and what prompted them to establish this foundation? What is their vision for the future? How might your organization play a part in making that vision become reality? Go beyond what's on the website by doing a Google search on the donors and the funding organization.

A little research will tell you even more about some of the funders whose mission statements are provided in the sidebar. Everybody knows who Bill Gates is. As CEO of Microsoft, he was famous for demanding results, and he has carried that culture over into his foundation. To write a successful proposal to the Gates Foundation, you have to show what results you expect to achieve and how you expect to get there. Staff will look for evidence-based practices that guarantee success. The Kresge Foundation is famous for working to bolster the internal strength of the nonprofits it supports, as well as achieving community benefits. Although it has changed its grantmaking priorities over the last decade, it still wants to help its grantees become stronger organizations as a result of receiving a Kresge grant.

The First Bank Financial Centre is a state bank headquartered in Oconomowoc, Wisconsin. These days, there aren't that many state banks left—most have been taken over by national bank corporations. So this smaller state bank emphasizes community and neighborhood in its charitable giving mission—it

> **Example**
>
> ## Sample Mission Statements
>
> ### Bill & Melinda Gates Foundation
>
> We seek to unlock the possibility inside every individual. We see equal value in all lives. And so we are dedicated to improving the quality of life for individuals around the world. From the education of students in Chicago, to the health of a young mother in Nigeria, we are catalysts of human promise everywhere.
>
> ### Kresge Foundation
>
> Our mission: To promote human progress.
>
> We advance our mission by:
>
> - Creating access and opportunity in underserved communities,
> - Improving the health of low-income people,
> - Supporting artistic expression,
> - Increasing college achievement,
> - Assisting in the revitalization of Detroit, and
> - Advancing methods for addressing global climate change.
>
> ### First Bank Financial Centre
>
> The mission of First Bank Financial Centre's Charitable Giving Program is to help meet the needs of the communities we serve by supporting nonprofit organizations that improve overall quality of life. Our community bank also proudly sponsors events that enhance the vitality of our neighborhoods, celebrate our community's success, and support local charities.
>
> ### US Department of Education
>
> Our mission is to promote student achievement and preparation for global competitiveness by fostering educational excellence and ensuring equal access.

is clearly proud to be a local funder. Applicants need to demonstrate how they benefit their local community.

The federal Department of Education is the opposite—it is, of course, a national funder. Its mission statement sounds generic, but it strikes a couple of key notes. It views education in terms of global competitiveness—making sure America can excel over other nations in terms of business, especially. It is also concerned with equal access so that the educational system will give everyone opportunity, regardless of racial or economic background. These issues may or may not coincide with the priorities of every educational institution that considers applying for a grant to the DOE, so if you're planning to apply, think about how your program fits within the DOE's primary mission.

Read the grant application questions again in light of a funder's mission. How does each question help the funder promote that mission? How will your answers help determine whether your project is a good fit for what the funder wants to accomplish? As you write your answers, refer to the element of the funder's mission that you're addressing, and show how you can help carry that mission forward. To paraphrase President Kennedy, "Ask not what the funder can do for you—ask what you can do for the funder."

To Summarize...

- You can learn a lot just from imagining what it would be like if you were the funder.

- Funders want to use their money to make change happen, not to support nonprofit organizations.

- Your boss may see grants as a funding stream for your organization, but the funders see themselves as improving life in the community.

- Pay attention to what funders say about their missions, and reflect that when you're writing a grant proposal.

Chapter 6

Types of Grants: What Makes a Fundable Project?

In This Chapter...

- Why do funders like capital grants?
- What kinds of programs and projects do funders prefer?
- Is there a way to turn operating needs into fundable projects?
- Can you get grants for endowments?

Grants come in many categories: capital grants, program grants, special projects, seed money, pilot projects, capacity building, and others. Funders often use these terms in their guidelines when they describe the types of grants they are willing to fund. The terms also appear in database entries designating what kinds of grants are eligible for consideration by each funder. So it's important to understand what grant categories exist and what kinds of projects they usually cover.

Most grants focus on results, so the most "fundable" projects are those that have clear goals, objectives (preferably measurable ones), and outcomes. Also, you may find that a funder prefers a project that has a clear beginning, middle, and end, along with a plan for sustaining the gains that the project produces. But there are ways to describe results for ongoing programs that can make them more appealing to funders. Sometimes a change of focus can transform day-to-day operating expenses into well-defined projects.

In this chapter, we'll discuss grants in these and other categories, such as capacity building and technical assistance that can strengthen your organization's administrative aspects. We'll also explain why it's so hard to get grants for endowments, and suggest a better approach.

Capital Grants

Capital grants are frequently the largest grants that nonprofits receive in terms of dollar amount. They are often grants for buildings, sometimes described as "bricks and mortar." They can also fund purchases of land or remodeling projects. But capital grants are not always for multi-million-dollar facilities—they can be for anything tangible. They can include major equipment, vehicles, computer systems, or even smaller items such as copy machines.

Funders like to make capital grants because they can see what they're buying. There's no question at the end of the grant period that a building was completed, or a new MRI machine was purchased. However, it will be important in the proposal to explain how the capital project fits in with your overall mission and serves your constituency. Don't just tell them *what* you need—tell them *why* you need it.

Some donors like the recognition that can come with a major capital project—for instance, if they make a large enough gift, they can put their name on a building.

Have Your Name Engraved in Stone!

Not everyone can donate millions of dollars to name a building, but smaller donors can be publicly acknowledged in creative ways, too. In the '80s the Pike Place Market, a major tourist attraction in Seattle, needed to replace its wooden walkway with something more durable. For a gift of thirty-five dollars, donors could have their names engraved on a tile that would be part of the new outdoor flooring. The campaign was highly successful. From 1985-87, more than 45,000 tiles were installed and nearly $1.6 million was raised. The new walkway was paid for in a short time, and the names are still there, almost thirty years later.

Pure Genius!

Nonprofits frequently offer *naming opportunities* for rooms or public areas of a building where a plaque recognizing the donor can be installed. Gifts can also be recognized on a donor wall—look for one next time you visit a recently built or remodeled theater, hospital, or university building. Because building projects are so expensive, they usually have a large number of donors, including foundations, corporations, individuals, and sometimes government agencies.

Program Grants

Most grants that aren't for capital fund some kind of program. They are grants for something the nonprofit does, and usually include costs for salaries as well as materials and tangible items. Here are some of the kinds of program grants that funders frequently make.

Special Projects

Funders often like to make grants for "special projects"—something that goes above and beyond the nonprofit's everyday activities. The good thing about special projects from the funder's point of view is that they have a well-defined beginning and end. The need can be clearly spelled out—there's some reason why the nonprofit has

Can We Get a Grant for Our School Trip?

Lots of organizations hope to get grants for tours or travel. Maybe your youth choir is going to do a European tour or your team has been invited to compete in another state. This looks like a "special project," so is it grant fundable?

Unfortunately, the answer is usually no. Funders that accept unsolicited grant proposals see dozens of requests to fund tours every year. Given the sheer number of schools and youth groups that get involved in such tours, it would be hard to sort through the many requests that come in. As a result, most funders put tours on their "we do not fund" lists.

There are a few travel-related grant programs, mostly for individuals and with an emphasis on extended study. And of course, there are exceptions to every rule. If a member of the choir is related to a person connected with a grantmaker in the community, that funder may make an exception.

Uninspired

decided to undertake this particular project. The goals and expected outcomes are usually clear as well. The organization knows what it wants to accomplish, and at the end it will be possible to tell whether the project succeeded and met its objectives.

For instance, a music organization that has a regular season of offerings may plan something special for an anniversary. Perhaps this special concert will use more instrumentalists and singers than usual, or bring in a conductor of note. This production will be more expensive than most, but it will also be more exciting and provide a special artistic experience for the audience. It may bring in new people who don't ordinarily attend its concerts. This initiative is a good candidate for grant funding because it's a special project, not something you do on a regular basis.

Seed Money

One of the most popular metaphors in the nonprofit world is the idea of *seed money*. When you plant a seed, you need to fertilize the soil and water the plant carefully while it is young. Once it becomes mature and established, it takes less care and can grow on its own. Funders sometimes like to make *seed grants* to help a new and promising program get started. Their funding plays the role of the fertilizer, nurturing the tender young idea until it can prove its value to the community and stand on its own. The hope is that a successful program will eventually become self-supporting, either because its beneficiaries will be willing and able to pay for it, or because it will attract ongoing donations from individuals who believe in its worth and will continue to support it in future years.

Pilot Projects

Grants for *pilot projects* are similar to seed money. A pilot project is a new, experimental idea that a nonprofit wants to try out on a small population to see if it works. This might be a new approach to teaching reading or a new way to prevent gang violence. If the project works well with its first group of participants, it can be expanded to other organizations and cities, perhaps nationwide. This is appealing to funders, because their grant is *leveraged*—a small initial investment results in benefits for a much larger group of people. Organizations can approach a wider field of funders, reaching beyond their local community, because a successful pilot project will potentially end up benefiting a national or international population.

Chapter 6—Types of Grants: What Makes a Fundable Project?

Expanding or Improving Existing Programs

If you have a program that works so well that you can't meet the demand with current resources, it's a good candidate for a grant. A funder may be interested in helping you extend it to more clients or new groups of people. Or maybe your program director has new ideas for improving the current offerings. You can seek a grant to make your good program even better. Anything new or innovative can attract grant funding.

Turning Operational Needs into Fundable Projects

But what about funding for *operational expenses*—the good, solid work you do week in and week out? Is it possible to get grant funding for these activities? Yes, nonprofits get grants for their ordinary activities all the time. But sometimes they have to be a little inventive to make "operations" sound more like "special projects."

Think again about that arts organization with a regular season of performances. In one sense, every production is a separate project, and you may be able to find sponsorships for each, whether as grants or as more direct gifts. Some grantors, including

---

"Please Send Money!"

There are some proposals that say essentially, "Here's what we do—please send money!" Of course, they're not as blunt as that. The organization describes its mission, clientele, and services, and makes a strong case for the value of its activities. At their core, these types of appeals boil down to saying, "If we had more money, we could help more people." Yet, to a funder, every organization could make the same appeal. As a result, such proposals don't give funders a good way to choose which requests to fund and which to decline.

These appeals are really better suited for individual donors via a solicitation for the annual fund. For grants, funders want to see those goals and objectives we've been talking about. Just describing the meals you serve homeless people or the after-school programs you run may not be enough, unless you can talk about how you improve your clients' lives in the long run.

Uninspired

corporations, like to have their names associated with culture, and will be especially thrilled to see their names projected on the curtain before your performance. (When public television was new to the US, some wits suggested that PBS stood for Petroleum Broadcasting System, due to the frequency of sponsorships by oil companies.)

What about an organization with an educational component? You may offer a series of classes or workshops every year, but you can make them more grant fundable by describing goals and activities for the coming year, and describing the schools with which you're collaborating. Many grantors want to reach out to minorities and people with low incomes, so if you're working with schools that have a diverse student body and a high proportion of students eligible for free and reduced-price lunch, funders may be interested. Or maybe you're an environmental organization trying to get kids more interested in the outdoors, for science, recreation, or understanding the need for conservation. If you can demonstrate the goals and benefits of your programs, they become much more fundable.

Organizational Grants

There is a third category of grant funding: grants that benefit the organization itself. Although funders tend to prefer capital

> ### So You Need a Grant to Pay Your Director's Salary
>
> Nonprofits often want to write grants for salaries: "We need to get a grant to pay our executive director." Funders are usually not too keen on these proposals, because they see them as black holes. "If we fund your director this year, how are you going to find the money to pay her next year?" Also, just paying a salary is not going to produce results, apart from keeping the organization going.
>
> A better approach is to think about what this staff person will be tasked with accomplishing in the next year. Will your director be developing a new program? Then write a proposal to fund the new program, and include the portion of the director's salary that will be spent on the project. Focusing on what staff will accomplish, rather than on the salary itself, will create a better opportunity for grant funding.
>
> **Inspiration**

and program grants over those that support the administrative aspects of a nonprofit, there are certain kinds of grants that will fund the back-office activities of an organization.

Capacity Building

Capacity building is a term of art that means expanding the capacity of an organization to carry out its mission more effectively. Capacity building includes looking at all phases of an organization's operations. For example, a growing organization knows that a key part of its future growth rests upon raising a third of its budget from individual donors through an annual campaign and special events. Staff may know that it lacks the ability to efficiently track the donor data needed to achieve that level of giving. Many funders would see a grant to install donor software and provide related staff training as an important capacity-building activity for an organization in that situation. If an organization is more efficient, has better systems and management, and has better-trained personnel, it will be able to serve its clients better.

The Campion Foundation explains its capacity-building program in this way:

> *We believe that an organization with a strong vision, effective governance and leadership, a robust fundraising program, and sound internal systems is better positioned to achieve program goals. Moreover, we believe that organizations build their adaptive capacity—the resilience and flexibility to adapt during times of stress as well as to be able to respond to new opportunities—when the critical building blocks of organizational health are in place and functioning smoothly.*

So a nonprofit might be able to get a capacity-building grant to pay for board development or assistance in developing a strategic plan. Or a capacity-building grant might pay for additional staff dedicated to marketing because these new staff members will be able to strengthen the organization financially to enable it to reach more people or provide improved services. This looks a lot like getting a grant to pay for salaries, but in this case, the new staff members will strengthen the organization in the long term. With capacity-building support, the nonprofit will soon have more revenue with which to pay staff in the future, after the grant period ends.

Technical Assistance

Technical assistance is support that helps a nonprofit do its work more effectively. It is closely related to capacity building, but the grants tend to be smaller and more limited. A technical assistance grant might pay a consultant to facilitate your board retreat or offer a workshop in grantwriting for your staff. It might pay for training in cultural competency so program staff can better understand clients from other cultures. Or it might pay for someone to help you learn how to use your organization's new database. The short-term training will result in long-term improvements in your organization's ability to serve its clients.

Process Grants

There are other kinds of grants that can be characterized more by how they're given rather than for what they're given. They come with certain conditions that recipients must meet to receive the funds.

Challenge Grants

Some funders will make *challenge grants*, which are contingent on the applicant raising a stated amount of money for the project. This is a common approach for capital projects such as buildings. The funder agrees to give a certain amount if and only if the nonprofit has raised *x* amount of dollars within the agreed-upon timeframe. The nonprofit can use this challenge grant as an incentive to encourage community donors to give by a

---

Are You Requesting Funding for a Means or an End?

Sometimes a request for a specific cost can be more fundable if it's reframed as part of a larger program. On a listserve, a grantwriter new to the field wrote, "I've been researching to find funders who will accept a grant application for funding background checks for volunteers. Any advice, experience, feedback would be most welcome."

An experienced grantwriter replied, "Rather than trying to find a funder who would support this specific expenditure, I would suggest applying for grants to support the program that uses the volunteers and include the cost of the background checks as a line item in your program budget. That way, each program grant will support a portion of the background check expense."

This is excellent advice, because then the background checks can be seen as a means to the end of providing excellent—and safe—service to the clients.

Inspiration

certain date. "Please send in your donation by November 1 to help us secure a $1 million grant from the Goldmine Foundation."

Matching Grants

Matching grants are also offered on a contingency basis. The recipient must raise x dollars from other donors to qualify for a matching grant from the funder. The match can be 1:1 (for every dollar from other donors, the End of the Rainbow Foundation will match it with another dollar), or in higher ratios such as 2:1 or 3:1 (the nonprofit must raise two or three dollars, respectively, for every one dollar in matching funds from the grantor). Government grants often require matching funds and contain very precise requirements for what kinds of income can be counted as a match.

What about Grants for Endowments?

An *endowment fund* is a sum of money (the principal) set aside to generate income for a nonprofit organization. The principal is not to be touched and is sometimes legally restricted. The income generated by the fund's investments can be used to support the organization's activities. Some private universities have large endowments—Harvard's was up to $32 billion as of September 2013. Universities often have endowed professorships and scholarship funds. Sometimes

Sorry, Volunteer Work Isn't a Match

A community orchestra made up primarily of volunteer musicians was applying for a grant from the National Endowment for the Arts. It hadn't read the directions very carefully and was surprised when it got to the part about required matching funds. At first, the orchestra thought it had an easy solution: Assign a dollar value to the time and expertise donated by its volunteer musicians, and that in-kind donation could serve as a match for the federal funds. But then the orchestra read the directions one more time. They said the matching funds had to be in cash—in-kind donations of time and effort (no matter how expert) did not count. The orchestra had to go back to the drawing board to construct a budget for its proposal.

Uninspired

arts organizations and other nonprofits also have endowments. Even though most endowments yield only about 5 percent of asset value per year, they are very valuable because the income they generate is unrestricted and dependable (unless the stock market crashes).

So can you apply for grants to be used for endowments? Usually not. Many funders specifically state that they will not support endowments; others may do so on a limited basis. But for the most part, funders want to see their grant money used immediately. They want to be able to see what their money accomplishes in the short term. Also, many foundations have endowments themselves and don't want to see money transferred from their endowment to yours.

Planned Giving

A more promising source for endowment money is planned giving. When individuals make gifts through their wills or set up charitable remainder trusts, their motivation is to continue to support an organization they love after they have passed away. They're looking for a kind of immortality, and in that case, an endowment is an excellent choice, since it is a sum of money that will generate interest in perpetuity. Grants are for right now; bequests are for the future.

To Summarize...

- Capital grants appeal to funders because they're buying something tangible and the funder can get public recognition for it.
- Program grants need to be able to show results, and most likely a plan for sustainability.
- To get funding for your operational needs, reframe them as programs with goals and outcomes.
- You can get funding for the administrative aspects of your organization through capacity-building and technical-assistance grants.
- To build your endowment, planned giving is better than grantseeking.

Chapter 7

Grants and Your Organization's Budget

In This Chapter...

- How do grants fit into the overall fundraising picture?
- What's special about grants for capital campaigns?
- What about grants for operating budgets?
- What is a revenue model and why is it important?

Ten or twenty years ago, we'd come across new groups expecting to start and sustain themselves primarily through grants. We even had people ask if they could write a grant for the cost of formalizing their organizations—for example, the cost of a lawyer to complete the application for 501(c)(3) status and to pay the application fee. We see this pattern less now, as most nonprofits realize that they can't support themselves solely with grants.

Understanding the role of grants in your organization's fundraising is still a challenge. The grants you can get vary, based on the services your organization provides. They can also vary from program to program: Some programs may be more attractive to funders than others. Your ability to find and get grants will depend on the type of funding sought, from operating funds to special projects to major capital campaigns.

In the last chapter, we discussed the different types of grants that funders make. In this one, we'll look at them again and discuss how each affects your fundraising strategy. Your grant success depends on the relationship between your project and the types of grants a funder prefers to make.

Grants and Your Fundraising

Grant opportunities vary with each type of request. A mistake that many new grantwriters make is looking primarily at only two factors in their grant research:

- Who makes grants to organizations in our area (geographic focus)?
- Who gives grants to organizations like ours (program focus)?

Grant research needs to include one more factor—*the type of grant you need*. You can be in a funder's geographic area and offer a service it supports but be turned down if you ask for operating support from a funder that doesn't make grants for operating support. Many funders make some combination of capital, project, or operating grants. Each has its own possibilities and limitations.

Grants and Capital Campaigns

Capital grants are usually for building projects. While any campaign to amass money (capital) could be called a capital campaign, the general usage of the term implies a major initiative that involves facilities, which can range from a building to a playfield.

There is a saying in the capital campaign world that "buildings are built by constituencies." This means that the core support for a capital campaign usually comes from contributors who've been with you for years. That includes funders who've funded you in the past.

Most major capital campaigns begin with a handful of individual donors. One or more of these donors may make gifts in the range of 10-15 percent of the total campaign. These *leadership gifts* are critical. And most often, these lead gifts come from dedicated individuals who've supported your efforts for years.

Chapter 7—Grants and Your Organization's Budget

This base of support is critical to attracting grants. Funders realize that few capital campaigns succeed without significant support from individual donors. Even though grants may eventually compose 40 or 50 percent of a project, funders often rely upon seeing commitments from individual donors before they commit to a campaign.

Project Grants

Project grants are a lot like capital grants. They are smaller, but like building projects, they have a beginning and an end. That's a key feature that makes them different from operating grants. Project grants can support the short-term costs for expanding a program or starting a new one. They can also help acquire

---

Uninspired

Leadership Gifts

In a standard capital campaign pyramid, the top gift should equal around 15 percent of the total effort. That is the *lead gift*. It is your largest gift and influences other top-level support. You will often find that funders will hesitate to commit their grants until the lead donor is in place.

If you plan to create naming opportunities for a project, be sure to do that before you begin accepting gifts. Some donors are highly motivated by naming opportunities and some only care that they are recognized appropriately. One error that inexperienced organizations sometimes make is agreeing to name a facility or portions of a facility without adequate planning.

For example, The Kids Place is a small rural child care facility that struggled for many years to develop a capital campaign to open another badly needed site. The board decided to take a leap of faith and start a $2 million campaign, kicked off by a board member's $100,000 gift. In the rush of excitement that followed, the board decided to name the new center after that donor.

What's the problem? By making the $100,000 the naming gift for the new building, the organization effectively put a lid on the size of gifts from there on out. Few donors were excited about making a gift of $100,000 or more to the campaign at that point. A successful $2 million campaign usually needs one gift at $200,000 and three or more at the $100,000 level.

new equipment, such as a computer system or software, and pay for staff training to use it.

Project grants can be a way to build rapport with funders. Many funders like a first grant to a new organization to be relatively small. That way, the funder can test both how you carry out projects and how you handle grant reporting. A small grant or two can create a track record that may open the door for larger grants. What's "small," of course, will depend on the funder's giving range.

Project Grants to Support Operating Costs

Project grants can support costs that otherwise might end up in your operating budget. When an organization needs a piece of equipment or has a special office expense, the first reaction can be to just pay the expense out of the checkbook. But with planning and foresight, you can turn some of these expenses into fundable projects.

The key to this approach is planning far ahead. In June or July of a given year, look ahead to the following year. For example, let's say you know that your organization plans to emphasize volunteer recruitment next year. That could be an opportunity to approach a funder to support redesigning and printing of volunteer materials and other costs associated with this one-time emphasis. That's the kind of project some funders will support rather than regular operating costs.

> ### Equipment Is a Means, Not an End
>
> One pitfall of equipment grants is that it's easy to focus on the equipment itself and fail to emphasize why you need it. For example, a computer is a tool. It may be a tool to better serve clients or a tool to help increase the organization's giving from individuals.
>
> Telling a funder what you plan to accomplish builds ties with a funder's sense of mission. Always focus on the purpose first, whether it's helping clients search job listings to find employment or building your capacity to support your work for years to come. If the funder likes what you're trying to accomplish, you may be surprised at the tools it may help you secure.
>
> **IMPORTANT!**

There's another reason why it's important to plan ahead. Funder timelines can stretch over several months. You may need to start pursuing grants in late summer or early fall to secure support for next year's project.

Grants and Operating Budgets

There are many foundations that make grants for operating expenses. Most of those are among the two-thirds of foundations that don't accept applications. A quick Foundation Directory Online search shows that there are just over 35,000 United States funders that give more than $100,000 a year. Out of those, only 11,500 accept applications. The ones that don't accept applications are often obligated to do so by conditions of the benefactor's gift.

Funders that accept applications understand that to be meaningful, operating support has to be significant and consistent. A $25,000 grant that isn't repeated doesn't have much impact. But $25,000 grants year after year to the same organizations will limit the number of charities a funder can support. That is the dilemma funders face when considering operating grants.

Grants and Your Revenue Profile

You can bolster your appeal for annual support by showing funders the role that grants play in your operating budget. One key to that is your *revenue*

Didn't Get the Memo

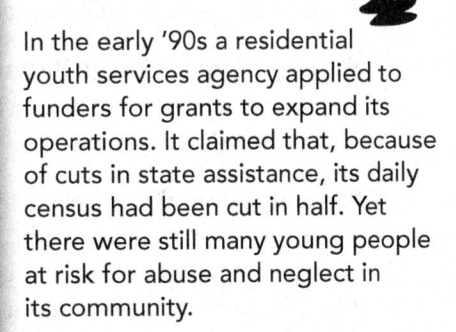

In the early '90s a residential youth services agency applied to funders for grants to expand its operations. It claimed that, because of cuts in state assistance, its daily census had been cut in half. Yet there were still many young people at risk for abuse and neglect in its community.

What this agency's appeals ignored was a key policy change. State family workers were now instructed to place abused and neglected young people into foster care instead of group homes.

If the agency wanted to make a case for an alternative approach, it had to at least acknowledge the policy shift first. Without that, its appeals created an impression that it really didn't understand its business.

Uninspired

profile. What is a revenue profile? It outlines the various sources of revenue that support your organization.

Your organization's revenue profile is heavily influenced by the type of services it provides. In fact, the revenue profile can vary from program to program within an organization. Here are three examples of revenue profiles from different types of public charities:

- A typical profile for a K–12 private, nondenominational school will see 85 percent of the operating budget come from tuition, leaving only 15 percent per year to come from fundraising.

- A nonprofit repertory theater will usually have around 50 percent of its operating revenues come from tickets and other earned income. The annual campaign, which includes many season ticket holders, raises another 30 percent or so. This leaves only 15 percent to 20 percent to be raised from outside sources such as grants and sponsorships.

- A food bank will usually have all of its cash revenues coming from contributions and grants while handling four to five times that amount in in-kind, donated food.

These are general examples. There can be special situations that make the case for a different revenue profile. A private K–12 inner-city school might be such a case. Since the families it serves can't afford to pay tuition at the full rate, it may have to raise 50 percent of its budget to subsidize its sliding-fee scale for tuition. The school may find funders that will find the school's mission compelling and be willing to make grants to support that tuition model. It also means that this school needs to build the capacity to raise much more money than its peers.

If you share your revenue profile with funders, you show them how their dollars make your organization's work possible. Grant funds may bolster a private school's ability to give scholarships that ensure diversity among the student body or help families that have fallen on tough times. The theater group may show how grant funding can defend against the vagaries of ticket sales when a marketing campaign falls short or bad weather cuts attendance. And while a food bank's volunteer coordinator salary is a core operating cost, a grant can leverage food for families in the community. After all, that employee musters volunteers who collect and sort donations. In turn, each grant dollar can mean tens of dollars in food to families in need.

Chapter 7—Grants and Your Organization's Budget

Understanding Your Organization's Revenues

To recognize how each type of grant may fit your organization's needs, you need to understand the role of grants in your organization's budget. That understanding begins by looking at your organization's IRS Form 990. Before you write a grant, familiarize yourself with your organization's 990 as available on GuideStar. Many funders will go straight to an applicant's 990, especially if they haven't worked with that applicant before. The 990 is one face of your organization, and you need to know what it is saying to funders and others who might look it up.

We'll address parts of the 990 throughout the book, but for now focus on page 9, titled "Statement of Revenue." This page outlines where the organization got its revenue during that fiscal year. A nonprofit uses this section to summarize the sources of its income by three main types: contributions and grants, program service income (fees), and other revenue.

The pattern of revenues for a particular program tells you something about the role of

Start with the Usual Suspects

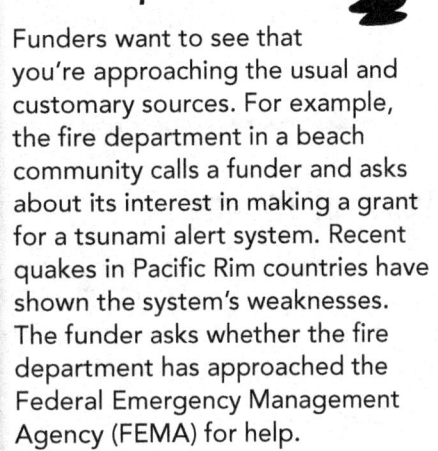

Funders want to see that you're approaching the usual and customary sources. For example, the fire department in a beach community calls a funder and asks about its interest in making a grant for a tsunami alert system. Recent quakes in Pacific Rim countries have shown the system's weaknesses. The funder asks whether the fire department has approached the Federal Emergency Management Agency (FEMA) for help.

The applicant says it really doesn't want to get involved with FEMA, and so this hasn't been explored. That answer would concern many funders, which see more good requests every year than they have funds for grants. They don't want to fund organizations that haven't explored key resources.

If there is a FEMA grant for tsunami warning systems, local funders might provide important matching funds to leverage that grant. That information can make the difference between a nonstarter and a compelling request. If there is a valid reason for the omission, be able to tell a funder that you've checked that possibility.

Uninspired

Part 2—Laying the Groundwork

fundraising and grants for that program. For example, child care agencies usually have significant revenues from fees. But nonprofit child care agencies tend to offer sliding-fee scales. Child care agencies usually use fundraising as the major source to fill the gap between the cost of service and fee income.

Page 9 of the 990 provides an organization-wide summary. Somewhere in your organization, there is information on how revenues support each program. For example, when you get a grant for a particular program, those revenues

> **Example**
>
> ## Types of Income
>
> Below is a general outline of how the various types of revenue show up on your IRS Form 990. This will help you understand where revenue comes from and how grants fit into the organization's budget.
>
> - Contributions and grants
>   - Allocations or designations collected from federated campaigns such as United Way and the Combined Federal Campaign
>   - Individual giving from annual campaigns and special events (except for the net from large special events shown in Section 3 of the Form 990 under "Other Income")
>   - Government grants, including grants for services to specified populations as opposed to providing services for specific individuals (for example, Medicare reimbursements are considered program service fees)
>   - Grants from private funders
>   - In-kind contributions
>   - Program service revenue such as fees for service
> - Other income
>   - Rents, if you rent your facility to other groups
>   - Sales of inventory
>   - Income from gambling, such as organizations that run bingo games or other ongoing activities

are credited toward that program's budget. Grantwriters need that information so they can understand the impact of grants on a program-by-program basis.

When you understand the role of grants in your organization and for each program, you can understand what type of funding might be needed for each component of your services. If you understand this approach, there are ways to look at next year's operating budget and create one-time grants for key items.

Finding Models

One useful purpose for revenue profiles is to find a model for developing or expanding a program. For example, a group of community volunteers sees a need for a place for children to play and learn. They create the Village Children's Museum. At first, it's just an idea. Their ideas take shape as they look at other children's museums across the country.

Often this research focuses on programs and facilities. But savvy groups go one step further. They look at the budgets of those groups and ask how they are put together. They might ask, "Once the Village Children's Museum gets going, how much money could we expect from memberships and admissions?"

The information the museum gathers on budgets helps them understand the revenue models for children's museums. There isn't just one revenue model, just as there isn't just one program model. But since they work hand in hand it's important to understand both.

Revenue models provide a vision for what a group wants to attain over the long run. A new organization or a new or expanded program takes time to get up to speed. A vision of where the organization or program needs to be in three to five years helps to guide your work. Let's say the Village Children's Museum commits to a revenue model that says it will need to raise 80 percent of its annual income from donations once established. In the early years, this figure may be 100 percent. But having a model and sharing it with funders helps you show them what you are working toward. It will also guide your work building organizational capacity. Any organization that plans to rely upon raising 80 percent of operating revenue year after year must invest in building that capacity.

Where do you find models? One place to start is by looking at organizations that provide services similar to yours. Look online for organizations both local and nationwide. That includes both organizational models and a model for a program.

You can find some information through GuideStar or other sources for looking at 990s. The first two pages offer information about programs while page 9 gives more detail about sources of revenue. But the 990 has limitations—donations and government grants are lumped together.

What can you do? Pick up the phone and talk to a development officer at that organization. Ask about the organization's revenue sources. Does it get grants, and if so, from what sources? Where does individual giving come from: an annual campaign, special events, a few major donors, or some mix of those? So long as the other organization doesn't see you as competition (a good reason to call someone from another geographic area), it'll probably be happy to answer your questions.

The Big Picture

Learning about your organization's revenue profile and the profiles of each program may seem like a lot of work. Yet funders are asking about revenue profiles because they want to support organizations that have solid prospects for sustainability. And new organizations need to show that they have a plan for the future so that funders understand that their start-up efforts are worth supporting.

To Summarize...

- Grants have a particular role in your organization's funding.
- The amount you can raise from grants will vary by service area and type of grant you want.
- Funders that accept applications have to balance ongoing commitments with the number of organizations they can support.
- Understanding how other funding supports your work is vital in finding the right role for grants in your development plan.

gifts
family
donor
charity
direct
costs
term
achieve
means
type
GRANT
needs
staff
results
plan
care
apply
groups
fund
year
budget
501 C 3
state
time
goals
accept
approach
pay
amount
key
giving
endowments
company
nonprofit
eligible
exempt
model
provide
funding
questions
charities
matching
annual
difference
website
tax
corporations
receive
board
example
guidelines
agencies
campaign
contributions
individuals
educational
dollar
community
support
future
services
grantmaking
deductible
programs
private
assistance
sources
process
clients
benefit
members
government
independent
research
education
profile
money
income
people
status
bank
purpose
terms
capital
volunteer
applications
mission
funders
organization
revenues
raise
foundations

Part 3

Getting Ready

You'll save yourself a lot of time and write more successful grants if you prepare well before you begin writing. It's important for your organization to be ready to win grants and to use the grant monies responsibly. We'll talk about how to identify funders that are a good match for your organization, and how to meet and develop a relationship with those funders, often before you submit your first proposal. We'll help you see the whole process from the funders' point of view, so you can understand their interests and priorities.

Chapter 8

Getting Your Organization Ready to Write Grants

In This Chapter...

- We have our 501(c)(3)—can we start writing grants now?
- What is a fiscal sponsor?
- What's the best way to get start-up funding?
- What organizational elements do you need before you begin writing?

Grant consultants often receive calls that go something like this: "I've started a nonprofit organization, and we've just received our 501(c)(3) recognition from the IRS, so now we're ready to write grants. Would you be interested in working with us?"

Just because you have your 501(c)(3) doesn't mean you're ready to write successful grant proposals, though it's certainly an important start. In this chapter, we'll talk about what your organization needs to have in place before you start writing grants.

Part 3—Getting Ready

In **Appendix D** we provided the cover pages from the Chicago Area Grant Application Form. This form is provided by Forefront (formerly the Donors Forum). It asks a few more questions than some cover sheets, but it's a good example of the organizational information you should have on hand. The information it contains is key to any grant request, whether a funder wants it on a cover page, in an online interface, or within a letter of inquiry.

This includes things like the full legal name of your organization, the names of your officers and board members, number of clients served, and the total annual budget for the previous year. At least annually, or when there are major organizational changes, this information should be updated.

Nonprofit Status

To be eligible for most grants, your organization needs to have federal tax-exempt, nonprofit status, usually in the form of a 501(c)(3) designation. (We discussed this in **Chapter 3**.) The reason most funders require it is that they want their donations to be tax deductible.

What If We Don't Have Our 501(c)(3) Recognition Yet?

Even if you don't have your 501(c)(3) recognition from the IRS, you can still apply for grants if you have a *fiscal sponsor*. A fiscal sponsor is an organization in a related field that does have its 501(c)(3) and agrees to act as an umbrella organization for your group. The fiscal sponsor will apply for the grant in its own name and agree to

---

Fiscal Sponsor, Not Fiscal Agent

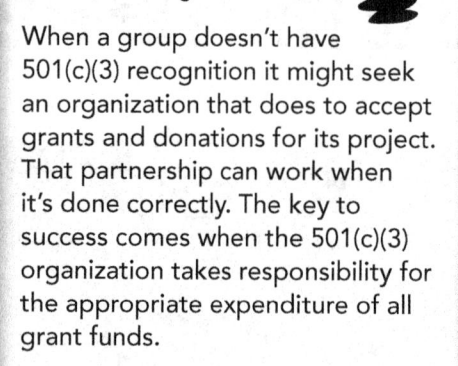

When a group doesn't have 501(c)(3) recognition it might seek an organization that does to accept grants and donations for its project. That partnership can work when it's done correctly. The key to success comes when the 501(c)(3) organization takes responsibility for the appropriate expenditure of all grant funds.

This partnership can go awry when the 501(c)(3) organization accepts grants but then simply turns the money over to the group that does not have confirmed charitable status. In that case the IRS deems that the grant was really made to the group without the 501(c)(3). That has negative implications for many funders.

There are a variety of ways to set up fiscal sponsorships, and Gregory L. Colvin's book *Fiscal Sponsorship: 6 Ways to Do It Right* is a great guide to setting them up.

Inspiration

receive and manage any grant funds awarded, but it will pass those funds on to your group or organization. Sometimes the fiscal sponsor will take a percentage of the grant as its fee for serving in this role. This arrangement is acceptable to many funders and can work well for fledgling organizations. However, the fiscal sponsor will usually not want you to apply for grants from funders that might be willing to fund the sponsor's own organization. It's important to understand the legal and ethical implications of using a fiscal sponsor.

Start-Up Funding

Nonprofit status is essential for most grants, but it's far from the only thing you need. Grantmakers rarely supply start-up funds for a brand new organization, unless they already know you. Your first dollars should come from your board and other individuals who believe in the mission, know the people who have started the nonprofit, and have faith in their ability to create a successful organization.

Pure Genius!

Getting Started through Crowdfunding

Nonprofits often get start-up funds these days through crowdfunding, which can be an effective way to get contributions from many small donors who like your idea. Some of the popular crowdfunding websites for nonprofits are Indiegogo, GoFundMe, and CrowdRise. Kickstarter provides funding for creative projects.

Here's how it works. You post a page on the crowdfunding website, explaining and promoting your project. (The website host will charge a fee, of course.) Let your friends and other supporters know about your crowdfunding campaign—social media is great for this. Maybe some people you don't even know will see your project online and get interested. Your supporters can donate via the website, and you can let them know how the campaign is going and what their dollars are accomplishing.

Crowdfunding has been very successful for a lot of organizations and causes, and is a great way to get started. It will also help when you do start applying for grants, by demonstrating that your organization has wide appeal.

If some of these people are closely connected with a foundation, they may invite you to apply, or simply write you a check that comes from their family foundation. This will be helpful later when you apply for competitive grants because you will be able to show that you've already been funded by a foundation. But that process is more like cultivating major gifts than writing grant proposals. You know people who have a foundation, you convince them that you're going to do something worthwhile, and they agree to support you financially. The process is more personal than a formal grant application.

With start-up funds from the people who are closest to you, you can get to work and create a track record that will stand you in good stead when you're ready to apply for your first grant.

Be Sure to Keep Records of What You Do!

Many nonprofit organizations start as informal associations of volunteers. They may run for years without paid staff and with little or no funding. It's important for these associations to keep records of their volunteers: who they are, what they do, how much time they put in, and what the group accomplishes. Even though these dedicated volunteers are not being paid, they are donating time and expertise that have a potential dollar value, and can be viewed as in-kind donations. You can create a budget based on what these activities would cost if the volunteers *were* being paid. What would that videographer charge to create your promotional video if you were a paying customer? What about the techie who developed your website? Keeping track of these things will be very important in establishing a budget when you want to write a grant to pay people to do the things that your volunteers have been doing for free all these years.

Mission, Vision, and Strategic Plan

Every nonprofit needs a well-written mission statement, created and approved by its board. Your *mission* explains your organization's purpose for existing and what it plans to accomplish—not just for the next few years, but for the foreseeable future. Make sure your mission statement really defines you, and is not just a hodgepodge of the latest buzzwords. (To cure yourself of writing meaningless mission statements, spend a few minutes clicking through the computer-generated mission statements on this website: *http://www.laughing-buddha.net/toys/mission*. They're based on corporate mission statements, but it's easy to substitute nonprofit jargon to get the same effect.) Along with the mission statement, explain why the organization was formed and what community needs it addresses.

Most organizations also create a *vision* to go with their mission—an image of an ideal future world that reflects the changes they hope to create. For instance, a human services organization might say, "We envision a world in which all children are wanted, loved, and well cared for. It will be a world in which no one is homeless or unemployed. All people will be able to use their abilities and feel valued by society." In other words, the vision statement is often utopian, but it creates a mental picture of the organization's long-term goals.

To approach that vision, an organization needs a *strategic plan.* This is a statement of long-range goals—usually projecting three to five years into the future. It states a series of goals that are achievable within the stated time range, and within each section, it states shorter-term steps or objectives that will be taken to reach the goals. The document is usually reviewed annually so that objectives achieved can be checked off, those that are no longer relevant can be removed or revised, and new ones can be added. A strategic plan is very helpful for keeping an organization on track with its mission. Many funders will ask if you have a strategic plan. The plan can be extremely useful in writing grants because it will outline goals and objectives your organization wishes to accomplish, and it will tie them to your mission. You'll be able to use this language in your proposals.

Track Record

In addition to money, of course, a nonprofit needs a track record of accomplishment in order to be eligible for most grants. Many funders will not give to an organization that is less than two or three years old.

If your nonprofit itself is brand new, you will need to rely on the track records of your founders, board, staff, and volunteers. Who are the people involved in this new organization? What do their résumés look like? What are their training, expertise, and history of accomplishment in the field of the new nonprofit? If the actual founders are young and stronger on enthusiasm than expertise, make sure you have a board of experienced advisers who can help make up for their deficits.

To establish your track record, be sure to document your activities, your clients, and most of all, your accomplishments. What do you do on a day-to-

Uninspired

Can We Hire a Grantwriter on Commission or Contingency?

If grant consultants are willing to consider working with brand new organizations, one of the issues that often comes up is payment on commission or contingency. New or small organizations sometimes want to pay the freelance grantwriter a percentage of the grant, if and only if the grant proposal is successful. This is considered unethical by most people and organizations in the profession.

The Grant Professionals Association (GPA) says in its Code of Ethics: "Members shall not accept or pay a finder's fee, commission, or percentage compensation based on grants and shall take care to discourage their organizations from making such payments." (See **Appendix C** for the full GPA Code of Ethics.) Other organizations in the development field such as the Association of Fundraising Professionals have similar codes.

The rationale behind these policies is that a grantwriter working on commission will not necessarily have at heart the best interests of the nonprofit and its clients. A grantwriter needs to be working for the good of the nonprofit, not primarily out of self-interest. Grantmakers seldom allow a grantwriter's fee to be included in the program budget, and hiding the fee in another line would be dishonest.

But how is that fair? an organization may ask. *Why should we pay the grantwriter if we didn't get the grant?*

Grantwriters are professionals who are paid for their skill and their time. Proposals succeed or fail for a number of reasons, many of which are out of the grantwriter's control. These include the strength of the project, how well it fits the funder's interests, and many others.

We're a small organization, just starting out. How are we supposed to pay a grantwriter if we don't have any money?

If you don't have any money, you're not ready to apply for a grant. Grants should never be an organization's first dollar. You need to raise funds from individuals first: people who believe in your organization and are willing to make a contribution to get you started. A good place to begin is your board.

For all these reasons and more, percentages and their ilk are a bad practice for freelance grantwriters. To preserve your reputation, whether you are an organization or a writer, stay away from them.

day basis? How does it support your mission? How many people do you serve, and in what ways? Who are your clients in terms of geography, income, ethnic background, level of education? What special projects or events have you mounted? How many people came? This information will be essential when you start writing grants.

Board

To be grant ready, an organization needs to have an effective board. You must have a board in order to obtain your 501(c)(3), usually with a minimum of three members. Your founder will be one, and often a spouse or partner will also be involved. But look beyond your family and close friends to establish a board that will be successful in governing your organization. You'll want to look for people with business skills—financial, legal, and managerial. And of course, you want board members who can contribute and raise money. Board members should understand that a certain level of financial support is expected, though the level can be assessed on a sliding scale, depending on the individual's financial capacity. Foundations often ask what percentage of your board donates to your organization, and anything less than 100 percent is unacceptable. (Even small donations count.) Well-connected board members who can open doors to foundations, corporations, and wealthy individuals are highly desirable to any organization.

Budgets and Financial Statements

Every grantmaker asks to see some kind of financial information from applicants. Of course, you'll have a project budget, but the grantmaker will also ask to see organizational financial information. Audited financial statements are ideal, but smaller and newer nonprofits may not have these, and even many organizations that are decades old may not have an official audit.

There are two other levels of financial statements. One is a review. Reviews are compiled by CPAs and can provide a limited assurance about the accuracy of the statements. Another level is a compilation. For a compilation, a CPA puts your information in the format of a financial statement, but the CPA does not make any assurance as to the accuracy of the information in the statements.

All of these statements are done after the books have been closed on a year of business. During the year, the organization should be producing statements that help staff and the board monitor financial affairs. That means a statement of assets and liabilities, and a statement of income and expenses. Software like QuickBooks can make it easy to keep proper financial records and generate these statements when you need them. But ask someone with an accounting background to help you set up your systems, and explain exactly what's meant by "restricted" and "unrestricted" funds. Grantmakers usually have someone on their board or review panel who will look first at the financial information before reading the narrative parts of the proposal. Disorganized or poorly kept records will doom your proposal from the start. On the other hand, a small or young organization with impeccable financial statements can make a very good impression.

Collaboration

Collaboration involves a variety of arrangements that focus on common outcomes and the good of the community. When nonprofits hear about collaboration, they often feel that it involves formal agreements between groups. But true collaboration can run from informal working agreements to contracts that spell out the relationship between two or more organizations in legal terms.

When funders ask about collaboration, they are usually interested in the broad view. You don't always have to have formal agreements with other organizations to answer that question. Simply being able to explain how your organization works with others in the community can show collaboration:

- How do the people you serve find your organization? Are they referred by other organizations or networks?

- Where do your clients go for services your organization doesn't provide? Does your organization actively make referrals?

- Is there a next step for people you've worked with? Do people need to move on to other service providers after working with you?

The answer to any of these questions can begin your story about how your organization collaborates in its community.

Why Funders Ask about Collaboration

Funders ask about collaboration because they often see requests for services that seem quite similar. We've often heard funders express frustration with what seems to be organizations providing overlapping services. This confusion often comes from funders not understanding the funding patterns that create these situations. But why is that?

Funders rely upon organizations in the community to help keep them informed about trends in services and funding. For example, government funding can be very specific in who is eligible for certain services. But people who don't qualify for those government programs may also need those services.

At other times government may contract with several providers for the same services. For example, there may be several organizations licensed by the state to provide foster care in your area. A funder could hear from several nonprofits that provide similar services. You can anticipate those questions and answer them up front by explaining your organization's unique niche in the community. The difference between what your organization does and what other organizations do may include geography, demographics, or other factors. The explanation may even be that the volume of service needed requires two organizations in the same area.

Collective Impact

Over the past several years, the term *collective impact* has been getting more and more attention. The term gained popularity as a description of efforts by funders to collaborate on their funding in concert with each other. Collective impact might be described as formal collaboration by funders. It is based on five key attributes:

- *A common agenda.* The organizations involved agree on a vision for change.

- *Shared measurements.* The organizations involved agree on what will be measured and how it will be measured when looking at progress toward the vision.

Informal Collaboration

There may be many activities that your organization participates in that may not seem like collaboration, but really are. For example, emergency services providers such as food banks or homeless service providers may meet on a regular basis. These discussions can lead to great examples of informal collaboration.

Funders will value hearing about those informal collaborations because it tells them that organizations that provide similar services are coordinating their work.

IMPORTANT!

- *Mutually reinforcing activities.* Organizations look at their activities in light of the whole project instead of just looking at individual programs.

- *Continuous communications.* Organizations realize that the only way to abide by the other commitments of collective impact is to maintain a free flow of information between all of the partners.

- *A strong backbone organization.* A key element in collective impact is that there is one organization that serves as the focal point for the work. This organization rallies funders on one side, garnering resources, and distributes those resources to a variety of community partners based on their ability to contribute to the shared vision.

What Collective Impact Means for Grantwriters

If you hear about a collective impact initiative and you think it might be an opportunity for grant funding, you should keep three things in mind:

- The strong backbone organization will usually be the conduit for funding to other nonprofits. Your relationship with that backbone organization, usually another public charity, may be your link to funding.

- Funding will be prioritized according to the common agenda and shared measures. As a result, you should participate in any community discussions that help develop that vision and those measures.

- Your communication with others in the general area of service is critical to being a part of collective impact.

The concepts of collaboration and collective impact recognize that many issues are multifaceted and require the work of more than one organization. Even if the work your organization does is unique in the community, the people you help or the community issues you work with are often touched by more than just your organization. If you fail to share how your organization fits into that picture, you may create the impression that your organization doesn't really understand its community.

To Summarize...

- You need more than a 501(c)(3) to get started writing grants.

- Working with a fiscal sponsor can be a good way to go if you don't have your 501(c)(3) status yet.

- Get your first dollars from your board and close supporters. Crowdfunding can be a great tool for this.

- Before you start writing grants, you need to have mission and vision statements, and preferably a strategic plan.

- Many funders encourage collaboration among nonprofits.

Chapter 9

Researching Funding Sources

In This Chapter...

- What are the best databases for researching grants?
- What can you learn from IRS 990-PF tax forms?
- How do you research corporate funders?
- How do you find federal and local government funding opportunities?

If you're going to start a grants program, you naturally want to know who is making grants that you can apply for. That's why it's important to learn how to research funding sources. There is a wealth of information online and in libraries, some of it free, some of it by paid subscription. In this chapter, we'll give you an overview of what's out there, and help you find your way to potential funding sources that will be a good match for your organization and project.

If you just google "grants in [your state]" or "grants for [your type of organization]" you'll get plenty of hits, but the data will contain unfiltered information that's difficult to wade through. It will include a mix of government and foundation grants, databases, and advertisements. It may also include deceptive information like the grant scams described in **Chapter 3**. You're better off starting with authoritative databases that will give you accurate information.

Researching private, public, and corporate foundations is relatively easy, using one of the many subscription databases available. Finding grants made directly by companies that don't have a corporate foundation is a little trickier, but there are ways to do it. Federal grants are researched primarily through a separate government website. For state and local government grants, you may need to go directly to the websites of the agencies providing the funding. We'll help you find your way through this forest of information so you can discover the hidden (and not so hidden) treasures.

Foundations

The world of foundation grant databases in the U.S. is dominated by two major players: Foundation Directory Online and FoundationSearch. These are two different products that provide similar information. Both these subscription databases derive most of their information from the same source: the 990 or 990-PF forms that all foundations must file with the IRS. These forms are public information, available to anyone on the Internet.

So why pay for the information when you can get it for free? What you're paying for is the ability to search the database. Search parameters help you narrow down potential grantmakers by fields they're interested in, where they fund, how

---

The Foundation Center (foundationcenter.org)

The Foundation Center is one of the oldest and most highly respected sources of information about grants in the United States. Established in 1956, it seeks to make information about grants and philanthropy available to a broad audience. Through its website, you can get training in grantseeking and grantwriting (some free, some paid), find information about funders, read about trends in philanthropy and grantmaking, and sign up for free newsletters. The Foundation Center focuses on private foundations and some corporate giving, but not government grants.

One of the many no-cost, helpful parts of the Foundation Center website is the "Funder Data" tab. If you know the name of a foundation, you can enter it into the search box and get basic information. This tool is actually a teaser for the full Foundation Directory Online, which requires a subscription.

Perspiration

much they give, and many other characteristics. The results are essential for developing a list of funders who will be a good match for your organization and its programs. Without a searchable database, you can wander in the woods of grant possibilities for a long time without coming up with useful information.

Foundation Directory Online (*https://fconline.foundationcenter.org*)

Foundation Directory Online (FDO) is a product of the Foundation Center. It is published as an easy-to-use, online database, including private, public, and corporate foundations. You can search grantmakers by parameters such as name, location, fields of interest, types of support, geographic focus, and more. You can also search the grants themselves. At the Professional level, there's a tab for searching companies, and you can search 990s directly.

With these tools, you can enter a multitude of parameters that will result in a list of funders well matched to your organization and projects. You can save your searches and results in either list or Excel format. FDO has recently added a new feature, Workspace, which allows you to organize your searches by project and track your progress with each foundation.

FDO comes in three different subscription levels, ranging from Essential to Professional. Subscriptions are offered by the month or by the year. If you need to do grant research only occasionally, you can subscribe for a month, save the results of your searches, and then cancel your subscription till the next time you need it. At the Professional level, FDO covers over 140,000 grantmakers and almost four million grants. It also displays information in maps and charts that make it easy to visualize the data.

If you live near a Foundation Center library collection, you can use FDO Professional for free at the library and save the results on a thumb drive, or email them to yourself. To find a Foundation Center collection (now called Funding Information Network location) near you, visit this website: *http://foundationcenter.org/find-us*.

How to Search on FDO

On the Grantmaker tab, it's important to start with Geographical Focus. If a funder is perfect for your organization except that you're in Iowa and it funds only in Indiana, it's not a match for you. So start by putting your state in the Geographical Focus field. Later, you can repeat the search, replacing your state with "national," which means the foundation makes grants all over the country.

After that, go to Fields of Interest. Click on "view index" to get a list of possible terms. Be creative in thinking of terms that might be helpful to your search. If you can't find the term you're looking for, enter it into "Keyword Search." You can further limit your search by Support Strategy (capital campaigns, curriculum development, etc.), but if you enter too many restrictions, you won't get many hits in your results list.

In fact, the trick to effective researching is to experiment with parameters and search terms until you come up with a results list of manageable size. Usually, a list of twenty to forty foundations is a good place to start.

At the bottom of the search page is a tiny box labeled "Exclude grantmakers not accepting applications." You may want to check it before you search so that you won't experience the disappointment of finding a foundation that looks perfect for you, only to see those discouraging words, "Applications not accepted." But after that first search, uncheck the box and try again. While foundations that don't accept applications will be far from the top of your to-do list, you may want to be aware of those that make grants in your field, just in case you can find a way to get an invitation to apply. (See the discussion of ways to do this in **Chapter 10**.)

Don't forget to search on "Grants" too. This will allow you to find lists of grants made in your field or to similar organizations. For example, if you know of an organization that provides similar services in a nearby community, search on its name. You may find funders that share a program interest.

Be sure to check the sidebar that shows a list of Recipient Types. You may find subject areas that differ from those under the Grantmakers tab, and they may be more relevant to your search. You may discover that an organization similar to yours has received grants from funders you were unaware of.

FoundationSearch/BigOnline (*foundationsearch.com*)

Foundation Directory Online's primary competitor is FoundationSearch (FS), produced by a Canadian company named Metasoft. Like FDO, FS derives almost all of its information from the 990 and 990-PF forms that foundations must file with the IRS.

FS has many helpful features and is constantly adding more. It lists newly registered foundations and provides a map search for them. It has a very useful chart showing what proportion of a foundation's grants are given to new versus past recipients. (If you're thinking of applying to a foundation that's never given you a grant before, it's important to know whether it funds a substantial number of new grantees each year or just gives to the same organizations every year.) FS also has ways to search foundation deadlines and news about foundations.

FS has an extremely useful tool called "My Foundation Manager" that allows you to generate prospects for your project, save your searches, create a calendar and alerts, and keep notes on your progress with grant prospects. (FDO's new Workspace tool appears to be designed to provide functions similar to "My Foundation Manager.") FS is sold together with BIG Online, a detailed training tool.

FS does not post its prices on its website; for pricing information, you need to call an agent and negotiate the amount. It's expensive, but if you sign up for a five-year contract, the annual costs are similar to those of FDO's Professional level. It is not available in libraries. FS has many wonderful features, and if you work for a large organization that can afford it, it is well worth the price.

In addition to these two "heavy hitters," there are many smaller companies that put out useful grant databases. One of the best:

GrantStation (*grantstation.com*)

GrantStation is a smaller and less expensive database than the ones discussed above, but it is still useful for finding potential funders. It has frequent sales that offer annual subscriptions at discounts of over 70 percent off the regular price. Some libraries make it available to their patrons for free.

GrantStation includes some government grants and even government loans. It also covers some international and Canadian grants. It limits its funders to those that accept unsolicited proposals or letters of inquiry, so while it covers fewer foundations than FDO and FS, the ones it does list may be more relevant to most grantseekers. GrantStation includes extensive tutorial and educational sections on grantsmanship, and it publishes a weekly newsletter listing grant opportunities. It's an excellent value for the price.

990 and 990-PF Forms

Every private and corporate foundation in the U.S. must file an annual form with the IRS called a 990-PF (PF for "private foundation"). Funders classified

> ### NOZA
> (nozasearch.com)
>
> NOZA is different from most grant databases. Instead of deriving its information from 990s, it gets its data from annual reports and donor lists posted on the Internet by recipient nonprofit organizations. NOZA scans these with its web bot and enters the information into its database. It then makes this information available to subscribers in searchable form. You need a paid subscription to search for gifts from individuals or corporations, but the foundation section is available for free. (You do have to register, but no subscription is necessary.) You can search by cause and several other parameters. NOZA is a rather blunt instrument compared to the searches you can do on databases with paid subscriptions, but it's a start.
>
> NOZA, which is owned by Blackbaud, is not the only database that searches donor lists. Several databases aimed at prospect research for individuals, such as DonorSearch and Wealth Engine, use the same technique. But most of these other products do not have the free foundation section provided by NOZA.
>
> **Perspiration**

as public charities, described in **Chapter 4**, file Form 990. (For purposes of this discussion, we include both 990s and 990-PFs when we talk about 990s.) These forms are public information, by law, and can supply a wealth of information for grantseekers.

There are many places to access 990s on the web. One is the Foundation Center's "Funder Data" tab described earlier, available via the *foundationcenter.org* web page. Another is GuideStar (*guidestar.org*). Both these sources will let you see the past two to three years of 990s for free, but you have to subscribe to their paid databases to see earlier years. You can find 990s going back to 2003 for free at Economic Research Institute, *http://www.eri-nonprofit-salaries.com/?FuseAction=NPO.Search*.

So what are you looking for in a 990? It may look a little intimidating at first, like one of those dreadful schedules on tax returns that only accountants understand. But with a little practice, you'll find 990s to be some of the most useful grant research tools out there.

On page 1, you will find the total revenue and expenses for the tax year. You'll want to take note especially of "Contributions, gift, grants paid." This is the total amount actually disbursed in grants. On the next page, you'll find a figure for total assets at the beginning and end of the year. Did the assets go up or down? That will tell you something about how the foundation's investment portfolio is doing.

Under Part V, you'll see a schedule of "qualifying distributions" (i.e., grants) and net assets over the previous five years. This chart makes it easy to see whether the foundation's financial position is improving or declining. Another thing these charts will tell you is whether the foundation has an endowment, or makes its grants on a pass-through basis. By law, a private foundation must distribute 5 percent of the fair market value of its assets for charitable purposes each year. Endowed foundations have a body of money (the principal) that is invested to produce income for grantmaking activities. So if you see a foundation with assets of $100 million that is giving away about $5 million in grants each year, it has an endowment. But sometimes you'll see figures in the 990 that show relatively low assets, with a much higher level of giving. For example, in 2012 the Xerox Foundation received $558,204 in gifts (all from the Xerox Corporation) and made grants of $558,220. It ended the year with a balance of $344 in assets. Many corporate foundations function this way. The company's executives determine how much they can afford to deposit in the corporate foundation that year, and then the foundation makes grants out of its current income.

Keep scrolling down until you get to Part VIII, which lists the officers, directors, and trustees. Here's where you'll find the names of the board members who control the foundation. An address will be listed, but it's often the address of the foundation or the family attorney, not the directors' or trustees' home address.

Finally, in Part XV, you'll come to the most valuable part of the 990: the list of grants. Every private foundation must list the recipient and amount given for every grant made in that fiscal year. While not required, many foundations also list the purpose for which the grant was made. So it may say "A Better Tomorrow Services, Oxford, MS. ESOL Program. $12,500." Invaluable information to the grantseeker!

Why is this list of grants so important? Because it gives you specific information about where the foundation spends its money. Most foundations have websites, or at least an information page that lists their giving interests, but it's in the 990 where the rubber meets the road. Sometimes there may be surprises—the 990 may list donations that don't seem to match the interests stated on the website. There are several reasons this happens. First, the 990-PFs that you can get online will be around a year old. Take a foundation that operates on a calendar year. Its 2016 990-PF isn't due until May 15, 2017. But due to the paperwork it has to file on investment holdings, it may file for and get extensions until November 15. By the time a source such as GuideStar puts this online, it can easily be January 1, 2018.

Another reason is that the funder doesn't get its website updated. Many funders run with very little staff. Those are the ones where you might see a difference between what a website says and what you find on a 990-PF. Also, don't be surprised if you see large donations to schools attended by donor family members, even if education does not seem to be a priority in the guidelines.

What exactly are you looking for in this long list of grants found in the 990? Look for grants made:

- In your geographical area
- In your organization's field (e.g., arts, early childhood education, youth services)
- To nonprofits with budget sizes similar to yours

These will provide the best indication of where your organization may fit in the foundation's giving priorities, and what grant size you might reasonably expect.

Researching Corporate Giving

Corporate funders pose a special problem to the researcher. If a company gives through a corporate foundation, it must file a 990-PF just like a private foundation, and its information will turn up in the same databases as other foundation data. But

---

Turning Guidelines into Priorities

Databases provide funder guidelines, but what you need from your research is a list of priorities. For example, under "types of grants" in a database listing, you might find scholarships. However, a list of actual grants might show that all the scholarship grants were made to private colleges. In such cases, the funder probably isn't interested in scholarships for your K–12 school.

Also, a grant list can help you pinpoint a funder's interest. Databases often use general terms such as senior services. A look at the grant list can help you see the types of senior services that interest the funder.

Finally, comparing the amount of grants and dollars by category can put a finer point on the funder's priorities. A look at past grants may show that one or two program areas stand out while the rest received much smaller amounts of funding.

In this way you can take the general list of guidelines and turn it into a picture of what the funder truly values, that is, a priority list.

Inspiration

if the corporation gives directly from the company coffers, it is not required to file any forms with a government agency, and it may reveal only as much as it chooses to about its corporate giving program.

Just finding the website of a corporate giving program can be a challenge. From the main corporate website, try searching under "community responsibility" or "corporate citizenship." A database like FDO will also link you to corporate giving sites. Enter the corporation's name under "Search Companies," and then click on the Grantmakers tab. A company may give through several different entities.

If the company does not have a corporate foundation but does do direct corporate giving, it can choose how much information it wishes to disclose. It may have a website or annual report containing information about its grantees, together with beautiful photos of smiling children and graceful dancers. But often these sources will say nothing about the size of grants given, and may not even mention the names of most grantees.

Here is where NOZA comes in. Since it derives its information from nonprofit donor lists and annual reports instead of 990s, NOZA allows you to search for a company's grants and gifts. Even smaller businesses that don't have formal corporate giving programs may make donations to local nonprofits, and these will show up in NOZA if the nonprofit includes them in its online donor lists. Since these lists often quote gifts in ranges rather than specific amounts, you'll see entries like "Bartell Drugs. $2,500-4,999." While the foundation section of NOZA is free, you must have a subscription to search for individuals and corporations.

The other way to research corporate gifts is through Google or other search engines, or by searching the archives of your local newspapers, especially business journals. But whether the grants will be listed at all, much less the amounts, is hit or miss. Often you'll only be able to find the really large grants that bring the corporate donor favorable publicity.

Search Tip

To search for corporate grants on Google, search on <corporate name> grant OR gift OR donation. Also try this: <name> site:org OR site:edu. This limits your results to websites with the suffixes .org or .edu, which is where you are most likely to find gift reports.

Perspiration

Board Members: Your Best Research Source

While databases and websites provide essential information about funding sources, it's important not to overlook your best source of information: your board members. Foundations and corporations with whom your board members have associations or connections are your best grant prospects. All those foundations that accept applications "by invitation only"? If one of your board members knows one of theirs, you may be able to get an invitation. Corporations often explicitly state that they will give preference to nonprofit organizations where their employees volunteer. If the corporate employee is a board member of your nonprofit, he or she will have even more influence in steering corporate grants your way.

So make sure your board members know how important their connections are, and know where you're looking for funding. Have a list of the companies where they work, and ask your board members to support your grant requests to their employers. They might be able to introduce you to those who make decisions about grants or write a message to community relations staff describing their relationship to your nonprofit and their admiration for your work. Board members who are executives or owners of their own companies may be able to make corporate gifts to your organization directly, without going through the grants process. Find out if your board members have family foundations that could make grants to your organization.

When you've put together a list of foundation and corporate prospects, make another list of all their trustees and directors. Distribute this list to your board members, and ask if they know any of these people.

Researching Government Grants

Most government grants will not turn up in the grant databases described above (except for a few on GrantStation). You will need to research them on websites provided by the government entities themselves.

Federal Grants

In the world of federal grants, everything starts with *grants.gov*, the official website for finding and submitting government grants. *Grants.gov* covers the twenty-six federal agencies that make grants, with more than one thousand grant programs. The website is fairly easy to navigate; the "Search Grants" page allows you to search by category, agency, eligibility, or funding instrument type. Another good website for researching federal grants is The Catalog of Federal Domestic Assistance (*cfda.gov*) which contains a full listing of all types of federal assistance programs.

It's also essential to visit the website of the agency that makes grants in your field to get a sense of its mission and priorities. The website will give you an overview of the department's programs, discuss its current budget proposal, and list its initiatives. You'll get a much better idea of what it funds, and why.

Making Sure You're among the First to Know

Federal grant opportunities often have very short timelines—the deadline for a large and complex grant application may be only a couple of months after the date when the announcement appears on grants.gov. For this reason, it's important to stay on top of grant announcements. There are several ways to do this:

- Go to *http://www.grants.gov/search/email.do* and sign up for the mailing list in your area of interest.

- Subscribe to grants.gov's RSS feeds here: *http://www.grants.gov/web/grants/rss.html*.

- Most importantly, contact the federal agency that is expected to release the funds, and ask to be put on its distribution list. Often federal departments send out "heads up" notices that funding opportunities are coming, and it's worth getting on that list.

Many government grant opportunities are cyclical—a particular government program may post opportunities in the same month every year or two. It's important to sift through past announcements in your field to find grants you'd want to apply for if they come up again. Most experienced federal grant applicants don't wait for the announcement to start planning their grant proposals. They know what's likely to come up and have much of their information, material, and collaborative relationships lined up beforehand.

Finally, many professional associations have inside lines on when funding will be released, or have staff tracking the progress of federally allocated funds through the release process. Nonprofits that want to apply for grants should be watching their professional/issue associations for this news.

Researching State, County, and Municipal Funding

Unlike federal grant information, which is centralized in *grants.gov*, grants from more local levels of government are not always advertised in a consistent way. Some states may have a central website that you'll find by searching on <[your state] grants>. But in others, you may have to hunt for grant opportunities under the various agencies that provide them.

Here it's essential to make contact with the individuals who manage the specific funds you are interested in. Almost all maintain email lists, and some have listserves where they'll share the release of funding information. It's important to find out who these people are, and make sure they know who you are. If you establish a relationship before you apply for a grant, you'll have a much better chance of getting funded.

To Summarize...

- To do targeted grant searches, you'll need a fee-based database, but you may be able to use it for free at your local library.

- You can find out a lot of important information about foundations by checking out their IRS Form 990s.

- Corporate grants can be hard to research unless they're made through a corporate foundation, but a database like NOZA can help.

- If you're considering applying for federal grants, find ways to anticipate funding opportunities even before they're announced.

Chapter 10

Increasing Your Chances of Success

In This Chapter...

- What's wrong with shotgun proposals?
- Why do some funders accept applications by invitation only?
- How can your board help you get grants?
- Why is it important for grantwriters to develop people skills?

Some people think grantwriting is a numbers game—the more proposals you submit, the more money you'll bring in. One key to becoming a successful grantwriter is disabusing yourself and your superiors of this concept. Fewer, more carefully targeted proposals will produce better outcomes.

To avoid being overwhelmed, some funders restrict applications by limiting them to those who are invited to apply. While this can be frustrating for nonprofits, it's important to position your organization in ways that increase your chances of getting on the "A-list." Other funders take control of the application process by issuing Requests for Proposals (RFPs). The criteria can be narrow, but if your idea fits, it has a good chance of success.

At this point in our discussion, it's a good time to look at pressures a grantwriter may experience on the job. When you're the only grantwriter on the staff of an organization, you'll find that not everyone understands the nature of your work. Your boss may pressure you to produce more proposals, or spend more time in front of your computer screen, instead of talking to coworkers or funders. On the other hand, coworkers who don't understand what you're doing may think you're just "filling out forms" and wonder why you don't make yourself useful in more visible ways.

In this chapter, we'll suggest ways to involve your boss and coworkers so they will help rather than hinder your work. Even if you're an introvert, you need to develop your people skills as well. They will make your job more enjoyable, and you'll write better and more successful grants.

Don't Shotgun Proposals!

Now that you know something about how and where to look for potential funders, you can start putting together a prospect list. But don't assume that once you have a list of thirty prospects, you can just send them all the same proposal letter (a practice known as shotgunning). In fact, this is an area where technology can be a dangerous weapon.

Funders recognize proposal spam just as you recognize spam in your email. Each grantmaker has its own criteria, its own preferred method of approach,

> ### Stop the Presses!
>
> A young, technology-savvy new board member heard that the grantwriting efforts of his organization were being hampered by a staff change. On his own initiative, he created a list of local grantmakers and entered the names and addresses into an Excel spreadsheet. He told the executive director he'd like to see "the kind of stuff" they sent to funders. Unaware of his plan, the executive director gave him a copy of a past proposal letter.
>
> Using that letter as a model, the board member set up a mail merge and, on his own, sent out a flood of letters to local funders. Soon, several past funders contacted the executive director to find out what was going on. Other funders sent denial letters, while some inquiries went completely unacknowledged. The executive director spent several days making calls to funders to repair the damage to the organization's reputation.
>
> **Uninspired**

and its own guidelines. You can't send funders a general form letter describing your needs, hope something will catch their interest, and expect them to write you a check. Not only is this a waste of time—it will actually damage your chances of receiving grants later. The funders will see you and your nonprofit as interested only in the needs of your own organization, rather than as a group seeking to create a beneficial partnership to help achieve mutual goals.

Shotgun proposals undermine your credibility with funders because they begin and end with a key assumption: that you can treat all funders the same way. But some things your organization does may fit with certain funders while different aspects of your work may fit better with others. That's why you can't send them all the same letter.

Two different funders might ask for background on your organization in much the same way. But one may be interested in the senior services aspect of your project while another may care about its impact on economic development. A good proposal will emphasize different aspects of your work depending on each funder's interests.

Interpreting Funder Websites

Database entries will give you a lot of information about a foundation, but your next stop needs to be the funder's website. This is where funders tell their own stories—who they are, how and why they were founded, what their missions and goals are, what they're interested in funding. They may provide a list of past grants they've awarded. The website will also provide guidelines for writing letters

Letters of Inquiry

Letters of inquiry (also called letters of introduction or intent or just LOIs) are a brief summary of your request for funding, usually limited to two or three pages. Many funders require grantseekers to submit an LOI first, before submitting a longer proposal. The funder screens the LOIs, and notifies organizations that pass this first step that they may submit a full proposal. Some funders pass any LOI that fits their guidelines, but then go on to fund a far smaller number of full proposals. Others use the LOI system as a more rigorous screening test: fewer applicants pass, but those who are invited to submit a full proposal have a fairly high chance of getting funded.

In **Chapters 14** and **15** we will go into detail about LOIs, which we introduced as the "Planning the Letter" in **Chapter 1**. We revisit them here as part of our discussion of the application process.

Definition

of inquiry and/or grant proposals, and may provide application forms or an online portal for applications.

In addition to reading the text carefully, be aware of the nonverbal messages the website is sending. What is its visual look and feel? Is it text-heavy, or does it emphasize photos and stories? What kinds of pictures does it include? Is a photo of the founder prominent? Are there primarily pictures of business people in suits, or of community members who have benefited from the grants? Or does it emphasize pictures of scenery from the areas where it funds? Is the website formal and heavy on compliance with guidelines, or more casual and creative? Is there a section on stories about people who have benefited from its grants? These indicators will help you craft a proposal that appeals to the funder's own values and culture.

No Unsolicited Applications

Many smaller foundations, especially family foundations, may state on their database entries, "applications not accepted," "no unsolicited applications," or "proposals by invitation only." You can also find this information on a private foundation's 990-PF form in Part XV, Line 2. (This information has been on page 10 of the form for many years.) These restrictions can arise for two reasons:

- There may be restrictions as part of a will or trust set up by the donor that provided the assets.

- There may be temporary restrictions by a living donor and/or a board of directors/trustees. Those restrictions can be changed if the decision makers so decide.

Many small foundations are an extension of personal or family giving. They may not have the staff (or the desire) to deal with the deluge of requests that even small foundations receive if they accept open applications. They prefer to give only to nonprofits they already know.

Unfortunately, there is a trend for larger foundations with professional staffs to be more directive regarding who can apply and how. This practice falls into two general areas: invitation-only submissions and RFPs.

Invitation Only

Funders use an invitation-only method primarily because they know what types of needs they want to address and have a good idea of what organizations can carry out the programs to address those needs. But if you're not on the A-list that gets invitations, it can be hard to get a chance to apply.

What can you do about this? The burden is on nonprofits to market themselves through media, including social media, and exploit their connections. Make sure you have an active Facebook page, Twitter account, etc. Try to get stories published about your organization in local media. Do individual prospect research on board members of foundations that show an interest in your field, even if they require invitations. Try to find connections between people who care about your organization and the funders. Then maybe someone will mention you to the right person at a dinner party, and you'll get an invitation to apply.

Your media work should focus on making the issue or need you address a community priority. That means highlighting both the direct impact of that issue and impacts on other community issues.

For instance, Salt Lake City, Utah, has recently gotten a lot of publicity for its Housing First program, which provides apartments for the chronically homeless even if they still have problems such as drug abuse and alcohol addiction, which usually disqualify people from public housing. It turns out to be cheaper to provide housing than to pay for the multiple emergency room visits and jail time often incurred by the homeless. The program not only helps homeless people, but also saves public money, relieves pressure on hospitals, reduces crime, and

How Your Board Can Help

A board member for an arts organization met a friend at a dinner party. She knew he was the president of a fairly large family foundation that was interested in the arts, usually with an emphasis on K–12 education. She mentioned a project that wasn't a perfect fit, but the foundation president was receptive anyway. "Sure," he said, "Tell your people to send us a proposal."

The foundation's website said it was not accepting proposals from new applicants this year, and for previous grantees, the deadline to submit a letter of inquiry had already passed. The nonprofit in question had never received a grant from the foundation. But because the president gave the go-ahead, none of that mattered. The arts organization was invited to skip the LOI and submit a full proposal. Two months later it received a grant of $20,000. What a lucky dinner party that was! And how nice that the board member was willing to use her connections!

Pure Genius!

makes the city more pleasant for everyone who lives there. (Programs like this exist in many other cities too, including New Orleans, Seattle and Los Angeles.) Favorable publicity for an innovative program like this can attract the attention of funders, leading to an invitation to apply.

Sometimes organizations can become synonymous with an issue. In the early '80s, Ruth Velozo became executive director of Northwest Harvest, a food bank and distribution center. Her passion for feeding people went beyond the concerns of her own organization. She was a tireless advocate for food issues, constantly addressing donors and government funders. As a result, when a food issue came up in the news, media called her for a comment. And when an organization has that level of visibility it gets invited to apply for grants.

Requests for Proposals

RFPs are one step more directive than invitation-only grant programs. Funders use them because they are convinced that they already know what issue they want to address and what needs to be done about it. As a result, responding to an RFP is something like bidding on a contract. RFPs usually outline the work to be done, the amount of money available, and the outcomes—sometimes called deliverables—that are expected. Many government grant opportunities—especially at the federal level—are essentially RFPs.

The key to success with RFPs is to be sure that your organization and the work it does fit all the criteria of the RFP. It may also mean that you are required to do your work in a manner that differs from how you do it now. At the same time, you can't abandon your core values. It is better to pass on an RFP that doesn't really fit than to chase funding. But if it's a good fit, it can be an excellent opportunity.

Institutional Pressures

Once you start developing prospect lists and planning your grantwriting program, you may have to resist pressure from your boss to churn out large numbers of proposals, even if they have little chance of success. To understand why this is a bad idea, it helps to look at the issue from the funders' point of view.

Funders are often asked, "How many grant requests do you receive and how many do you fund?" The implication is that, if a funder receives a thousand

Chapter 10—Increasing Your Chances of Success

requests in a year and funds one hundred grants, applicants have a 10 percent chance of being successful. Yet it really doesn't work that way. If you put in the work to learn about potential funders and develop relationships with them, you can increase that ratio from one in ten requests to a much higher rate of success—maybe seven or eight in ten.

It won't be easy. First, you'll write far fewer proposals. They should be better proposals if you've done your homework. But you may feel pressure from your superiors—from the executive director to the board—to produce a lot of visible work. You may find that there is pressure for you to crank out one hundred proposals to get ten grants, rather than allowing you to complete fifteen proposals to get ten. This pressure may come from the fact that pushing out a hundred proposals looks like more work than submitting fifteen well thought-out and targeted grants.

While either approach might produce ten grants, the ten grants out of one hundred will likely be smaller grants that fail to build real relationships with those funders.

Getting a grant doesn't always mean success. A $10,000 grant from a funder that has the means and interest to give $50,000 for your project is less than a total success. A funder may make a less than optimal grant because it feels pressure to do something. Sometimes this happens when the influence of a board member or key contact gets a request considered even though it may not really fit. But the funder may not be enthusiastic about making another grant for a future project.

The Quota System

An experienced grantwriter once had a boss who thought she wasn't producing enough work. To enforce increased productivity, the boss made a new rule: Every week the grantwriter would be required to write at least five inquiries and two or three full proposals. At least once a month, she would submit a grant to a government agency or a major private funder for $100,000 or more.

These requirements did not come with any promises of increased support from executives or board members who might identify and cultivate the recipients of these requests. There was no time built into the schedule for the grantwriter to research and develop relationships with the funders. She was simply supposed to crank out proposals and get them out the door.

The grantwriter knew that the only way to meet these quotas would be to submit numerous inappropriate proposals that would have little or no chance of success. She resigned her position shortly thereafter.

Uninspired

Get Out from Behind Your Desk

Grantwriting is in many ways a solitary profession, and many grantwriters think of themselves as introverts. But grantwriting, like every other aspect of fundraising, involves people. You need to get to know a wide variety of folks in your organization, including others in the development department, program providers and managers, the accounting and marketing departments, executives, and (in some organizations) the board.

If you get out and observe programs in person, you'll have a better understanding of what your organization does, and you'll feel more enthusiastic about it. You might even ask if you can spend time volunteering to provide service to clients. Once you have a firsthand knowledge of what your organization is all about, you'll be able to write better grants with fresh language, instead of just recycling the same old-same old that's been used in your organization's grants and solicitation letters for the past decade.

You'll also need people skills in getting to know funders and developing relationships with them. This is an essential part of the process that can be overlooked by those who think grantwriting is just about researching and writing. In the next chapter, we'll talk about how you can approach and cultivate funders.

To Summarize...

- In grantwriting, quality is better than quantity.
- A good media presence may get you an invitation to apply from a funder.
- Don't let your boss pressure you into sending out proposals that don't fit the funders' priorities.
- Get to know other people in your organization, and observe their work firsthand.

Chapter 11

Approaching Funders

In This Chapter...

- How can you meet funders before you submit a proposal?
- What's the best way to use your contacts?
- How can you make a good impression when you talk to funders?
- Why are ethics important in dealing with funders?

You often hear that it's always best to ask in person. Whether asking for a favor or special consideration, meeting a person face-to-face personalizes the situation. It simply makes it harder for someone to say "no." While this is true, funders don't have the time to meet everyone who has an idea for a proposal. Even funders that make it a point to meet with grantseekers generally reserve meetings and site visits for those whose proposals they've already screened.

Getting to know a funder before submitting a proposal is often less about a particular proposal than it is about putting a face to your organization, and there are a variety of ways to do that. Don't delay submitting a proposal just because you haven't been able to talk to a funder about it in advance. Sometimes it's the first grant to an organization that begins a nonprofit's relationship with a funder.

The hallmark of a solid grant program is the good work your organization does and proposals that showcase that work. The tips we share in this chapter will help you understand how to create and maintain relationships with a funder, which can only increase your grants success.

Meeting Funders before You Have a Grant in Hand

Grantmakers are constantly asked for help by people and groups they don't know. That's why a big part of their jobs is reviewing requests, declining some, and pursuing others. But when asked by people and organizations they do know, they can be more flexible and trusting.

While funders often act like institutions, the person who reads your proposal is an individual. That's why it's important to get to know that person before you even have a proposal in hand, so you can get a general sense of personality and preferences. Is this someone likely to favor an appeal that features facts and statistics? Or do you feel that you might connect best on an emotional level? You can write a compelling appeal either way. And it can be much easier to write your request when you have a sense of the person who will be reading it.

Making a Good Impression

Funders talk among themselves in a variety of venues such as Regional Associations of Grantmakers (RAGs) and informal funding groups. They talk to each other about applicants just as grantseekers talk about funders. Many grant applications ask you to list other funders supporting your project or whom you plan to approach. A funder may call a peer on that list and ask for perspectives on your organization. For this reason, your work with one grantmaker can either help or hinder your work with others.

Also, don't forget that the people who make funding decisions are a part of their communities. They can hear about your work from family and friends. When someone shares an enthusiastic reaction to your work, it makes an impression. That's why well-run organizations realize that their day-to-day work in the community can be as important as a well-written grant request.

Inspiration

Places to Find Funders

So where can you find funders? Do they ever mingle with grantseekers in public? Yes, they do. There are a number of venues and events where you might be able to sight and even meet the elusive funder.

Grantwriters' Associations and RAGs

Many areas of the United States have grantwriters' associations. In Seattle and Tacoma, we have the Puget Sound Grantwriters Association (PSGA) (*grantwriters.org*), founded by Goodwin. Nationwide there is the Grant Professionals Association (*grantprofessionals.org*)—see if there's a chapter in your area. These associations offer regular membership meetings, conferences, and other events where funders are invited to speak. And while we urge you to join your local grantwriters group, many of the educational programs are open to nonmembers. In some communities, the RAGs themselves hold events where grantwriters are invited to meet grantmakers and hear them speak.

It's very helpful to hear funders speak in person, even if you're just a member of the audience. They'll usually talk about what they fund and why, how they like to be approached, and how they make funding decisions. Afterward, there may be a chance to speak with them one on one, briefly, and to exchange business cards. Of course, this is not the place to talk about a specific proposal, but you may be able to ask if you could call later to discuss a grant.

Speed Dating with Funders

Some associations such as PSGA hold funders' forums or roundtables. These events invite funders to sit at tables where there will be spaces for seven to ten grantseekers. Each funder will talk for a while and then allow time for questions.

You may get fifteen to twenty minutes at a table, and then everyone will be asked to move to another table. In the course of a morning, you might get to visit with three or four funders. The roundtables usually have ground rules such as not pitching proposals to funders. You can ask questions about the funder's guidelines or terminology it uses.

Manufactured Events

Sometimes nonprofits have heard that if a funder visits them, it's likely to make a grant. They figure that if they create an event and invite funders, the funders will show up and be more inclined to make a grant to them. We've been asked about this approach by board members, staff, and a few grantwriters from nonprofits.

Usually these events attract few, if any, of the invited funders. Funders aren't callous, but they get invited to far more events than they can ever attend. Events that are compelling and worth doing for their own sake are important. But events designed solely to gets funders to visit you usually don't work.

Uninspired

Special Events

Funders frequently attend grand openings of projects they've supported. Often those events are open to the community. Also, funders may speak at community forums open to the public or simply attend them. You should make it a point to attend significant events that may attract funders.

But don't corner funders and pitch projects. Your purpose is to be seen and to listen. By being present, you may have the chance to say hello and start a friendly conversation that may result in the funder asking you about your organization.

By being present, you may hear things you didn't know about a funder or even learn of a funder that's new to you. Don't expect to hear details so much as to learn about what motivates the funder's decisions.

Using Your Contacts

You need to build your grant program around solid funder research and good writing. Those are the key elements for building compelling proposals. Yet there are times when contacts among your board and volunteers can help you open the doors to a funder. Your stakeholders' participation can help a funder understand your organization better.

One good way to use board members is to ask them to help set up meetings with funders for new staff hired for key positions. New executive directors, development directors, or grantwriters should review the organization's list of funders for the past three to five years. Then get board members involved in helping to set up and attend introductory meetings with those funders. That shows grantmakers that the board is involved in the organization's work.

It also gives key staff a chance to meet funders before asking for a grant.

Be clear that these are "getting to know you" meetings. Funders will often schedule such meetings when they know that you're not coming to push a grant proposal. Even though you're not there to sell a particular proposal, the funder might ask about the organization's current projects and future plans. In that case, it's appropriate to discuss those.

Another reason for these meetings is that someone may have dropped the ball on grant reporting in the past. Usually, funders will share such a lapse during an introductory meeting. New staff people can apologize and promise that it won't happen again. But without this kind of meeting, your proposals may be rejected due to that past error and no one would know why that was happening.

Almost every funder makes a few grants based upon a special connection. And you should pursue those chances when you can. But don't let that keep you from doing the important work of researching prospects, crafting proposals, and building your relationship with funders. A special connection may get you one grant, but a lasting relationship results from connecting the organization's work to the funder's mission and activities.

How to Talk to Funders

Funders are busy people, and many grantseekers want to talk to them in

---

Pay Attention to Process

We understand why shortcutting a funder's process can be so attractive. When you keep getting turned down, you look for other ways to get in the door. But consider the funder's job. Shortcuts may save you time or get you past barriers, but they can create problems for the funder. And more important, shortcuts don't necessarily solve the problem that's been keeping you from getting a grant.

Generally, if a funder has an application process clearly spelled out, it's best to follow that process. It can be tempting to ask board members to use their contacts to help your proposal along, or board members may just charge off and do this on their own. Yet that approach can backfire.

Decision makers at funding organizations often don't want to be approached with proposals outside the funding process. They don't want to be put on the spot by people with requests in hand. That's why their giving programs have staff and processes. As a result, taking a shortcut can create negative feelings among the decision makers as well as the staff at a funder's office.

WATCH OUT!

person, call, or email to advocate for a grant proposal. That's one reason processes evolve the way they do.

We suggest some basic rules for communicating with busy funders:

- Keep your communications to the point.

- Share your knowledge about your community and the needs you serve. Be an asset to the funder.

- Focus on where your organization's values align with the funder's.

Pick Up the Phone!

We've cautioned you about trying to short-circuit the application process by going around the program officer, but that doesn't mean you can't make your own contacts with the funder. If the grant guidelines provide a contact person and phone number, pick up the phone and call that person before you write your proposal. The instructions generally won't tell you to do this, and it may seem intimidating, but it can pay off in a big way.

If you've spoken with a person at the foundation, you've improved your chances of being given serious consideration. If you've had a conversation, then the person you talk to will think of you as a human being rather than just a piece of paper or an online submission. When your proposal arrives, you want the program officer's

> **More Than a Summary Budget**
>
> Once I was writing a letter of inquiry to a local corporation that asked for a "summary budget." I wasn't sure what that meant, so I called the corporate foundation manager. When I explained that I was calling on behalf of the Seattle Chinese Garden, she sounded thrilled and said, "Oh, a Chinese garden! I've been to the one in Portland, and I loved it! I'm so excited to hear that someone is building one in Seattle." After that I felt like I was talking to a friend. It was easy to tell her about our project and ask her advice on how best to approach her corporation. I found out a lot more than I'd originally expected.
>
> —Goodwin
>
> **Pure Genius!**

first impression to be, "Oh yes, this person called last week. Let's see what her proposal looks like." You've already stood out from the crowd.

Do Your Homework First!

How do you make sure your phone call leaves a positive and lasting impression? First, make sure you've carefully read the material the foundation publishes about its history, giving programs, and application process. Usually, these items will all be available on the foundation's website. If you have any substantial questions about the application process or guidelines, you have a reason to call and ask for clarification. For example, is there a question you could ask about the grantmaker's funding policies or what exactly is meant by a particular question in the guidelines? Avoid trivial things like how wide your margins should be or what size type to use. As you read through the application process and the guidelines, you may still have a question such as, "What does the grantmaker mean by that?" or, "Which category would our project fit into?" Those are the types of questions that you can pose to funders.

Grantwriters Need to Make the Call

If there are important questions to be asked, the grantwriter or development staff needs to hear the answers and be a part of the discussion. Don't delegate these calls to volunteers or clerical staff. Even asking a simple question such as, "Are the guidelines on your website up to date?" can lead to a deeper discussion that would benefit a grantwriter or other development staff.

If a funder specifically says on its website or guidelines, "Don't call us," then don't. Or if the funder doesn't provide a phone number on its website, don't hunt one down through the IRS Form 990 and then call a board member at home. This kind of sleuthing will not produce the results you want. If there's an email address but no phone number, try to make contact via email.

How to Ask Productive Questions

Asking good questions can open the door to a greater discussion about the funder's interests and how your idea might fit those interests. As we discuss in **Chapter 15**, part of your challenge is turning a funder's guidelines into a listing of its priorities. A phone call or email exchange is another tool for doing that.

Let's say you provide live music performances in suburban schools. You can ask what the funder means by arts education and whether that could include

There Really Is Such a Thing as a Dumb Question

A program officer picked up a call at her desk when the administrative staff person was out one day. The caller asked, "When is the next date for submitting applications?"

The program officer answered, "June 30th. It's right at top of the 'How to Apply' page."

The caller responded, "Oh, I didn't read that."

Since the funder only wanted letters of intent by that date, the program officer asked, "What kind of document were you going to submit?"

"A full application," came the reply.

The program officer told the caller that he should read the application process page on the funder's website so he would be clear on what was needed, the kind of grants the funder would consider, and how the process worked.

When you ask questions that are clearly answered on the funder's website, you leave a bad impression of yourself and your organization.

Uninspired

---

taking performances into schools. That would be a great question if the website didn't address that level of detail. And it might elicit some back and forth between you and the person at the funder's office about geographic priorities.

Another approach is to say (after introducing yourself and your organization), "I've read your guidelines and looked at your giving history, and I believe our program is something your foundation would be interested in. We'd like to submit a proposal, and I'd just like to tell you briefly what it's about and make sure it's something your foundation might consider funding. Is this a good time to talk?"

The emphasis here is not, "We need money, and we're really hoping you'll support us," but rather, "What we're doing is the kind of thing you appear to support, and I think you'll find it interesting." You're hoping that the foundation will want to partner with your organization to achieve goals you both share.

With any luck, the person you speak with will be friendly and helpful. Once the conversation gets going, the program officer may tell you things you'd never thought to ask. You may learn specific information about the foundation's interests that isn't explained in the guidelines, or that one of the directors has a personal interest in your organization or in something your organization is doing. You may learn that if you emphasize a particular aspect of your program, you're

The Golden Phone Call

At my first meeting with a new client, I asked how recently it had been in touch with funders who had supported the agency in the past. In some cases, it had been several years. I recommended that a call be made to tell each of these funders about the organization's latest plans and invite the funders to visit.

One foundation had been sending a gift of $15,000 each year. The development director called the board member to whom the requests were usually sent and invited him to visit. He declined but said, "Why don't you call our foundation manager, Nancy? I'm sure she'd like to hear about your program."

The phone call to Nancy went remarkably well. Near the end, Nancy said, "Tell you what—why don't you ask for $50,000 this year?" So the development director submitted a request for $50,000, and it was funded in full. Without that phone call this agency would never have received a grant of that size.

—Goodwin

Pure Genius!

---

more likely to catch the attention of the foundation board. Lastly, you may learn how much money you can reasonably ask for in your grant proposal.

There's no guarantee, of course, that the program officer will be encouraging. You might be told that all the foundation's funds are already committed for this year, but if you apply in a few months, you might have a better chance for next year. Or you may hear that the funder has changed its priorities but hasn't updated the website yet. Finally, you may learn that while the foundation supports what your organization does, its funding in that area is already tied up in multiyear commitments. Even in such cases, you've had a valuable conversation. Maybe you've saved yourself from spending a lot of time on a proposal that would have no chance of being funded.

That's another reason funders use screening processes such as LOIs. They believe that a quick "no" helps you more than a drawn out process that will probably end in a denial anyway. It also means they can focus their time and energy on proposals that fit. This is especially true with funders that do site visits or invite you in for a meeting about your request.

Using Email

Sometimes you may find that a contact at a funder prefers email to phone calls. A busy program officer can handle your questions during down time on the road or other times that a phone call isn't convenient.

Uninspired

Dishonesty Doesn't Pay

In the late '90s a public television station decided to get the jump on new technology by purchasing equipment for high definition broadcasting. The economy was booming and the station was doing well financially, so it started raising money for a High Def Fund. It got a large grant from a well-known foundation that wanted to help move the station into the twenty-first century.

Then came the dot-com crash of 2001. After many new Internet companies created a stock market bubble in the late '90s, scores of them went bust, and the market went down with them. Wealthy investors lost millions. Donations plummeted.

Suddenly the TV station was in trouble, and was even having difficulty making its required payments to the Corporation for Public Broadcasting (CPB)—the equivalent of paying rent. The board and the executives looked at all that cash sitting in the High Def Fund, and thought, "If only we could 'borrow' some of that money to pay the CPB!" But the fund was restricted by the donors, and couldn't be used for operating expenses.

The organization's accountant came up with an ingenious idea. The station owned some undeveloped land that had been donated by a supporter. If the accountant moved the property (or its estimated value, at least) into the High Def Fund, the station could temporarily withdraw the equivalent in cash from the foundation grant and use it to pay the CPB. Then when its cash flow improved, it could put the cash back in the fund, take out the property, and no one would be the wiser. Problem solved!

Unfortunately, a reporter got wind of this and the whole story turned up on the front page of a local newspaper. The station executive had to go sheepishly to the foundation, admit what he'd done, and beg forgiveness. The foundation cancelled the rest of its pledge to the High Def Fund. Eventually the station was able to repair its relationship with the foundation, but the breach of trust was serious.

Remember, being direct and to the point is still a key. And, as already suggested, make sure you've read the website information.

Ethics in Dealing with Funders

It should go without saying that it is crucial to be honest and truthful in all your dealings with funders, whether before, during, or after a grant award. Things can go wrong in the grants process, and most funders will be sympathetic if you explain the problem and tell them what you are doing to fix it. But if you try to hide a problem from funders and do something behind their backs, the consequences can be disastrous for both you and your organization.

The situation in the sidebar illustrates this point. What could the public television station have done instead? It could have asked to meet with the foundation executives, and included them in the process of trying to solve the cash flow problem. This would have given the foundation the opportunity to be part of the solution, perhaps through a low-interest loan. Of course, the foundation might also have refused to help, and then the station would have had to raise the funds elsewhere. But that still would have been better than the embarrassment the station experienced when the story appeared in the newspaper, and the humiliation of having to confess to the foundation about what had happened.

Funders can be your allies in hard times. The last thing you want is to make them your enemies.

To Summarize...

- Make an effort to meet funders at public events.
- It's okay to approach funders; just be sensitive to their limitations and feedback.
- A well-handled phone call to a funder can help you write a better grant proposal.
- It's always best to be honest with funders, even if you're in a difficult situation.

SUSTAINABILITY
INFORMATION
CHANGE
RESULTS
TARGET
EXAMPLE
CONTACT
MISSION
STATEMENT
OBJECTIVES
PLANS
QUESTIONS
SUPPORT
OUTCOMES
GRANTWRITERS
STATISTICS
GOVERNMENT
ACTIVITIES
PROVIDE
CAPITAL
IMPACT
FAMILIES
FUNDERS
PROCESS
PURPOSE
DO
ACTIVITIES
OUTPUTS
WE
WHEN
GOALS
UNDERSTAND
RESOURCES
COSTS
BUDGET
APPLICATION
GRANT
NEEDS
WHO
CAMPAIGN
CLIENTS
FUNDRAISING
SERVICES
APPROACH
ASK
DESCRIBE
GUIDELINES
NARRATIVE
REQUEST
EQUIPMENT
HOW
OUTLINE
WHY
NEEDS
EVALUATION
KEY
WANT
NONPROFIT
501C3
INCOME
PROPOSAL
ARTS
PROGRAMS
COMMUNITY
ORGANIZATION

Part 4

Writing: The First Stage

You're almost ready to start writing, but there are a few more hurdles to jump over. Before you can access a funder's online application, you may need to pass an eligibility screening test. You'll need to determine the submission requirements, and plan how to gather the information you'll need. For many funders, the first thing you write will be a letter of inquiry (LOI). We'll give you some tips on good writing, and then go into detail on how to write an effective LOI that will lead to an invitation to submit a full proposal.

Chapter 12

Preparing to Write

In This Chapter...

- What are online eligibility screening tests?
- What are typical submission requirements?
- How can you gather the information you'll need from your coworkers?
- How can you address funders' motivations for giving?

So you've chosen a fundable project, identified a likely funder, and made contact with the funder via phone or email. All systems are go. What happens next?

Before you can even look at a funder's application form, you may have to pass an eligibility screening test. That tool helps funders weed out proposals outside their funding areas, and it can also be helpful to grantwriters since you don't want to waste your time writing a grant that has no chance of success. But it's important to read the funder's guidelines before you complete any screening test.

It's essential to find out what you're going to need at the beginning of the grantwriting process, and ask your colleagues to help you gather it promptly.

One of the most important skills for a grantwriter is being well organized. Nothing will drive you—and your coworkers—crazier than being one of those people who is always in a panic before a grant deadline because you don't have the information you need.

And finally, before you start to write, reread the funder's guidelines and history one more time. Be sure you know why the funder is making grants and how it wants to benefit the community so that you can show that your proposal is exactly the one it's been waiting for.

Online Eligibility Screenings

Some funders require you to pass an eligibility screening before they even let you access the application form. If you answer something in a way that does not adhere to the funder's guidelines, the system will boot you out. Funders feel these online screening tools serve two purposes. First, they cut down on truly irrelevant letters and/or applications. Second, funders believe they are helping grantseekers by letting them know very quickly when their request isn't going to be a fit.

Grantseekers don't always agree that this system is helpful. Online screening forms can be a bit clumsy. They also require careful reading of the guidelines before you start them. In fact, if there is one critical piece of advice we can offer about online screenings, it is to read the guidelines carefully before you start. Be sure your organization and your request fit all the major requirements, because there may be some pitfalls ahead.

The eligibility screening may ask you to select which program areas you serve, out of a multiple-choice menu. On occasion, these can be "gotcha" questions. The list may include areas of service the funder does *not* fund, along with those it does. So it's okay to say "no" or leave an area blank. Grantseekers sometimes feel that clicking on every program area that their organization might offer is better. But a "yes" response may toss you out. You may receive an automated message explaining that the funder does not make grants in this area. The same thing can happen on a question about "types of support"—what type of grant you are seeking, such as capital, program, or operating.

These "gotcha" questions may feel unfair, but usually they are not the result of a funder being malicious. The companies that design online application software often set up boilerplate lists of program areas. When a funder buys the software, it's asked to check the program areas it funds. Rather than rewriting the list, the software assigns codes. If you check a program area that is funded, you move on to the next step. If you check one that isn't funded, you're told that your request doesn't fit the funder's guidelines.

Make sure to review the funder's guidelines before you begin an online screening. Don't expect to just dive in or you may make a misstep. However, if you do get thrown out of the screening and you think you really qualify, you can probably start over. You may need to close your browser and restart the process.

What if you don't see a match on the screening, but the guidelines seem to say that your project qualifies? This is another of those times when it's appropriate to pick up the phone can call the funder if you can.

Uninspired

What If Your Program Area Falls through the Cracks?

Because eligibility screening tools list only general categories, they can be especially frustrating for grantwriters whose programs don't fit into them neatly, even though a search of the funder's giving history shows that it actually does fund in that category. One grantwriter told us:

"These are my least favorite screening tools because our focus is mental health. Often, the funder may actually fund mental health services under 'health' or 'basic needs' but it is not clear in the online content whether it considers mental health as a health or basic needs focus area (many do not)—and an inquiry generates a vague or unhelpful, 'Submit and see what happens' response from funder staff. I can't pass the screening tool unless I just go ahead and select either category just to get into the system."

If this happens to you, and you know from your research that your program really is something the funder would consider, it's best to just go ahead and click on the category that seems closest to what you do. You'll get a chance to explain yourself more clearly in the proposal.

Confirming the Submission Requirements

Let's assume you've made it through the eligibility screening, and you're now ready to proceed with the application. These days, the vast majority of proposals (80-95 percent) are submitted electronically, either through an online application form or via email attachments. This has simplified the submission process in some ways and complicated it in others.

When working with an online application format, carefully read the directions for entering text and data, and saving your work. Often there will be a button at the bottom of each page marked "save." You may have to scroll down to see it. Don't forget to click on it frequently to save your work. If you move to the next page without clicking "save," your work will disappear. Run a test by filling in a few lines, saving, closing the document, and reopening, just to make sure you really will be able to return to your application after an interruption without losing the work you've already completed.

It's also important to figure out how to upload attachments. Run a test by uploading a sample document just to see if it works. You will probably need to upload many documents such as budgets, financial statements, 990s, and board lists.

Check the deadline, and plan to submit early if at all possible. As we mentioned in **Chapter 4**, large servers, such as those run by federal government agencies, can get clogged up if everyone tries to submit at the literal last minute. But even with smaller grantmakers, it's much better to submit early. If you run into technical problems, the funder's staff will usually be happy to assist you, but if it's the day before the deadline they may be overwhelmed with panicky grantwriters who are having similar problems.

Save Your Text and Data on Your Hard Drive!

When using an online application, it is crucial to compose your narrative and any other text in a Word document and save it on your own hard drive. Then copy and paste it into the online form. For parts of the application that are fill-in-the-blank or composed of numeric data, save each page as a PDF or screen shot as you fill it in.

Online applications can crash, and everything you've entered will vanish in an instant. If you've saved your text and data entries, this is merely annoying. If you haven't, it's a disaster.

IMPORTANT!

Early submission can benefit you in other ways as well. Sometimes staff at the funder's office will check to make sure your application is complete and will let you know if you've left something out. But since the deadline is usually firm, they can only give you this helpful information if you submit your proposal at least a few days ahead of time—a week is even better.

Getting What You Need on Time

As soon as you've figured out what will be required and when it must be submitted, the next step is to determine what information you need to collect and where you will get it. Go through the guidelines and the instructions for attachments. What information do you need that will have to be supplied by other people? Make a list, and then contact these colleagues right away.

If you show up in the finance office with complicated budget forms and demand that the staff supply the information immediately because the grant is due the next day, you won't make any friends. And you may not get data you need on time. So plan ahead and reach out to colleagues as early as possible.

Working with Coworkers

When you need your colleagues' help, call a meeting of the people who will be providing key information. This should happen very early on in the grant development process. In some organizations, the grantwriter may need to ask a superior such as the development director or the vice-president for advancement to call the meeting or to lend authority to your requests. If you don't have enough clout to herd the cats in your office, ask the chief lion to back you up.

At this planning meeting, give everyone a list of the information you need to answer the funder's questions. Ask for specifics—staff will be much more cooperative if they know exactly what you're asking them to produce. Be clear about who is expected to do what. Give everyone a deadline that gets you the information in plenty of time. Let them know you're available at any time to answer questions and help them complete their assigned tasks.

When it comes to the program staff who will help you define the proposed project, some people will be willing to write you a few paragraphs or at least jot something down in outline form. Assure them that spelling and grammar don't matter—polishing writing is your job, as the grantwriter. Other people may panic at the thought of writing anything down or say they're just too busy. Offer to meet with them and let them simply talk about their program—you can take notes and/or record the conversation. Do whatever you need to do to make it easy for your colleagues to give you the information you need in a timely fashion. Then send them follow-ups and reminders, if necessary.

If you're working with someone who is writing-phobic and can't seem to fit a meeting with you into the schedule, try writing up something yourself and sending it with a note saying something like, "I know how busy you are, so I took a shot at writing this myself. Is this right? Do I understand this correctly?" It may be easier for your coworker to correct and edit your words than to write the first draft.

Reading the Guidelines for Funder Motivation

Once you've set this information-gathering process in motion, it's time to start working on your own part of the proposal. Before you write, read the funder's materials again, paying special attention to the parts of the website that cover the funder's history and mission. Why was this organization founded? When and by whom? What were or are the founders' chief interests, and what are the issues they want to address? What are their assumptions and worldview?

Pay close attention to the language the funder uses, and reflect it in your own writing. If the materials say the funder wants to make your region a better place to live, show the funder how your project will help do just that. If the funder says it wants to develop each child's potential, use that language in your proposal. If the funder uses words like "empowerment" and "proactive," you can go ahead and use them too; otherwise, stay away from jargon. We'll discuss jargon in the next chapter.

To Summarize...

- When filling out online eligibility screening forms, pay careful attention to the wording of the questions and the funder's guidelines.

- Carefully read the submission requirements and plan ahead.

- Make it easy for your coworkers to give you the information you need in a timely fashion.

- Before you start to write, reread the guidelines to be sure you know what motivates this funder to make grants.

Chapter 13

Getting Your Message Across

In This Chapter...

- Why is it important to be aware of your audience?
- What is jargon, and why do writers use it?
- What are technical terms or terms of art?
- How can you format your proposals to make them more readable?

For a writer, it's important to know who your audience is and adapt your writing accordingly—neither talking down to your readers nor assuming they know more than they do. In grantwriting, that means adjusting your proposal to the interests of the particular funder you're addressing. All grantwriters want to write compelling proposals. But you have to remember that compelling is in the mind of the beholder.

The key to creating a compelling proposal is to frame your project in terms of what it will accomplish for the community and to make sure that accomplishment coincides with the funder's priorities. When you find funders that care about those same community needs, you have the chance to write a very strong proposal. But all of that can fall short if you fail to communicate clearly. Grant writing shouldn't be a writing contest, yet there are times when poor writing gets in the way of sharing your organization's vision and accomplishments.

We often see two elements that get in the way of sharing a powerful message. The first is jargon. Jargon is a common pitfall for all sorts of business writing and speaking, including grants. People use it because they think it makes them sound knowledgeable and important, but actually it obscures meaning. We'll show you how to recognize it and how to avoid using it.

The second is formatting. Grantwriters are tempted to play with formatting to squeeze more words into the space allowed. But those manipulations, such as small type and little or no white space around the text, often make the application hard to read. We'll give you some tips on how to use formatting to make a good impression.

Know Your Audience

How important is it to understand your audience? Talk to anyone who does marketing or website design about a project and the first question you'll hear is, "Who is your audience?" Even savvy businesspeople struggle when faced with that question.

Adjusting presentations to the audience is difficult for everyone. Yet it seems to be even more of an issue for people in the nonprofit sector. We want to appeal to everyone, and we find it hard to believe that someone isn't all that interested in our work. As a result, it's easy for grantwriters to fall into the trap of focusing on the tools that grant money will buy instead of the purpose of the project. This produces a proposal that becomes about the organization's needs rather than the community's needs. Look at the following two approaches:

- We need to install lights for the fields next to our school to create better playing conditions.

- We want to increase the community's use of the fields next to our school so we plan to install lights that will allow for longer playing hours.

There will be donors that find the first approach appealing, primarily alums who played on those fields in the early evening dark when they were enrolled.

But there may be funders you can engage if the school honestly wants to encourage and expand community use.

Whenever you approach a funder for a grant, you should ask yourself, "Why would this funder make a grant to us for this project?" If your answer is that the funder has made grants to organizations like yours, then you may be falling into the Willie Sutton trap, simply writing to that funder because it gives away money. If your answer is that the funder has supported similar types of projects, you may well have a case. Note, though, a similar project doesn't mean that since the funder bought a truck for another group, it will buy one for yours. Think about what the truck enabled that other group to do. The common thread is the result, not the tool.

When you're writing a grant to a funder that covers a variety of funding areas, assume that your readers are educated people who are not necessarily specialists in your field. Don't talk down to them, but don't assume that they know everything you know. Give them the information they need to understand the terms and assumptions on which your proposal is based.

If you're writing to a specialized funder, such as the Robert Wood Johnson Foundation (which focuses on health) or the Department of Education, assume that the readers are experts in their fields who will share a common vocabulary and knowledge of the subject matter of your proposal.

Jargon

Do you know what the following sentences mean?

- *Through a national enterprise community of practice, the organization will build regional representation and subject matter expertise with cross pollination to maximize dissemination of all collaborative materials.*

- *By the end of the project there will be a set of performance tasks with construct validity and rubrics that atomize the performance and levels of the skills and abilities.*

Neither do we, although we can probably tease out some kind of meaning if we work hard enough at it. (The first one seems to mean, "We'll share what we learn." The second one means something like, "We will establish an evaluation system.") But the writers knew what they meant, and they assumed their readers would too. If their audience were made up of people in the same field who shared their secret language, these sentences might have conveyed precise meaning. But they tend to leave the rest of us rubbing our eyes and wondering if they're really written in English.

Why Does Jargon Happen?

Jargon begins innocently enough. Someone comes up with a word or phrase that describes a recurring concept in a kind of shorthand. An example might be "best practices." This term describes recommended standards for a particular discipline. But lately, it seems to be thrown into almost any business communication, as a kind of guarantee that everyone is aware of the standards and is doing things right.

Other jargon infections begin when someone borrows a cool-sounding term from another discipline, often science or medicine, and uses it to make their own work sound more important.

One example is the word "ecosystem." Ecologists use it to describe the complex web within which a community of plants and animals interact in a natural setting. But now we're hearing about "the family ecosystem," "the nonprofit ecosystem," and a host of others. Soon another good word will be stripped of its meaning and turned into something vague.

That's the problem with jargon. A word that once meant something precise gets overused and watered down until it becomes nothing but a signal to other people that you know the latest buzzwords.

Jargon Vocabulary

Here are some currently popular jargon words. You can probably add a few more from your own field.

- Incentivize
- Disruptive
- Synergy
- Value-added
- Granular
- Empowerment
- Knowledge-based
- Drill down
- Impactful
- Win-win
- Bandwidth

What these words have in common is that they're overused and don't mean much. They are chosen because speakers and writers think this vocabulary will make them sound important and aware of the latest trends.

Example

Can Jargon Be Cured?

Yes, fortunately, a cure exists, and it's free. It comes in the form of three brilliant book-length essays written by Tony Proscio and published in 2001 by the Edna McConnell Clark Foundation: *In Other Words, Bad Words for Good,* and *When Words Fail.* You can read them here: *http://www.comnetwork.org/2010/08/jargon-books.*

A related website by the same author is the Jargon Finder at *http://www.comnetwork.org/category/jargon.* Here the words are listed in alphabetical order, with Proscio's incisive and hilarious commentary under each. Be sure to read what Proscio has to say about "paradigm" and "-based" (as in "community-based").

We promise you, after reading these books or spending time with the Jargon Finder, you'll be very nearly cured of using jargon. We still use a few jargon words occasionally ourselves, but we feel guilty every time we do it.

Technical Terms or Terms of Art

After all that negativity, is there ever a place for jargon? Yes, in a way. Every field has its own technical terms or terms of art that are well understood by other practitioners. In this book, for instance, we talk about "capacity building" and "logic models." We explain what we mean by these terms, and then we can use them to refer to a complex idea in an easy shorthand. Used in this way, and explained at first use, this kind of jargon is perfectly acceptable.

Another example is when you're talking or writing to people in your own field and they expect you to use a certain vocabulary to show that you're a member of their

---

Jargon Isn't New

Lewis Carroll was famous for skewering jargon in his time. This excerpt from 1871 shows how jargon was as much of a temptation to speakers in his era as it is now:

"When I use a word," Humpty Dumpty said, in a rather scornful tone, "it means just what I choose it to mean—neither more nor less."

"The question is," said Alice, "whether you can make words mean so many different things."

"The question is," said Humpty Dumpty, "which is to be the master—that's all."

—Lewis Carroll, *Through the Looking Glass*

Inspiration

intellectual club. This is often the case with federal grants, where reviewers expect grantwriters to use the same vocabulary and style used in the grant guidelines. If you don't write in the expected style and with the technical vocabulary—however impenetrable it may seem to the uninitiated—the reviewers will assume that you are not qualified to deal with the issues of the field in question.

Clarity Is the Goal

Good grantwriting is the same as any other good business writing: clear, concise, and easy to understand. It's somewhat formal, so you won't use contractions as we do in this book—we're striving for a friendlier, more colloquial tone. As you edit your work, take out the extra words that don't convey meaning but just make your writing sound stuffy. Don't use grandiose vocabulary. For instance, instead of saying "The youth in our community are in need of a secure recreational area," you can just say, "Our kids need a safe place to play."

There are many excellent books that can help you polish your writing. One of the great classics is Strunk and White, *The Elements of Style*. Another favorite of ours is Joseph M. Williams, *Style: Ten Lessons in Clarity and Grace*. Many websites also give good advice on clarity and eliminating wordiness.

No matter how good a job you do of matching your proposals to funders, you can still stumble if your writing gets in the way. That is why clarity is so important. The topics we cover in this chapter come from problems that get in the way of clarity. And when you understand these common problems you'll know where to look as you do the real work of writing: rewriting. Each time you reread your work you'll find ways to improve it.

Ask a Friend

One of the best tools you can have for dealing with your writing in general and jargon in particular is another person who is willing to read your work and give candid feedback. While we suggest a friend, be sure that it is someone who will not spare your feelings. Too often, others you ask to review your work will give you only bland encouragement. That happens because they don't want to seem critical. They also may assume that the funder you are writing to will know all about the subject matter and therefore anything that is unclear or confusing will be clear to the funder.

You need to let your reviewers know that the best thing they can say to you is, "I'm not sure what you mean by…"

Perspiration

Formatting Tips

Some of the formats that funders present to you will require particular typefaces, spacing, and word limits. If you're filling in an online form, you may have no control over format at all. But in many cases, your initial approach to funders will be in a more flexible format. When you can send a letter or use your own proposal format, you have to make some choices about form as well as function.

You shouldn't try to use fancy formatting to make your message seem more important. The power of your request is in what you say. But good formatting that makes your document easy to read will strengthen your proposal. You want to use a legible font, include plenty of white space, and break up long stretches of text with headings, bullets or graphics such as tables or small photos. On the other hand, if your layout looks messy or if you've used a tiny

---

Perspiration

Is It Ever Okay to Use the First Person?

It's almost never a good idea to use "I" in a formal grant proposal. The applicant is an organization, not an individual. The only exception might be in an LOI or cover letter, where the signer (your executive director or board chair) personally knows the individual to whom the letter is addressed.

But what about using "we" and "our" to refer to the applicant organization? For instance, you might write, "The Downtown Food Bank serves people in a fifty-square-mile area. Our clients come from all backgrounds and ethnicities. We provide basic groceries to two hundred families each week."

Many experienced grantwriters and funders (including both of us) think this usage of the first person plural is fine. It sounds more active and personal than using only "it" to refer to the applicant organization. But other grantwriters believe the first person plural is inappropriate. This is often the case for federal grant proposals, which require a higher level of formality.

By the way, we have written this book in the first person plural, in keeping with the less formal, conversational style of books in the For the GENIUS series.

font and narrow margins, you'll make a poor impression before the reader even begins to absorb what you've written. Your format should look clear, professional, and easy on the eyes.

Typefaces

The key decision in choosing a typeface is, "Is it readable?"

There is a debate regarding whether you should favor serif typeface over sans serif typeface. Some people contend that a serif type, like **Times New Roman**, reads better in blocks of text than sans serif types, like **Arial**. Others just prefer the look of sans serif fonts.

Generally, any typeface that isn't too fancy will suffice. Don't be like the historical society that decided to use **COPPERPLATE GOTHIC** for its application because it looks historic. As long as it's easily readable, almost any font will work. But don't use **Comic Sans MS**. It's very legible, but there's a reason why it's called "comic"—it looks silly. Save it for party invitations.

> ### Sometimes Details Are Critical
>
> Some funders use formatting criteria to make or break your proposal. This is especially true for government grant programs and organizations like United Ways. These funders set requirements for formatting such as margins, typeface, and attachments to maintain the readability of applications. If you fail on any of them, your application won't go to the next stage.
>
> Even some private funders will enforce similar requirements. Sometimes the staff at a private funder has the ability to help you correct your errors if your request is compelling. But don't take that chance!
>
> **Observation**

One other note about typefaces: Use an eleven- or twelve-point font. A smaller font will allow you to put more words in the same space, but it won't be as readable. Remember, funders read hundreds of requests. And some of your readers may be older folks who have trouble reading smaller type.

Margins

Use a one-inch margin on all sides. This guideline applies to both text and budget documents. While it will limit the number of words you can use, cutting margins too thin to squeeze in more words can work against you. One reason for this is that the white space around your text or numbers makes a document easier on the eye. Also, funders may make notes in the margins.

Letterhead

Letterhead is a must for any letter you send a funder. This includes letters of intent, grant reports, and any other correspondence. Even if you don't have a printed letterhead, create one in the header section of your word processing document. This information ensures that the reader will have your organization's name and key contact information.

You should also be careful with your letterhead. While there may be important names on a list of board members or advisory committees, you don't want to use so much space on the page that you have little left over for text.

Also, while this may seem obvious, don't use letterhead after the first page. To make sure the following pages match the weight and texture of your first page, use blank paper that matches the letterhead.

To Summarize...

- Understanding the audience you are writing to can be as important as understanding a funder's guidelines.

- The temptation of jargon is to make your request sound more important. But the real power of your request is in its clarity and saying something compelling.

- It's okay to use technical terms, so long as you explain them first.

- Make sure your format is clear, easy on the eyes, and not a distraction from your message.

Chapter 14

Letters of Inquiry: Part 1

In This Chapter...

- Why do funders ask for LOIs?
- How can an LOI help you build your case?
- What should you include in your letter?
- What are program models, and how can they help you?

Letters are a key to engaging many funders. They allow you to tell your story much better than an application form. They can help you organize your thinking and provide vivid language for completing online screenings or application forms. They can also help you flesh out your ideas and turn them into grantable projects. That's why we began with the Quick-Start Letter to get you started on an LOI. It's also why we provide a model LOI in **Appendix A**.

While you drafted an LOI with your Quick-Start Letter, this chapter will help you polish your drafts so they appeal to each funder you approach. We'll discuss how to make your request resonate with a funder's own interests and concerns. Then we'll go through the structure of a letter step by step. This will help you see how each paragraph in a letter builds upon the paragraphs before it.

This approach will also help you understand how all that you write in an LOI should relate to the key theme of your request. Keeping your key theme in mind is how you decide what needs to be emphasized and what can be summarized in your letter as well as what should be included and what can be left out.

Funders and LOIs

Here's an example from a funder's website about why it asks for letters as the first step in its process:

> *A Letter of Inquiry helps us learn about your organization and programs so we can assess your organization's potential fit with our grant priorities.*

Read that sentence again and ask yourself, "What should I stress and what should I leave out in a letter to this funder?"

> ### Ideas Alone Aren't Enough
>
> Early in my career with a private foundation, the executive director gave me some advice. He said that, as we attended events and meetings, people would share ideas for projects and grants. He suggested reminding them that the process starts with a letter. He also predicted that I would be surprised by how few of those conversations actually ended up in a letter to the foundation. And it has been true for many years.
>
> I'm convinced that the ideas that never resulted in letters probably didn't seem as good as they first sounded when put to paper.
>
> —Ken
>
> **IMPORTANT!**

The exact answer depends on that funder's grant priorities, and those change from one funder to another. The principle, which remains the same for all, is that you stress the programs and aspects of your organization that fit the funder's priorities. That is the guiding principle to what you include and what you leave out.

A fair amount of detail would be relevant on a program that fits the funder's priorities, while others can be summarized. You might think that is obvious. Yet one of the most common questions we answer is "How do I describe everything we do in such a small space?" Organizations with multiple programs can't expand on all of them. You'll want to focus on the program at the heart of your request and summarize the rest.

Chapter 14—Letters of Inquiry: Part 1   **155**

The Usual Approach

Most organizations start their grant search when they feel that "We need a grant to…" When grantwriters create LOIs, they know they want *to get a grant to fund something*. There's nothing wrong with starting there. In fact, it's a good place to begin putting your thoughts down on paper. But a compelling LOI comes from taking that idea and imposing some structure on it, one that anticipates questions that funders will ask and the goals that funders want to achieve for their communities.

Let's start by outlining what first drafts of LOIs often look like. Since grantwriters begin by knowing what their organizations need or what they've been assigned to raise money for, first drafts of LOIs often start:

> *Dear Funder,*
>
> *We are writing you to request a grant for $40,000 to purchase a new, walk-in freezer for our food bank.*

Since grantwriters know that funders care about an organization's nonprofit status, the next line is often, "XYZ was founded as a 501(c)(3) organization in 19xx. Our mission is to…"

Next, the letter goes into several paragraphs about what the project will do. In this example, it might be about how much food will be stored and distributed by using the new walk-in freezer.

The letter will begin to close with some mention of the total cost of the project and a repeat of the original request, "a $40,000

How Readers Read

Joseph M. Williams makes a key point early in his book, *Style: Toward Clarity and Grace*, about how structure influences your message. Williams points out that early on in any document (a letter, a term paper, a report, etc.), a reader looks for a theme. This theme summarizes what the document is about. If you fail to share a concise and memorable theme, readers will provide one based upon what they think you mean.

The first reader of your letter at a funder's office will often need to share a concise summary of your letter with other decision makers. You have a choice: You can shape that summary through your theme or you can trust that reader to figure it out. Your best approach is to have a clear theme for each funder that resonates with its values.

Inspiration

grant to purchase a new, walk-in freezer." Finally, the letter will conclude with a contact name and the signature of the executive director and/or the board chair.

As outlined, that's not a bad letter. But what's the first impression the letter makes? The words, "$40,000 to purchase a new walk-in freezer" create a lasting impression about the letter. For a funder, the fact you are writing to ask for a grant is not news. Funders that accept applications get a lot of requests for grants.

The only new information in that line is that your organization wants to purchase a new walk-in freezer. But how compelling is that? Of course, you have a good explanation of why you need the freezer. That explanation might start, "We need this freezer because…" Any parent will tell you that once you say "because," you're in trouble.

That's why we recommend getting right to the point. Strip away "We're writing for a grant…" and "We need this freezer because…" Begin with the words that would follow "because." Write a simple declarative sentence about what you want to accomplish and that reflects the funder's priorities. Some examples might be:

- We'd like you to join us in expanding the supply of food for…

- We hope you will assist us in maintaining our vital services for…

- The community is asking us to take on this new service to…

Your approach depends on the nature of what you hope to achieve and a particular funder's priorities. Later in the letter, after you've described what you need to do to achieve the vision of your project, you can talk about the tool(s) you need to carry out the project.

In short, the purpose of a grant is not to buy a freezer. A freezer is a tool. If you convince a funder that your project will accomplish something important, you may be surprised what tools a funder may help you buy.

Making Your Request Appeal to Funders

In other areas of the book, we've outlined how the various common grant applications (CGAs) used across the country ask the same questions even though they may use different formats. Even funders that do not use CGAs

Don't Bury the Lead

Nearly every charitable organization's activities are compelling to someone. The key to getting grants is finding the right audience and making sure your approach doesn't get in the way of your message.

Red River Child Care provides full-time care, before- and after-school care, and early childhood education services. When it writes an LOI to a funder it begins with a long description of all of its programs, including details on each program's staff and their credentials. Since much of that information rarely changes, the nonprofit has created boilerplate wording that it pastes into every letter.

With every letter using this boilerplate introduction, funders have to read well into the second page to find the real purpose of the request. In journalism they call this "burying the lead."

When you are clear about the purpose of your letter, put that first. Then let that purpose be your guide as to what gets put into a letter and what gets left out, what gets emphasized and what can be summarized.

Uninspired

---

ask similar questions of applicants. These similarities tell us what funders want to know, so we used them to structure the Quick-Start Letter, and thus LOIs in general. You'll see that in the model LOI in **Appendix A**.

CGAs are usually broken down into two main sections: background information on the organization and a project narrative. The background information includes key staff such as an executive director's name and title, the number of programs, the size of the organization's budget, and similar information. The project narrative focuses on what you are asking the funder to support. Our approach to an LOI takes key parts from both sections and marries them in a way that reinforces your request to make it succinct, memorable, and compelling.

Writing to the Reader-Funder

The starting point for personalizing each LOI is to find an opening statement that will resonate with the funder. A letter that begins "We're writing to request a grant of $40,000 to purchase a new walk-in freezer for our food bank," says one thing. An opening that says "We're writing to ask for your help to increase the amount of food available to low-income families in the rural areas of northern Minnesota," says something else.

Which theme do you think will resonate with funders: buying a freezer or increasing the food available for low-income families?

In the Quick-Start Letter, we asked you to put information in a slightly different order than you might have expected. Our approach is based on the commonalities we see in CGAs and our experience with grants and nonprofit organizations. First, you build your best relationships with funders when you make a connection based on mutual interests. Second, you can weave together the information funders care about to tell a story reinforcing that connection.

As you read the questions below, think about how you can answer them in a way that weaves in the important information for a particular funder and for your particular request.

- What is your organization and what does it do?
- What is the need/opportunity you want to address?
- How are you going to address that need/opportunity?
- What will success look like?
- What resources do you need?
- What do you want us (the funder) to do?

See how these questions flow together? That order comes from how most CGAs ask you to structure your project narrative. They also create a great structure for telling a story. This approach can capture funders' imaginations and incite their enthusiasm.

You may hear from time to time that a funder would rather you begin your letter, "We are writing for a $40,000 grant to purchase a cooler/freezer." Make a note of that funder and write your future letters just that way. With a few sentences, you can add that beginning to the model proposal letter. Here's how it might look:

> *Dear Ms. Jones:*
>
> *We are writing to the XYZ Foundation for a grant of $40,000 to purchase a cooler/freezer. This equipment will allow us to increase the amount of food available for low-income families....*

This beginning can be added seamlessly to the model letter approach. It provides what those funders want to know right up front, how much and for what. But it also helps you put the focus on what your organization plans to accomplish.

Telling the Funder What You Want to Accomplish

Funders see grants as tools to accomplish their missions and goals. And those are usually about helping people and communities. That's why you make your best connection with funders by showing what you plan to accomplish for your community.

We'll go through the basic sections of an LOI and show what kind of information needs to be shared and how you customize it for a request.

Inspiration

Telling Your Story

Over the past decade, the phrase, "tell your story" has become popular in books and classes for grantwriters. Even journalists are using the phrase, "controlling the narrative."

One tool to tell your story is through a client's experience, whether an actual testimonial or a composite of several individuals crafted to personify your typical client. If you use a composite client story, however, make that clear. Some organizations that have presented composites as actual clients have been accused of deceptive practices.

The point of a client story is to document the validity of your assertions. Think of it as anecdotal evidence. You use that story in the same way you use census statistics, service data, or any other set of numbers.

Like all evidence, the story must be to the point, clear, and related directly to your case. A simple concrete example does much more than generalized statements. Contrast these statements: *"I was failing until Big Brothers came to our school. They helped me a lot,"* or, *"I was failing because I felt all alone. When I got a mentor there was someone who cared. Now I care about school."*

While there are a few more words in the second example, it's much more compelling. It tells a donor both what your program does and what the impact is. You can draw out quotes like the second example if you ask the right questions about specific and meaningful experiences.

Who You Are and What You Do

Grantwriters understand that they need to tell a funder about their organization and what it does. But why do funders ask that?

Sharing your organization's history, mission, and activities builds your credibility. For example, the LOI in **Appendix A** shares the organization's history from starting as a food bank to becoming a distribution center for a network of food banks. It stresses that history and those activities because that is at the core of its project, distributing more food to low-income families.

Why You Want to Do This Project

Successful projects have four key parts. They begin with a need, then a plan to address that need. Then comes the actual implementation, and finally an evaluation or feedback on how the implementation worked. That structure parallels the questions funders ask outlined above: What is the need, how will you address it, and what will success look like?

> *A powerful way to introduce your concept of a need is a statement like, "In the course of our work, we've seen that many of the young people coming into our job training program lack basic computer skills. In today's employment market, even a job answering phones can require basic computer skills to manage a sophisticated phone system. The youth who come to us lacking those skills often fail to complete our job training programs. These youth need an entry level computer skills class so that more youth can complete our program and find employment."*

This approach tells a funder that:

- Your organization actively looks at why clients drop out.
- Your organization will structure the project to meet identified and practical needs.
- The project will serve clients who may not find help through other programs.

How the Project Will Work

You've described a need your organization sees in its day-to-day work. Perhaps it's a frustration program staff have shared such as, "We have some really good

Chapter 14—Letters of Inquiry: Part 1

> ### Describing Community Need
>
> If you've skipped a description of the need and jumped right into your project, you might confuse the funder. Your letter may seem like a solution in search of a problem.
>
> For example, your organization asks for a grant to provide more rental housing for low-income families. Yet the funder may still wonder, "How important is this housing?" Or, "How do we know this housing will go to the people who really need it?"
>
> You can anticipate those questions, and answer them in advance, when you share what led your organization to begin looking at this project and how that knowledge guided you in designing it.
>
> **Observation**

kids in our program who just can't keep up because they don't know…" An attentive reader may be thinking, "It sounds like they need a preclass for these kids before they go into the training programs."

Your task now is to outline the key aspects of the project in a way that follows along with the ideas you've already shared about the needs. Make sure that your project description is consistent with how you've stated what you want to accomplish and the community need.

If you crafted your need statement to highlight a particular geographic area that is a priority for the funder, make sure your project description touches on that geographic area.

Using a Model

As you describe your project, keep in mind that funders may wonder if you have the right approach. One way to address that is to cite a model.

Most likely your organization isn't starting the program from scratch. For example, a project might be developed because someone on your staff or board worked with a similar program elsewhere. Or perhaps your organization learned of a program at another nonprofit in the region or somewhere across the country. This existing program can serve as a model for the new one you want to develop.

Why do funders like models?

- Models show that your organization is willing to learn from others' experiences.

- Without models, every new program would be a new experiment.

- Models can serve as maps for how things could work.

- Models can help funders see how your activities can result in your stated goals.

That doesn't mean your organization has to follow a model in lockstep. What is important is that you show that you are aware of it and why it will work in your community. Phrases such as, "We think this program will work in our community because...." can show that you have thought through how your organization will use the model.

One type of model is an evidence-based practice (EBP). EBPs are programs that have been tested with rigorous evaluations that show they are effective. Often EBPs are very controlled models. They are great for programs that are supposed to have long-term impacts. Since the EBP has already been tested for its ongoing impacts, your evaluation work can focus on the short-term output objectives which are easier to measure. The theory behind an EBP is that, if you do all the steps right (something you can monitor and control), then the positive long-term outcomes should result. There will be more about goals, objectives, and EBPs in **Chapter 17** that covers logic models and **Chapter 19** that discusses goals and objectives.

One difficulty of using EBPs is that they can be expensive and complicated. Some ask you to use copyrighted materials that you must purchase from certain vendors. As a result, the cost of replicating EBPs can be difficult for a small organization to meet.

But a small organization can develop its own program that operates consistently with the principles behind the EBP. That requires a concise outline of the EBP and a description of how your program uses its principles. This approach doesn't ensure the long-term outcomes in the same way that completely following the model does. But it is a start in the right direction.

Finally, remember that the way you frame your project also determines your budget. We'll describe budgets in more detail in **Chapter 22**. The way you conceptualize your project influences what belongs in the budget and what doesn't.

To Summarize...

- Funders that accept unsolicited applications need a way to review a lot of proposals in summary so they can focus on ideas that really interest them.

- The letter format can help you complete screenings and applications with more compelling writing.

- Working section by section in the letter format, you can provide all the information funders ask for while creating a compelling story.

- Basing your project on a model can make success more likely.

Chapter 15

Letters of Inquiry: Part 2

In This Chapter...
- How do you build your project budget?
- Why are time frames important?
- How do you decide how much to ask for?
- How can you prepare for the step beyond the LOI?

While an LOI is a summary of a full proposal, an effective one must still include many details. And providing those details can be one of the biggest challenges for grantwriters. One of the most common questions we get about LOIs and grant applications is, "What do we put in and what do we leave out?"

In this chapter, we'll cover those key points that need to be included. Details can bring your request alive. They can anticipate questions that funders will ask. And by answering those questions, your LOI will feel complete. For example, usually when funders read requests for facilities, it's very clear how much money an organization wants to raise. But they are often frustrated that these requests fail to be clear about where the building will be and how big. Those details are important, and they add depth to your proposal. The location

> ### A Budget Is a Plan, Not a Prediction
>
> Grantwriters often feel overwhelmed by budgets. When we've talked with people in class sessions or at conferences one major reason for this seems to be feeling that the numbers have to be exact. One way to get past that feeling and feel a little less stressed by budgets is to remember this: a budget is a plan.
>
> The expense portion of your budget answers the question, "What will it take to do this?" The income portion of the budget answers the question "Where will you find those resources?"
>
> Funders understand that your budget is a plan, an estimate. They will accept minor changes and don't expect your final budget to be exactly the same as your plan. Your budget should be well enough developed that you won't have any major changes (variations of 25 percent or more), as that can undermine funders' faith in your planning.
>
> If you keep these thoughts in mind, you can reduce the stress that often goes with writing a budget or answering questions about it.
>
> **Pure Genius!**

of your building may say something about the needs it addresses, and its size may say something about the need for your organization's services.

Every project has hundreds of details. What's important is understanding which ones add to the case you are trying to make and which can, at least for now, be left out of the LOI.

What's It Going to Take to Do This?

If your plan seems to make sense in light of what you want to accomplish, a funder will wonder, "What is it going to take to do this?" The answer to this question comes from your budget.

In a letter, online screening, or the narrative section of an application, you'll probably only need to share the project's total cost. Application forms will ask for full budgets either on a form the funder provides or with your own form. It's a good idea to have your project budget completed so that you can share an accurate total.

You'll probably find that the expenditure portion of the budget is the easiest part to create. Most of it will be based upon assumptions you can control: How much space will the program need? What kind of materials? How many staff and/or volunteers? What will it cost to construct and furnish a building? All you need to do is put a price tag to those assumptions.

While you won't include all this detail in your letter, you should base your general remarks upon a solid idea about what the costs will be. This is the one area where you should have your background work done in advance even if you are writing your letter only to see if any funders are interested. Nothing kills a grant request faster than a big change in the budget. Funders can understand small adjustments; as we said, a budget is a plan. But a major change like an increase because you forgot to include the design fee or a major new piece of equipment undermines your entire proposal.

Where Will the Resources Come From?

The income portion of the budget may be the most difficult part of your LOI and the grant application. At a minimum, outline a plan. And that plan needs to seem attainable.

> **IMPORTANT!**
>
> ## A Budget Needs a Time Frame
>
> Don't forget to include a timeframe for key project steps as well as for income and expenditures. If you're starting up a new program, a funder will want to know when you will begin spending grant funds. If it's a capital campaign, a funder will look for key dates, such as groundbreaking and occupancy of the completed building.
>
> At the LOI stage, the budget timeframe can be more flexible. Generally, you should plan to raise all the money for starting or expanding programs by the time the project is completed. In this context, raised means having the money in hand since you'll need to pay all those costs by the end of the budget period.
>
> A capital campaign is different. You might break ground and even complete a building before the last 5 to 10 percent of the dollars are raised. In a capital campaign, by "funds raised" we mean both dollars in hand and binding pledges to be paid over time, which may be up to three to five years. Since capital campaign gifts are often larger than those for annual giving campaigns, pledges are often paid over several years. The gap between when you spend the campaign proceeds and when you collect pledges is covered by interim financing such as a bridge loan. We cover that in **Chapter 22** on project budgets.

One error some grantwriters make is that they don't have a full plan for the income portion of a budget. When you request a grant but don't have a full plan for raising the needed resources, funders may hesitate. They prefer to commit to projects that look like they will actually happen, even if you must estimate a good deal of the early-stage figures. You can base those figures on your understanding of the project, your donor base, and your prospect research. Also, the summary you present of the planned income sources should be built upon some level of detail. Say a funder calls and asks, "I see you plan to raise $1 million from foundations for this project. What big grants are you asking for to get you to that amount?" You should be prepared to answer such questions.

You'll describe your budget plan from the top down, assigning percentages to types of funding sources. What will that summary look like? It starts with the fact that nonprofits generally have five main sources of income:

- Fees for service
- Government grants
- Individual giving
- Private grants, such as foundation and corporate gifts
- Other, such as debt and miscellaneous income

Say you have a $12 million budget for a project. Your plan might call for $4 million in government grants, $3 million from individual donors ($1.8 million of which is from a naming donor), $3 million from foundation and corporate gifts, and up to $2 million in long-term debt that a bank has already approved.

While you should have detailed plans for each category, this general outline will usually suffice for an LOI. You can add a specific detail that strengthens your case, such as naming key amounts you already have in hand.

How to Determine How Much to Ask For

Once you've shared, in summary, how much the project will cost and your plan to accumulate those resources, a funder will want to know the amount of your grant request. It's important to cite a specific amount in your letter. A funder will look at that amount in light of its grants program and your fundraising plan.

How do you decide how much funding to ask for in a particular grant proposal? There are several main factors to consider:

- The size of your project budget
- The funder's grant range
- The funder's giving history to organizations of your size and in your field

The primary factor is, of course, the size of your project budget. We'll be discussing this in detail in **Chapter 22**, but early on in the grantwriting process, you need to sit down with your executive, the program director, and your financial person and determine how much the project needs for a successful execution.

The next consideration is the grantmaker's funding range. Sometimes this will be stated in the guidelines, or a database entry such as Foundation Directory Online. But just because the database entry says: "Grants: Low - $500; High - $100,000" don't assume you can ask for the high end. Sometimes the database will give a typical grant range—say, $5,000 to $25,000—in addition to low and high. The typical range is a better guideline.

If you have not received any previous grants from this funder, you will need to establish a relationship first. Often you'll want to request a modest amount the first time you approach a funder, to make it easier for the funder to give you a grant. After it gets to know you, a funder may invite you to apply for a larger grant next time.

Finally, you need to look at the funder's specific giving history to nonprofits of your budget size and in your field. If the funder's website lists previous grants, look through them to see what amounts it has given to organizations that look like yours. If there's no list on the website, go to the IRS Form 990 and look back through the past several years of grant listings. See what types of organizations receive the

> **Neither Cadillacs nor Kias**
>
> Sometimes grantwriters ask, "Should we ask for more than we need, since we probably won't get as much as we ask for anyway?" This is a dangerous road to go down. You don't want to think of a grant budget as a bargaining position. It should be an honest estimate of what you think the project will cost—neither padded with excessive perks (the "Cadillac version"), nor a bare-bones estimate that will be too low to fund a quality program. Funders have seen a lot of project budgets, and a budget that is unrealistic, on either the high or the low side, will undermine their confidence in your organization.
>
> **Observation**

majority of its grants. Is your organization in a priority field, or are you in a field for which the funder reserves a smaller amount of its giving budget? How does your annual operating budget compare with those of other grant recipients? An organization with a $500,000 annual budget will naturally be expected to request a smaller grant than one with a $5 million budget.

In most cases, you will not be asking a single funder for the entire amount needed for your project. Many funders specifically say they will not be sole donors, and some even limit their grants to 10 or 25 percent of the project budget. In that case, you'll need to develop a fundraising plan that will include grants and gifts from several different sources.

It's important to get the ask amount right. A request that is excessively high—or even low—may be rejected, because the funder will assume you didn't do your homework. On the other hand, a realistic project budget with an appropriate ask amount will tell the funder that your organization is well managed and has done the necessary research and planning to carry out a successful grant project.

While your organization's grant history is one guide, you can also pick up the telephone and ask a funder about an appropriate range for its grants. You need to tread carefully, though. A good approach is to ask about how much a funder gives to projects of a size similar to yours. Asking "What's the average grant size for a $2 million building project?" is a question that a funder can handle.

The Right Closing

When you send an LOI, you hope that it captures the funder's imagination. If it does, the funder will follow up in some way. That is why you identify a key contact person. Even though you've submitted your letter on letterhead, it's critical to identify the best contact for a prompt response to any questions. This may be the person who signs the letter or someone else. Whoever is cited needs to be a reliable contact, easy to reach and knowledgeable about the grant request.

We recommend including name, title, phone, and email for this contact. Also, provide as direct a phone number and email as possible. Don't assume that the information on your letterhead suffices. Many times the letterhead phone number is also the one people call when looking for help or it goes to an automated switchboard. If you haven't provided the contact's extension, then the funder has to struggle through the voice mail menu or wait for a human to

> ### Don't Mail Your LOI from the Airport!
>
> An executive director mailed several LOIs on his way out of town for a month's vacation. Although he worked for a moderate-size organization, he hadn't briefed anyone else on the project or the fact that he'd just mailed requests to funders.
>
> Over the next few weeks, three funders called his office, only to be told that the executive director was out of the office and no one else knew anything about the project. Who knows how many funders failed to follow up again or provided only token support when they might have enthusiastically embraced the project?
>
> **Uninspired**

answer, and we all know how frustrating that is.

The same goes for email addresses. Make sure you provide an email address that is actively monitored and that will get to a person who can respond to messages. For example, if the executive director doesn't use email or gets so many that an assistant screens them, perhaps another contact should be used.

Who Should Sign and Why

The signature on your letter is very important. A funder wants to be sure that the request represents an organizational priority. That can only be represented by the signature of an organization's executive director (or equivalent) and/or the board chair.

The executive director has a unique role working with the board of directors. The executive director is responsible to the board for both the revenue portion of the organization's budget and how revenues are spent. Also, the executive director and the board are responsible for program quality.

What if the executive director delegates signing to the development director? That's generally not a good idea. A letter signed by a development director only represents a commitment to raise money. The development director doesn't have control over how money is spent.

It's also in your interest as a grantwriter to have the letter reviewed and signed by the executive director because if the LOI leads to a full application, the director and/or board chair will need to sign it. You don't want your organization's leadership to decide suddenly to make major changes from what was outlined in the LOI because it wasn't thoroughly reviewed earlier

Uninspired

Be Prepared!

Many years ago I got a call from the director of a youth organization I didn't know. (Let's call him Jeff.) He explained that he'd submitted a letter of inquiry to a large, well-known foundation, and it had already come for a site visit.

Four days ago Jeff had received an email from the program officer saying he would like to submit the proposal to his board, but he needed Jeff to answer a few questions. Oh, and the due date was the next day. Could I come in tomorrow and help him write it up, in time to submit it by 5 p.m.?

In a fit of temporary insanity, I agreed. I arrived at Jeff's office early the next morning (which happened to be Oct. 31), prepared to knock off the answers to "a few questions." It turned out this amounted to writing a full proposal in one day.

The next several hours were a nightmare, trying to convert the organization's records into the statistics required by the foundation. I attempted to extract answers to questions such as, "If you hire another staff member with this grant money, what will that person be expected to accomplish? What are your goals for next year? How will you evaluate your results?" Jeff hadn't really thought about these issues—he just knew he wanted to expand his program.

It was the scariest Halloween of my life. In spite of tension, panic, and a computer crash that wiped out two hours of work in an instant, I somehow finished the proposal and submitted it by 5 p.m. Later I heard that the organization had received the grant.

After this traumatic experience I called Ken (because he was a funder I knew well and I could vent to him as a friend) and demanded indignantly, "How could that foundation have expected anyone to write a full proposal in just five days?" Ken admitted the timeline was a little short, but said the organization should basically have had a full proposal already written (or at least outlined) before it submitted the LOI. An LOI should be a condensed version of a full proposal that already exists, not a vague idea that you'll develop only if you get a nibble from the funder.

—Goodwin

Preparing for What Follows

If your letter or online submission gains a funder's interest, the next step may be a site visit or a visit to the funder's office. As you write, keep in mind that either one of those steps may follow. When funders make site visits or ask you to come into their office, their goal is to learn more about your request. Your letter can't provide all there is to know about your organization or the project in your LOI. What your letter should do is get the funder interested in your project.

When leaders in your organization review your draft letter, that process prepares them for the steps that may follow its successful submission, including site visits, which we discuss in **Chapter 25**. The organization needs to be committed to what you've outlined, and key people in your organization should be able to discuss that commitment at a site visit or a visit to the funder's office.

To Summarize...

- Funders that accept unsolicited applications need a way to review a lot of proposals in summary so they can focus on ideas that really interest them.
- A budget is a plan, not an iron-clad prediction.
- To determine how much to ask for, look at the funder's giving patterns as well as your own project budget.
- Working section by section in the letter format, you can provide all the information funders ask for while creating a compelling story.
- Be prepared for follow-up from a funder as soon as you send your letter.

Word cloud in the shape of the letter **I** containing the following words:

proposal, vocabulary, organizations, story, loi, style, font, budgets, fact, director, answer, meaning, describe, families, summary, eligibility, requirements, 501 C3, ask, inquiry, readers, audience, applications

money, provide, space, term, step, person, order, email, funders, history, word, amount, letters, page, clarity, structure, models, idea, submit

information, guidelines, application, grantwriters

process, contact, grants, see, writing, years, give, visit, program, serve, review, think, funder, time, first, text

nonprofit, community, CGA, jargon, asking, message, start, fit, data, site, terms, words, system, technical, resources, need, share, foundation, new, important, questions, write, income, screening, executive, purchase, deadline

Part 5

Writing a Full Proposal

Finally, in this section, we'll talk about what's involved in writing a full grant proposal. We'll go into detail about each section of a standard proposal, and explain what funders are looking for. By the time you finish this section, you'll be prepared to write the kind of grants that speak to funders' missions and will help your organization develop a long-term grants program.

In **Appendix B**, you'll find an example of a full proposal that follows the structure and advice we offer in this part of the book. It's a parody, originally written for a grantwriting class, but it's also a helpful illustration of the principles of grantwriting we advocate. You'll get a few chuckles from it and hopefully learn something as well.

Chapter 16

Cover Letters, Cover Sheets, Proposal Outlines, and Summaries

In This Chapter...

- What goes into a cover letter?
- What is the best way to fill out a cover sheet?
- How can a generic proposal template help you?
- Why is the summary so important?

At this point in the book, we are beginning an in-depth discussion of a full grant proposal, a stage that often comes after the LOI or initial application has been approved for the next round of review. The full grant proposal can range from a letter-type proposal, limited to four or five pages, all the way up to a federal grant proposal that may be hundreds of pages long. What makes it a "full proposal" is that it is the final document needed to apply for a grant unless the funder later requests further information. The specific sections of a full proposal will differ depending on the funder's guidelines, of course. But we'll cover the most common ones, so you'll know what to expect.

In the old days, when all grants were submitted on paper, it was customary to send a cover letter with most proposals. Now that most grants are submitted online, there isn't always an opportunity to include a cover letter (though you may be able to write a cover email). But when you have the chance to add one, it can be a very effective introduction to the proposal that follows.

Cover letters are usually optional, but many funders require applicants to fill out a cover sheet that gives the basic facts about your proposal. While it's mostly self-explanatory, there are a few important points to keep in mind. It's especially important to make sure that the figures on the cover sheet match those in the body of the proposal.

After the cover letter and cover sheet, the main body of the proposal narrative usually begins. The first section of the proposal is the summary or abstract. This is where you have your first real chance to make your case to the funder, so it's essential to make a good impression. We'll give you some tips on how to write a summary with maximum impact.

Cover Letters

A cover letter is a brief introductory note, *written on your organization's letterhead*, that allows you to address the funder directly. It should be formatted like a business letter, including the date, the funder's mailing address, and a salutation. It concludes with the signature of the authorizing official.

The letter should be short—usually no more than three paragraphs, and certainly no more than one page long. Remember, you don't need to repeat everything in the proposal. You're just trying to introduce your organization and call attention to a few key items.

What Kinds of Proposals Should Include a Cover Letter?

Full proposals to private funders, both foundation and corporate, usually have a cover letter if they're submitted in hard copy. However, the letter is not an integral part of the proposal, and may not be passed on to everyone on the grant review committee, so don't put anything essential into the cover letter that is not included somewhere else in the proposal proper. The letter is just a courteous introduction to your proposal.

Letters of inquiry and proposals that are already in letter form don't need a cover letter. Proposals to government funders should closely follow instructions and not include anything the guidelines don't ask for, so only add a cover letter if it's specifically requested.

What about online submissions? If the proposal format is fully electronic—you're filling in an online form provided by the funder—there's probably no way to include a cover letter. But sometimes you may be sending the proposal as an email attachment. In this case, you can turn your accompanying email into a cover letter, but keep it really short. You can mention any prior contact with the funder and make a brief statement of why you believe this proposal is important to the community. Another option, if the proposal is to be submitted as an email attachment, is to upload the cover letter, written on letterhead, as a PDF.

Addressing an Individual

It's always better to address the cover letter to an individual, rather than "Dear Grant Committee." If the funder's website or database information provides the name of the contact person for grants, then use that. (Databases can be out of date, however, so do check the website. Addressing your proposal to someone who left that position years ago is not a good way to begin.) You can also address it to the chair or president of the foundation. But if there's no individual listed and the guidelines clearly state that proposals should be submitted to a committee, you can go with "Dear Grant Committee."

Use Proper Form for Salutations!

If you use an individual's name, the salutation should read "Dear Ms. Johnson" or "Dear Mr. Rodriguez," not "Dear Barbara Johnson" or "Dear Juan Rodriguez." If the funder's website refers to this person as "Dr." or puts a doctoral degree after the name, make sure you use that honorific.

What if the gender of the individual isn't clear from the name? (People frequently assume incorrectly that I'm male on the basis of my first name, which is a family name. When I get mail addressed to "Mr. Goodwin Deacon," that tells me the sender has no idea who I am.) Do a little online research and see if you can find out the gender—just put the name into Google, or try to find the person on LinkedIn or Facebook. Ask your colleagues, or a professional listserve. As a last resort, you can email the funder's office—better to ask than to get it wrong.

—Goodwin

IMPORTANT!

The Opening Paragraph

If you've had any past contact with the funders, mention that in the first sentence. Thank them for their past support if they've funded you before, and say something about what their most recent grant accomplished. If you're approaching a funder for the first time, but you've spoken with someone from the office on the phone, thank that person for assisting you.

Even if you've had no prior contact with the funders, mention briefly why you're approaching them rather than someone else. For example, "The Goodworks Foundation has been a leader in making sure that homeless children get an education. Our project is part of that effort." Next, briefly introduce your organization and indicate its mission. You don't have to go into detail—just explain in a few words what you do and whom you serve.

The Middle Paragraph

This is the place to introduce your project and explain why it is important to the community. What are you planning to do? How will the project benefit the people it is designed to serve? How will their lives be improved through this project? Why is your nonprofit the best qualified to provide this service? But remember, you only get a few sentences to convey this message.

Make it clear why your organization believes in the importance of this project. You can let down your hair a little in this letter—it may have a more personal feel than the more formal language of the proposal. Let your enthusiasm shine through.

The Final Paragraph

Here you will mention the amount you're requesting, and state specifically how the funder's money will be used. Even if the request is part of a larger project, many funders want to know specifically where *their* dollars will go. So stating that you plan to use this grant to cover artists' fees or school supplies, for instance, is a good idea.

Acknowledging the Grant

You may also want to explain how you will publicly acknowledge the grant. This is more important to some funders than others. Some family foundations want no public acknowledgment at all because their funds are limited and

> **Will or Would?**
>
> When you're talking about what will happen if you receive a grant, you may be tempted to use the conditional "would": "If we receive an award, we would acknowledge it in our newsletter." But it's better to use the simple future "we will acknowledge it…" because it assumes that your proposal will be successful. "Would" sounds tentative; "will" implies confidence.
>
> *Perspiration*

they don't want to be besieged by requests they will have to turn down. Corporations, on the other hand, are usually eager for publicity, and their decision about whether to fund your request may depend to some extent on the amount of positive public recognition you can offer them. Other funders fall somewhere in between—they will appreciate an article in your newsletter or an acknowledgment on your concert program, but they don't ask for a major marketing campaign.

Recognition for capital gifts is another category altogether. Nonprofits raising money for construction usually offer donors "naming opportunities" calibrated to the size of the gift: $10 million to name the building, $50,000 for a classroom, etc. You don't need to go into detail about this in the cover letter, but you might say, "We will be pleased to discuss appropriate naming opportunities with you," or "A gift of $10,000 will be acknowledged on our donor wall in the lobby."

Contact Person and Signer

The rules for who should act as the contact person and who should sign the cover letter are the same as those for LOIs, covered in **Chapter 14**. If the contact person (for instance, the director of corporate and foundation relations) is not the signer, give that person's name and contact information in this concluding paragraph. Finally, thank the reader for considering the proposal. But don't say "We look forward to hearing from you," or "I'll call you next week"—that sounds presumptuous.

Cover Sheets

Many funders include fill-in-the-blank forms that function as cover sheets for the proposal. These help the reader at the funder's office see very quickly who the applicant is, what you're requesting, and how much you're asking for.

The cover sheet may ask for your organizational mission statement, and it may give you only a very small amount of space for it—sometimes one hundred words or fewer. So if you have a long, wordy mission statement (not a good idea anyway), you'll need a more concise version for the cover sheet.

It will also ask for the title of your project and a very brief description of what it's about. This is a good opportunity for you to make sure you can sum up the essence of your project in just a few words. If that's difficult, you may need to rethink the focus of the proposal.

Whatever figures you put on the cover sheet for the amount requested, total operating budget, and project budget should match the figures given in the body of the proposal. If you revise these amounts in the course of writing the proposal, make sure you change them on the cover sheet too. It's easy to let things like this slip by, and funders will notice if you're not consistent. They will also be confused.

> ### The Elevator Speech
>
> Fundraisers often talk about having an "elevator speech" ready. The scenario is that you find yourself in an elevator with an important potential donor who asks you what your organization does. You have only a few seconds to sum up what you do in compelling words that the donor will remember.
>
> A cover sheet is like an elevator speech for grantwriters. In just two or three sentences, you have to explain what your proposal is about, why it's important, and what it will accomplish. If you can convey this well on the cover sheet and pique the reader's interest, the funder will begin reading your proposal with a positive attitude.
>
> **Inspiration**

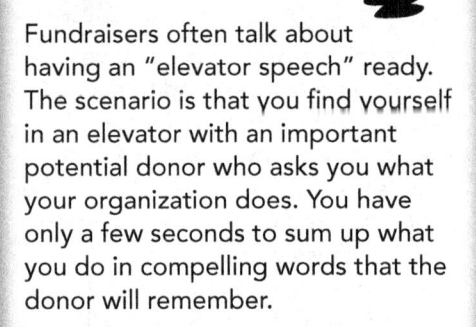

Revenue and Other Funders

The cover sheet may ask where your organization's revenue comes from and who else has funded you in the past. Usually, it's not asking for a list of individual donors (which would be much too long). Funders want to know about your institutional donors, including foundations, corporations, and government entities. The reason they're asking is that they want to see if you have broad support from funders like themselves. If they see that other funders believe in you, that makes it easier for them to invest in your organization as well.

Generic Proposal Template

Now that you've gotten all the introductory material out of the way, you're ready to start the proposal narrative itself. We'll go over each section in detail in the next several chapters. But before we start, we want to give you an overview of the narrative as a whole.

The outline in the sidebar is a generic template. When you write an actual grant proposal, you'll be answering the specific questions in a funder's guidelines. These may be worded differently, but almost all funders want to know some version of the issues covered in this outline. Knowing what the template looks like will help you interpret the questions asked in the actual guidelines. For instance, if the guidelines say, "What problems are you addressing?" you'll know they're asking for the needs statement, and you'll know that by "problems" they mean "community needs." If the guidelines say, "Describe your plans for assessing the outcomes of your project," you'll know they're talking about the evaluation.

> **Generic Proposal Template**
>
> I. Summary
>
> II. Needs Statement: Why?
>
> III. Goals and Objectives: What?
>
> IV. Work Plans: How? Where? When? Who?
>
> V. Evaluation: How will you measure success?
>
> VI. Budget: How much?
>
> VII. Organizational Information: Who is applying?
>
> VIII. Sustainability: What's next?
>
> **Perspiration**

Use the Funder's Headings

In providing this proposal template, we're giving you general section headings like "Needs Statement" and "Evaluation." But when you're writing an actual grant proposal, you'll be responding to the funder's specific questions. You'll want to use those as headings in your narrative.

When you're writing your proposal, you want to make it as easy as possible for the reader to follow. The funder has asked specific questions, and you need to make it clear that you're answering each one. So use the headings from the guidelines when you're writing your proposal. That way, the reader will be able to see which questions you're answering, which makes the job of evaluating proposals much easier.

As you draft the proposal, copy each question from the guidelines into your document—that will help you stay focused on the question at hand. If the questions are long, you may want to cut them down to a key phrase or two in your final draft, so they don't take up too much space. And of course, you don't need to include instructions to applicants. But make it clear which question you're responding to, and answer the questions in the same order used by the funder.

Summaries or Abstracts

Now we finally get to the beginning of the full grant proposal narrative. It is worth noting that some funders request letter proposals, formatted like business letters, with a salutation (Dear Ms. Goodrich) and ending with a signature, much like a letter of inquiry. Those proposals don't require a formal summary, though you may provide one in the opening paragraph. Lengthier full proposals usually begin with a summary or abstract section that encapsulates the rest of the proposal. We will use the terms "summary" and "abstract" interchangeably since longer proposals such as those submitted to the federal government are more likely to refer to this section as an abstract.

Write the Summary Last!

Although the summary comes first in a proposal narrative, you should always write it last. If you try to write it first, you'll find that it gets much too long. The reason is that, no matter how much preparation you've done, you rarely think your proposal through until you've written it all out. Once it's down on paper (or your screen), you'll be able to distill the essence of it. And that, in turn, may help you winnow out unnecessary passages or digressions that appear in your first draft.

Perspiration

Chapter 16—Cover Letters, Cover Sheets, Proposal Outlines, and Summaries

If you're filling out an online application form, you may be limited by space constraints, such as boxes with specific word or character limits. But we'll assume you're writing a proposal that gives you a fairly free hand in formatting your narrative. Remember, what we're providing here is advice on how to construct a generic grant proposal. What you actually write will depend on the specific guidelines of the funder to which you're applying.

Why Is the Summary Important?

The summary is the first thing the reader at the funder's office sees after the introductory material. You want to make sure your summary is clear and compelling. Include something that will catch readers' interest and make them think, "This sounds like an important project. I'm curious to see what this organization is planning to do."

A good abstract also makes the screener's job easier. The screener will submit a report to the board or committee that determines grant awards, including a brief summary of each proposal to be considered. If your abstract is concise and well written, the screener can simply use it in the report, and will mentally thank you for it. That's always a good foot to start on.

What Goes into the Abstract?

The abstract is a distillation of your entire proposal. Ideally, you devote one or two sentences to each of the key sections of your proposal. It tells the reader:

- Who is applying for the grant
- The nature of the project: what you plan to do
- Why the project is necessary and important
- A brief statement of goals and objectives
- Total project costs, including the amount already raised
- Why you are applying to this funder in particular
- Amount requested from this funder
- How you will use the grant money specifically

You may notice that you've written something similar to this before, in the LOI and the cover letter. Don't worry about repeating information from the LOI—you submitted that weeks or months ago, and the reader of the full proposal may not remember it. The cover letter is not a formal part of the proposal and may not be passed on to every reader.

The summary, on the other hand, is the gateway to your formal proposal. It clarifies what your proposal is about, and will make it easier for the reader to understand the much more detailed narrative in the following pages. So make it clear, and make it sparkle!

How Long Should the Abstract Be?

Usually, the abstract or summary shouldn't be any longer than a page, even for a large proposal like a federal grant. For shorter proposals, half a page is better. It shouldn't be more than a paragraph or two in most cases.

If your summary is clear, concise, and well written, the reader should be eager to turn the page and read the full proposal. It's the grantwriter's job to make that prospect exciting!

Maybe You Really *Did* Learn Something Useful in Middle School English

Remember those five-paragraph essays they made you write in middle school? There was an introduction, then three paragraphs describing different aspects of your topic, and a conclusion. In the introduction, you were supposed to write one sentence on each of the points you were going to develop in the middle three paragraphs. That's the same thing you do in the abstract, except that you have more than three topics. The point is to boil your essay (or grant proposal) down to its essence in the introduction, so your argument will be easier to follow. Maybe your English teacher was onto something important after all!

Inspiration

Chapter 16—Cover Letters, Cover Sheets, Proposal Outlines, and Summaries

To Summarize...

- The cover letter provides a very brief introduction to your proposal and allows you to emphasize key points, including your previous interactions with the funder.

- Make sure the information on the cover sheet is consistent with the rest of the proposal.

- The generic proposal template gives you a handy outline to follow as you develop your narrative.

- The abstract should encapsulate most of the major sections of the proposal, and make the reader want to continue to the detailed explanation that follows.

Chapter 17

Logic Models

In This Chapter...
- What does a logic model look like?
- Logic models and theory of change: Are they different or alike?
- How do funders use logic models?
- How do you show impact?

Logic models have been around for decades, but in the past twenty years, more and more funders have begun using them as a part of their grant applications. Funders use logic models for two reasons. Many use them as a way to understand your project. They feel that having applicants complete a logic model as a part of the application process allows them to better compare requests.

Other funders use logic models to make their priorities and preferences clear. These funders will outline the short- and long-term outcomes that fit their grantmaking. Then they allow you to propose what you plan to do to achieve those outcomes.

Not all funders ask for a logic model. Yet even if a funder doesn't ask for one, you may still want to craft one to help you refine your ideas or draft project. A logic model can help you start with a basic idea and think about what the immediate outputs will be. Will the project serve one hundred people or one thousand? Will there be something special about the people you should serve? And when you understand that, what will be the ultimate outcomes (impact) of your project.

When you share your logic model, or an outline of it, with other staff you may find that it generates some discussion. That discussion is great. It can help you clarify what you are trying to say. It can also help your colleagues understand the commitments that grants can entail.

In whatever situation you encounter logic models, you'll find that they can be great learning tools. They show the interconnection between your organization's programs, the impact they can have on your community, and the resources it takes to run those programs.

What a Logic Model Looks Like

There are dozens of books and articles detailing logic models, and funders use several different formats. Fortunately, those models vary only slightly. As we've done in other areas of this book, we'll focus on a format that illustrates the general principles of these models.

Also, we will do something that you won't see in most grants books or instructions from funders: We will describe how to take a project you seek funding for and show you how to put it into a logic model.

As you can see a simple logic model is laid out on a regular sheet of paper turned on its side and divided into five even columns. From left to right, the column headings are Resources, Activities, Outputs, Short-term Outcomes, and Long-term Outcomes. We've provided an example in the illustration. But even though this is the order of the columns from left to right, that isn't the order in which you fill them out.

Start with the Activities column. The activities you plan are your guide to the resources you will need. So you can complete the Resources column next. After that, you can begin filling in the Outputs column. Next, you can outline the Short-term Outcomes and Long-term Outcomes you hope will result from those outputs.

Simple Logic Model

Resources	Activities	Outputs	Outcomes	
			Short Term	**Long Term**
Four new full-time child care workers	Create fifty new child care slots:	Serve eighty families per year	Thirty low-income parents will gain employment due to stable child care	Families gain economic stability
Two new part-time child care workers	◆ Thirty full time	90 percent of families served will have incomes below 120 percent of poverty level	Twenty low-income parents will report increasing earnings due to stable child care	Children have better grades and are more likely to graduate from high school
Add 1,000 square feet of space for full-time program	◆ Ten part time			General economic condition of the community improves
Add 550 square feet of space for part-time before-/after-school care	◆ Ten before/after school			
Add part-time billing assistant				
Add furnishings for 1,550 square feet of new space				
Run an outreach campaign to actively enroll low-income families				

Putting Your Project in a Logic Model Format

| 2. What you'll need to carry out your activities | 1. What you want to do | 3. What you think the results of your work will be (outputs) | 4. The immediate impacts you expect your outputs will have on your community | 5. The long-term impacts you expect from your outputs and the short-term outcomes of your work |

> **Reading a Logic Model**
>
> When you look at a logic model template, the temptation is to read the information from left to right. But funders tend to read logic models from right to left, looking at three basic chunks of information: the outcomes you hope to produce, the activities and outputs you will undertake to produce those outcomes, and finally, the resources you'll need to carry out the activities you plan.
>
> **IMPORTANT!**

Let's assume your nonprofit has been providing child care in your community for many years. As a result of inquiries from local families, the organization has decided it needs to open fifty additional slots to respond to these needs. You have a plan outlined; you know what resources you'll need and why it's important to the community that you expand your services.

But how do you plug that information into a logic model?

Begin with a succinct statement such as: Provide fifty more slots for child care. You write that in the second column of our five-column model, headed Activities. You might refine this activity by specifying the types of slots. For example, your plan might be to provide fifty new child care slots: thirty additional full-time child care slots, ten more part-time, and ten new before/after-school child care slots.

Child care programs are regulated by a variety of state regulations. The variables of your activities, such as the number of full-time child care slots you add, have a big impact on the resources the project needs, including staffing levels, amount of space, and meals/snacks. All of those factors will influence the resources you'll need.

Resources

Your next step is to list the resources you'll need to carry out the planned activities. Put those in the column to the left of Activities. At this point, you need to list the items, not the cost—for example, four new child care workers.

You'll determine the cost of these items later when you build a budget. It's also a good idea to divide these items into two groups: items that are ongoing costs and those that will be one-time expenses. For example, furnishings for an expanded child care space will be a one-time need. Salaries for staffing will be an ongoing cost.

Those differences can be important when you are building a budget and making requests to funders. As we've pointed out in other chapters, some funders prefer to fund projects and some will fund ongoing program costs. The one-time costs to expand the child care can be presented as project costs.

When you list the resources needed, make sure to ask key people about resource needs beyond direct program costs. For example, a program working with low-income families conducts billings each month. Staff may be billing government programs that assist parents or families on a sliding-fee scale that allows them to pay what they can afford. Adding fifty slots of child care for low-income families means certifying more families for government programs on the sliding-fee scale, producing the billings, recording payments, etc. While costs like these may have to be met out of fee income rather than grants, you still need to outline them.

Outputs

The next three columns sometimes cause confusion because their titles, Output, and two variations on Outcomes—short term and long term—appear to be similar. *Outputs* are the things your activities produce that you can observe. *Outcomes* are the results that you expect to see from those outputs, both short term and long term.

In describing your outputs, you might describe different levels of completion. For example, a parenting class might cite three outputs:

- One hundred parents will enroll and attend an introductory session of the parenting class.

So What's Your Fundraising Plan?

Sometimes organizations approach funders with community needs and plans for meeting those needs, but no plans for raising the resources. For example, a community group cited a need for more soccer fields because teams and leagues had a hard time finding a place for games. It planned to build a complex of several additional fields.

But when it approached grantmakers without a plan for raising the resources, it put the funders in an awkward position. The lack of a good fundraising plan raised doubt about whether the organization could really pull off the project, even in the eyes of funders that were otherwise enthusiastic. As a result, the project failed to go forward.

Uninspired

- Eighty-five parents will complete all five class sessions.

- Eighty parents will show significant improvement in parenting knowledge and skills, based on precourse and postcourse testing.

The outputs you cite may create special obligations for your work. As a result, you may find that as you list the outputs, you may have to go back to the Resource column and add resources that didn't occur to you earlier.

For example, you might cite as an outcome for the thirty full-time child care slots, that 90 percent of the families served will have an income level below 120 percent of the poverty level. You've already noted that you'll need more staff to enroll, screen, and bill the additional families. But you may also have to work at recruiting the new families.

A targeted outreach campaign might reach the families you hope to serve and get them set up before the expanded program even opens. That costs money.

In small ways like that, the logic model helps you both articulate why you're taking on the project (to assist more low-income families) and what that might imply for the resources you need. It also helps you anticipate funder questions. Funders often wonder if "just putting a program out there" really meets the needs of the community. If you simply enroll parents on a first-come, first-served basis, a funder might ask if the program is really reaching the parents who need it.

To really demonstrate impact, you may need to think about how you can focus on the clients who most need your services. Working with the Department of Family Services or another organization in your community may help you see that 70 or 80 percent of the parents in your parenting

Call If You Have Questions

Outputs and outcomes can be very confusing. And you may even find that the language funders provide in their instructions confuses you more than it clarifies. If so, call and ask for a clarification.

Also, you may need to ask funders about the level of detail they want in each portion of the logic model. Is a statement such as "additional furnishings for new space" sufficient, or do they expect more detail?

Asking funders what they mean by output or outcome and how that might apply to your project is the kind of question that can help you in creating rapport.

Observation

classes are people who would not have attended the class without your outreach or other motivation.

When you pay attention to these details and note them on the logic model, you may discover resources you had previously overlooked. Also, it paves the way for making your case for short-term and long-term outcomes.

Short-Term Outcomes

Some people have described outcomes as being the "what if" question that begins most program development: "What if we had more child care, so that low-income, single working mothers could get and keep jobs?" That question could be the kernel of the idea that led to adding fifty slots for child care. When you looked more deeply at what those working mothers needed, that analysis may have driven your decision to create a combination of full-time, part-time, and before/after-school slots.

These "what if" questions can be recorded in your logic model, usually as short-term outcomes. They address the immediate impact that you expect of your outputs. They also show funders why your work is important in the community.

Long-Term Outcomes

We began with our idea of increasing the amount of child care an organization can provide. We summarized the kinds of resources needed to expand and continue to offer services at that level. We then showed what the outputs of that child care might be, along with goals for those outputs.

Assuming that the project can produce those outputs, we plugged in some short-term benefits to the community. These short-term outcomes are the kinds of things that should happen and can be measured over the next one or two years.

Yet a funder might still ask about the importance of achieving those short-term outcomes. The funder might ask, "But even if that all happens, what difference does it make?" The answers you provide are the long-term outcomes.

Your organization may not be able to measure long-term outcomes, but you can still cite them. The answers fall into two categories: common sense and evidence-based programs. The ideas we've sketched into our model promise that, over the short run, many families will gain employment or increase earnings based on our successful project. Those short-term outcomes indicate that families will gain economic stability, children will do better in school, and there will be a positive impact on the general economic condition of the community.

Can we ever absolutely prove any of this? Probably not. But as laid out in the logic model, the steps from the activity to the outputs and to the short and long-term outcomes should make sense. How far you have to go to substantiate long-term outcomes depends on a funder's level of faith. Some funders will believe that families getting jobs and increasing earnings equates to economic stability. Others will want more proof. Where does the proof come from?

There are a couple of tools for proving long-term outcomes. First, research or studies done in the field may document the validity of your approach.

Second are evidence-based practices (EBPs), which are programs that have been heavily studied and documented. The theory is that, if you carry out an EBP in line with its design, then you should be able to count on certain outcomes resulting.

A logic model provides a structure for testing your project against the key elements of an EBP. If you have the resources to provide the program described in the EBP and produce the outputs, then you should see certain outcomes result.

Logic Models and Your Theory of Change

A *theory of change* connects your programs to your mission statement. In some ways, a logic model is a way to formalize your theory of change. Asking applicants to outline their work and the goals they want

---

Theory of Change

Sometimes funders ask applicants to describe their "theory of change" in a proposal. This question can confuse applicants because they aren't sure what a theory of change is and whether they have one or not. But there are few charitable organizations that don't have one, even though they may not call it that.

A theory of change can be as simple as, "If we do this…, then this will happen…" In other words, it's a simple if/then statement. It connects the organization's day-to-day work with the change in the world that the organization would like to see (its mission statement).

If you keep this simple idea in mind, you will be prepared to deal with the various ways in which theory of change might appear in grant applications.

Definition

to reach in a similar format helps funders compare requests. Be aware that some funders will use the terms "logic model" and "theory of change" interchangeably. So it's important to pay attention to how the funder asks you to respond to either format. Those directions will provide clues to what the funder is really looking for.

Challenges of Logic Models

Logic models present certain difficulties. While they can be great tools for thinking about program design, they can also be burdensome. The simple model earlier in the chapter outlines a plan to expand a child care agency serving low-income families. It plugs our child care example into a logic model framework.

Remember, we started with simply describing a program your nonprofit really wants to carry out: expanded child care. When you complete a full logic model, it should contain all of the major reasons why your organization considered the project. Those reasons will be among the outputs and the outcomes.

Logic models present a formatting challenge. Look how one simple statement in the Activities column creates much more information in each of the other columns. There comes a point where so much information gets jammed into the model that it confuses people rather than enlightening them.

As you complete a logic model for a funder, pay close attention to the directions

Logic Models and Budgets

A logic model provides the context for your budget. Once you've completed each column, make sure you have the resources you need for each activity and any work you need to do to measure outputs and outcomes.

When you have a full list of the resources you'll need, you can create the budget. The first step is to put a price on each item. While that price will usually be expressed in dollars, there are times when in-kind donations are key. You may want to figure out what those in-kind donations are worth in dollars, such as the value of food distributed by a food bank.

Remember that some costs might be one-time costs, especially for a start-up, while others will be ongoing. A funder that only awards project grants might fund a one-time cost to start or expand a program. Another might be more likely to fund the ongoing costs of a new or expanded program. In either case, you can use this information to plan your future fundraising efforts.

IMPORTANT!

and examples. Usually, they will be good clues as to the level of detail you need. For example, under Resources, our example states, "Add furnishings for 1,550 square feet of new space." For some funders, that description may require additional detail, including tables, chairs, etc. Others may be happy with a summary that merely lists furnishings as a broad category and other facility requirements.

Learning to Love Logic Models

Many grantwriters see logic models as impediments that only complicate the application process. While there is a seed of truth to those feelings, logic models usually clarify a funder's thinking and charitable commitments. When you understand how a funder views the world, you can quickly identify how your organization's work fits or does not fit with a funder's priorities. While that may be an impediment to your current request, it can also be a clue to future opportunities. Over time, a funder's interests may change. And when a funder uses a logic model to convey those interests, you can quickly determine whether your organization's work is a fit or not. Being able to make that assessment quickly can be a great help to you in your work.

To Summarize...

- Logic models begin with the project you want to undertake.
- Filling out a logic model will help you see which resources you need to achieve your stated outcomes.
- Your logic model shows funders how resources connect to activities, what those activities will achieve, and how the project is important to the community.
- Logic models can help you show impact in your community beyond the participants in your program.

Chapter 18

Needs Statements

In This Chapter...
- What is the relationship of the project to the need?
- Whose needs are you presenting?
- How can you find relevant statistics?
- Who else is working on your issue?

The needs statement is a key section in your proposal. It's here that you explain why the community you serve needs the project you propose to carry out. You guide the reader through the process that led your organization to conclude that such a project or program was needed. You answer the question, "Why are we proposing to do this?" If you write a strong and compelling needs statement, you are half way to convincing the funder that this project should be funded.

It's important to show that this project grew out of a recognized community need—that it's not just an idea conceived by your marketing department. Even if the project you propose will improve your organization's image or prestige, you need to focus on how it will benefit the people you serve, not on how it will make you more competitive in the marketplace. (This is one way in which the nonprofit world differs from that of for-profit businesses.)

A strong needs statement will include local statistics that demonstrate community problems or gaps. It will also be proportional to the goals and objectives of your project. You want to concentrate on problems that can be solved (or at least mitigated) by the resources you are likely to have.

You also want to show that you're aware of other nonprofits that are working on the same issues. You can indicate where you fit in your field—your niche. If you're collaborating with other organizations to solve a common problem, this is a good place to mention it.

Which Comes First—The Project or the Need?

In an ideal grant development world, a project arises out of a need identified in the population served by a nonprofit. It's even better if leaders in the community approach the organization to help them solve a problem. For instance, a nonprofit may provide after-school care for elementary-aged students only, while middle school kids are considered old enough to take care of themselves. If those middle schoolers are getting into trouble in the late afternoon while their parents are still at work, their parents may approach the nonprofit with a request to develop after-school programs for older kids. The nonprofit and the parents can work together to design a suitable program, and then the organization can write grants to fund it. In this case, the need is clear and arises out of a well-defined gap in services articulated by the clients themselves.

But sometimes the project arises in a different way. Perhaps the project was proposed because the leadership in your organization got excited about doing it or wanted to be able to compete with similar organizations. Maybe the board of your university concluded that it needed a new engineering building, or the museum wanted to bring in a traveling exhibit.

In these cases, when you plan the grant proposal, you'll need to stop and think about the needs that the funder will care about. These may be different from those discussed in the board or staff meeting that led to the project.

Whose Needs Are They, Anyway?

When beginning grantwriters see a question in the guidelines that asks, "Why is this project needed?" they may be tempted to answer regarding their organization's needs: "We need this grant because our science labs are outdated." But what the funder is asking about is why the community needs the project, not why your organization wants to pursue it.

Many years ago, Goodwin had a grantwriting student who worked for a highly respected institution that provides therapeutic day care to low-income, high-risk children. (Let's call it Springfield Children's Daycare, or SCD.) This organization had been around for almost a hundred years, and its buildings were many decades old. A few months earlier, the Department of Health and Human Services (DSHS) had inspected SCD's facilities, and the charming but antiquated buildings had come up short. They failed to meet code on a number of levels and were close to being deemed unsafe. SCD was told that, unless it corrected these deficiencies within three years, the organization would be in danger of losing its accreditation.

> ### Waiting Lists Prove the Need
>
> A nonprofit that works with developmentally disabled adults realized there were very few opportunities for its clients to socialize, so it started holding a monthly dance for adults with developmental disabilities. The program was hugely popular, and soon there were more people wanting to attend than the venue could hold. The nonprofit applied for grants to allow it to rent a larger facility. The fact that it had a waiting list was proof in itself that the community it wanted to serve was enthusiastic about the program.
>
> **Pure Genius!**

Needless to say, this created a sense of urgency at SCD. After considerable research and discussion, the leadership decided to launch a capital campaign to replace its aging facilities, rather than trying to upgrade them. One of the reasons the student was taking Goodwin's class was to learn how to write grants for this campaign.

The first draft of her needs statement began something like this:

> *The facilities of Springfield Children's Daycare are badly in need of repair. A recent inspection by DSHS resulted in a failing grade. We were told that, unless we correct the deficiencies soon, we could lose our accreditation.*

Now this is a dramatic statement, and it certainly grabs the reader's attention. But it gives the wrong impression. This sounds like an organization on its last legs, in danger of imminent failure without an immediate infusion of cash.

That's not a good way to attract grants because, as the old fundraising adage goes, "Nobody wants to give you your last dollar."

But there's another reason why this needs statement is wrong-headed. It focuses on the needs of the organization, not the needs of the community. And in this case, the community had far-reaching needs, and the organization was doing a very good job of serving them.

Accentuate the Positive!

Instead of focusing on the drawbacks of its facilities, SCD should describe the needs of the community it serves. Its clientele is the children of struggling families in desperate need of help. These are children under five years old who are victims of abuse and neglect. Often they are on the verge of being removed from their families and placed in the foster care system. SCD provides the loving care that has been missing in these children's lives and works with the parents to teach them better parenting skills. SCD is often the last hope of keeping these families together, and the organization has an excellent track record of succeeding.

So, in its needs statement, SCD could describe the needs of this population and the organization's track record of success. After it has convinced the reader that it is providing a valuable service, it could then go on to talk about why it is launching a capital campaign to replace its facilities. The emphasis needs to be on the clientele, not on the organization itself. SCD needs to explain that the current facilities do not allow it to provide the level of care that its clients need and deserve. At this point, the proposal may list some of the deficiencies that were noted in the DSHS report and that SCD has been aware of for a number of years. All of this is a prelude to the goals and objectives section, where SCD will explain its plan for new buildings that will enable it to provide outstanding services to vulnerable children and families.

Circles of Need

One way to think about the various stakeholders is in terms of "circles of need." The largest circle is the community as a whole, and this is what the funder cares about primarily. Within that circle is the clientele served by the organization, in this case, small children whose lives have started out with a lot of disadvantages. The next smaller circle is SCD, the organization serving these children. And at the center is the facility, without which SCD cannot deliver its services. This figure illustrates a hierarchy of needs. Each level depends on the next, but if you jump right into the center, your proposal will sound as though you care only about the needs of your organization, not the needs of the community and the people you serve.

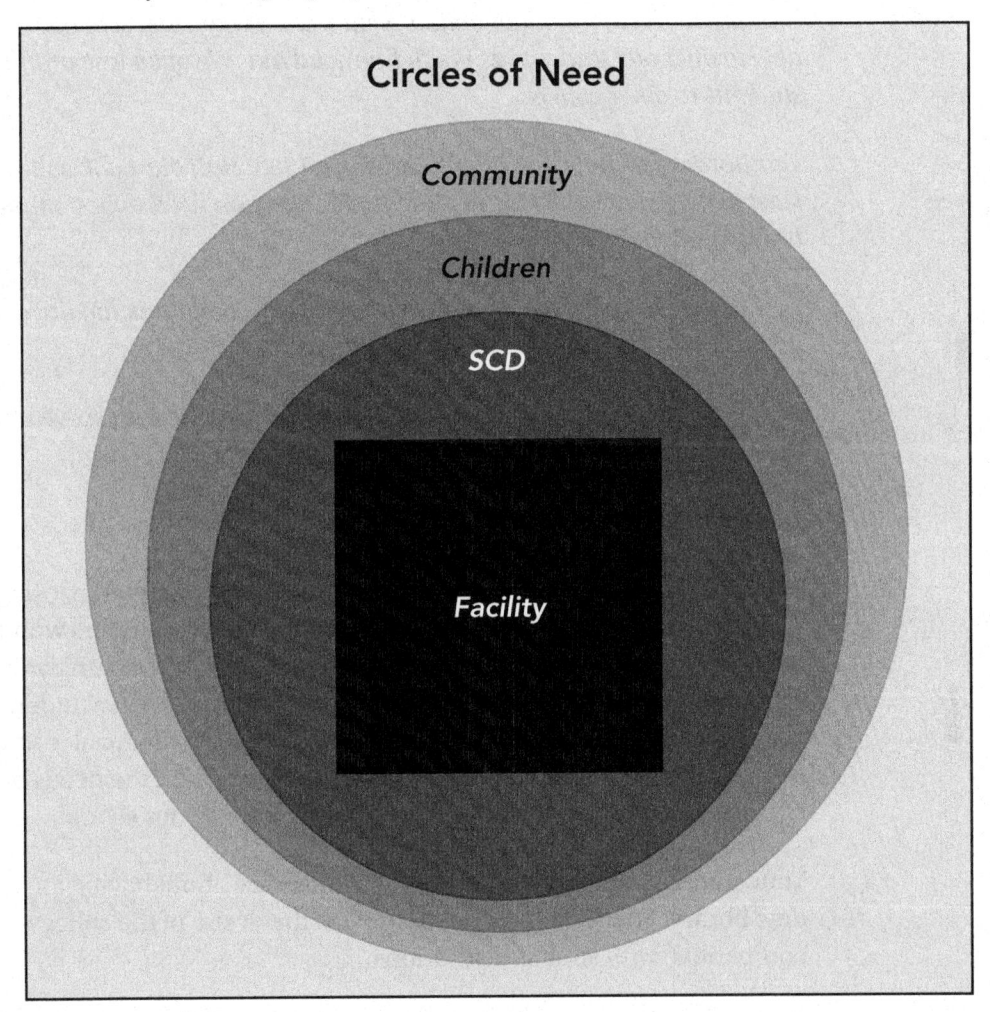

Circles of Need

- Community
- Children
- SCD
- Facility

Who Cares?

A good way to test whether needs are those of your community or your organization is to consider the question, "Who cares?" Look at the statements below, and think about who would care about them. Would these challenges concern the people you serve, or the community at large? Or would these be an issue only for your board and staff, and maybe your alumni? If you want funders to care, you must present needs that speak to a group beyond your immediate organizational family:

1. *Because we have a smaller endowment than many other schools, we are not able to offer our students as much financial aid. We often lose promising students to other colleges.*

2. *Our library has not been remodeled since 1982. Half our book collection is at least twenty years old. Our facilities and collection need to be enlarged and brought up to date.*

3. *In the current economic downturn, requests for food bank aid have doubled, while donations have decreased by 30 percent.*

4. *Due to financial and management difficulties over the past six years, both admissions and fundraising revenues have fallen by 20 percent.*

Here are some possible answers to "Who cares?" about these needs:

1. Only your board, staff, and alumni care about whether you're losing students to other schools due to lack of financial aid. Funders won't care, because these top-rated students are going to get snapped up by the best schools no matter what. But funders *do* care about whether students have the opportunity to attend college, regardless of their financial resources. In writing a proposal for scholarship funding, focus on the needs of your current and prospective students, not the needs of your school.

2. Your students, current and future, certainly care about having an up-to-date library. Focus on their needs, not on the desire of the college to be competitive with similar institutions.

3. This is clearly a community need that funders of human services organizations will care about.

4. This is a purely in-house problem. Your board, staff, and close supporters care very much about your financial difficulties. But funders who aren't already involved with your organization probably won't care. Pleading financial need will rarely get you funded by outsiders unless your nonprofit is seen as indispensable to the broader community.

Vital Statistics

A compelling needs statement will include a good core of well-researched statistics. It's not enough to say that too many people in your area are hungry. You need an estimate of the number of people suffering from food insecurity (the industry term for people who aren't sure where their next meal is coming from) and their percentage of the population of the area. What are the trends? Has this number been growing over the past several years? If so, why? Is it the economy, and the rate of unemployment? Is it the number of single-parent families? Some graphs or charts can illustrate the situation in a way that is easy to grasp.

It's important to make your statistics as local as possible. The national unemployment rate is only marginally useful. To make a strong point, you need to know the rate in your local area, and among the demographics you serve. Do your homework, and make your statistics as specific as possible.

Where to Find the Statistics You Need

One excellent place to start is the Census Bureau. Its American FactFinder website (*http://factfinder.census.gov*) gives detailed data on demographics, housing, employment, and many other elements of the economy in astonishing detail, down to zip codes. (Look up your own to see who your neighbors are.) The Census Bureau frequently offers in-person training in the use of its website at affordable prices—contact your local bureau to see if one is planned soon in your area. Training is also available online.

There are many other private resources that give excellent demographic and economic data. One is the United Way. In many areas, it provides a Community Needs Assessment, often on an annual basis. School districts offer demographic reports on their students, showing ethnicities, languages spoken at home, and the proportion of students receiving free or reduced-price lunch. Universities may report the number of their students receiving Pell grants, a federal needs-based financial aid program available only to low-income students.

Whatever field your organization works in, look for reports made by government agencies or well-known organizations that produce credible statistics. There is a wealth of information available if you do some research.

Make Sure You Have a Problem That Can Be Solved

Another term for needs statement is problem statement. You are describing a problem in your community, and soon you will propose a solution. So the problem you describe needs to be one that can be solved, at least in part, with the resources you are likely to have.

Many nonprofits work heroically to solve problems that, on a large scale, are never going away. As Jesus said, "The poor ye have always with you," and no one expects poverty to vanish entirely in the foreseeable future, even in a country as rich as the United States. Unemployment, homelessness, alcoholism, drug abuse, and a myriad of other social ills are not going to disappear any time soon. Still, these are the kinds of problems that nonprofits are working on. Some social and health issues may be large in scale, but your organization is going to try to improve the situation for a small, defined population. Describe the needs of that group in particular, so later you can move on to propose a solution that will work.

When you write your grant proposal, it's important to describe the need in a way that's proportional to the solution you will offer in the goals and objectives section. Maybe there's been an economic shift in your community, and many workers have been laid off from jobs that have been shipped overseas. You describe the distress that has been caused by this situation, and the need for workers to acquire new skills. Then you'll go on to propose a retraining program. This is a manageable approach to unemployment on a community basis.

Do You Need a Course in Statistics to Be a Grantwriter?

It certainly wouldn't hurt, and if you're dealing with studies of large scale populations, it is a good idea to take a statistics course. (Check your local university extension or community college.) Grantwriters working with school districts, large health organizations, or major social service organizations, for instance, will find a solid knowledge of statistics extremely useful. However, if you're working with a smaller clientele or in a field that doesn't deal with large populations, you can probably learn what you need to know about statistics on your own. One old but still relevant and highly entertaining book is Darrell Huff's *How to Lie with Statistics*. Another readable introduction to the field is Larry Gonick's *The Cartoon Guide to Statistics*.

Perspiration

Need for the Arts

Arts organizations often struggle with the needs statement. How do you describe the community need for a performance of Beethoven string quartets? Nobody's going to die if the ballet doesn't perform *Swan Lake*. Arts organizations often get an inferiority complex when they compare their work to the essential human needs tackled by social service organizations. As we used to say at the opera, "Starve a child and feed a tenor."

Because of this insecurity, arts organizations often try to justify themselves by asserting that involvement in the arts helps solve other kinds of problems. You hear statements such as:

- Studying music helps kids do better in math.
- After-school arts programs keep at-risk kids from joining gangs.
- Art therapy can help people suffering from mental illness learn to express themselves.
- Music in senior centers can help people with dementia be more alert and engaged.

All these things may be true, but the programs they justify use the arts in the service of something else. What about the value of art for its own sake?

The world does need the arts, and if you're someone who creates or enjoys them, you know this in your heart. For many people, the world would be a barren place without music, dance, theater, or visual arts. And the lives of many more people would be enriched if they had more contact with and understanding of the arts.

Fortunately, you usually don't need to make a case for the core value of the arts in a grant proposal, because you're writing to a funder that already believes in them—otherwise, the arts wouldn't be listed among its funding interests. So draw your circle a little smaller than the universal question, "Why do people need art?" Ask instead, "Why does this community need a live performance by world-class artists?" or, "Why does our town need a youth symphony?" Maybe you are bringing the arts to people who may not have access to them for reasons of cost or distance. Maybe you're giving children a chance to develop and showcase their talents. Whatever the situation, be assured that people need the arts because they feed the human soul.

Who Else Is Working on This Problem?

Somewhere in the proposal—often in the needs section—you will need to discuss other organizations that are working to solve the same problems you describe. Funders frequently remark that, in each funding cycle, they get proposals from several organizations, each claiming to be the only one in its area working on a particular issue, or with a certain population. "How can these nonprofits think they're the only ones dealing with this problem?" the funders will say. "Don't they know there's a similar organization just a few blocks away?"

If you're not part of a consortium of organizations in your field, do your homework and find out who else is out there. Apart from simply doing a Google search, you can get this information by going to a database like Foundation Directory Online and searching in the grants section. Use search terms that bring up grants received by your own organization, and see who else comes up within the same parameters. If you're not familiar with these nonprofits, go to their web pages and find out who they are and what they do.

You want to assure the funder that you are not duplicating services provided by another organization. Chances are, you have your own niche. The population served may be large enough that there's plenty of room for several nonprofits to assist with its needs. You may be working with a particular segment of the population, or your approach may be different from that of other nonprofits. In the needs section, let the funder know

Circular Reasoning Not Allowed!

One student in a grantwriting class was writing a proposal to build an adult day center for seniors in a rural community. His reasoning went something like this:

There are no adult day centers in our town. Therefore, our organization proposes to build a day center.

The problem with this thinking is that it assumes the need for adult day centers is self-evident. Instead, the student needed to describe the plight of isolated seniors who sit in front of their TVs all day with limited social contact. He could elaborate on the risks of this situation to their health and well-being. After establishing their need for companionship and stimulation, he could then have gone on to propose the adult day center as the solution.

WATCH OUT!

you're aware of what other organizations are doing and describe your own place within this sphere. But don't criticize others—just describe what's special about your organization. And if you're collaborating with some of these other nonprofits to meet community needs, that's even better.

To Summarize...

- The needs statement is crucial in explaining why your project is important and should be funded.

- Funders care about the needs of your community or clientele, not the needs of your organization.

- Arts organizations can describe needs in terms of how they will bring enrichment to their communities.

- To show that you're not duplicating services, describe other organizations that address the same areas of needs as yours and show how you are different, how you serve a particular population, or how you fill a unique niche.

Chapter 19

Goals and Objectives

In This Chapter...
- Why use goals and objectives?
- How do goals and objectives influence your grant applications?
- What are SMART objectives?
- What's the difference between process and results?

Even if your organization doesn't formalize goals and objectives, it still has them. Think of it like this: Your organization has a reason for existing, a mission. It carries out activities because its leadership and supporters feel those are the right things to do in pursuit of that mission. And when an organization begins looking for grants it will often need to put that work into a goals and objectives format in order to respond to funder questions.

In this chapter, we'll describe how your organization can describe its work in that format. As you read, keep in mind that while your organization has only one mission, the goals and objectives structure can be used at a variety of levels. For example, an organization might create a strategic plan with three goals for the next several years. Those goals are the main themes of the work the organization is going to do to support its mission. And each goal may have several objectives that need to be attained to meet the goal.

When goals and objectives are written down, they become tools to ensure that everyone in your organization is working toward the same purpose. They impose a level of planning upon organizations; they encourage everyone in the organization to ask, "Are we doing what is best right now to pursue our mission?" If you understand how mission, goals, and objectives fit together, you can deal with the variety of formats you may see in grant applications.

The Mission, Goals, Objectives, and Work Plan Structure

Many organizations formalize their mission, goals, and objectives in a strategic plan. They use that plan to help develop work plans year by year in line with the goals and objectives. But even if your organization doesn't use a strategic planning process, it can still write down its mission, goals, and objectives. If the organization does even that level of planning, it helps a grantwriter build the case for support for any specific grant request.

If the goals and objectives are not written down, a grantwriter will have to ferret out that information from staff, volunteers, and board members. Without that information, it will be hard to make a case for how a specific request helps the organization pursue its work. We've seen cases where

> **What Is Your Charitable Purpose?**
>
> When your organization completed its application for charitable status with the IRS, it had to state a purpose for the organization. That purpose had to fit the definition of "charitable" in the law. According to the IRS website, "The exempt purposes set forth in Section 501(c)(3) are charitable, religious, educational, scientific, literary, testing for public safety, fostering national or international amateur sports competition, and preventing cruelty to children or animals." As we said in **Chapter 3**, the IRS also includes arts and environmental protection among these purposes.
>
> Your organization's mission needs to fit that purpose. Likewise, your organization's goals and objectives must work toward your mission. It's important that mission, goals, and objectives work together toward your charitable purpose.
>
> **Observation**

grantwriters have rewritten LOIs several times because each time they talked to a different staff person, they got a different message about what the organization did and why the grant was important.

So here is a structure for understanding mission, goals, objectives, and work plans. If your organization already has a strategic plan, compare the structure outlined below to how that plan is organized. If your organization only has an informal outline of goals and objectives, use this framework to formalize it. Then vet your goals and objectives outline with others in the organization. When you have an outline that people agree on, you have a base of information for building grant requests. That outline doesn't have to be shared or made public so long as the organization's leadership agrees with it.

Goals and Objectives Framework

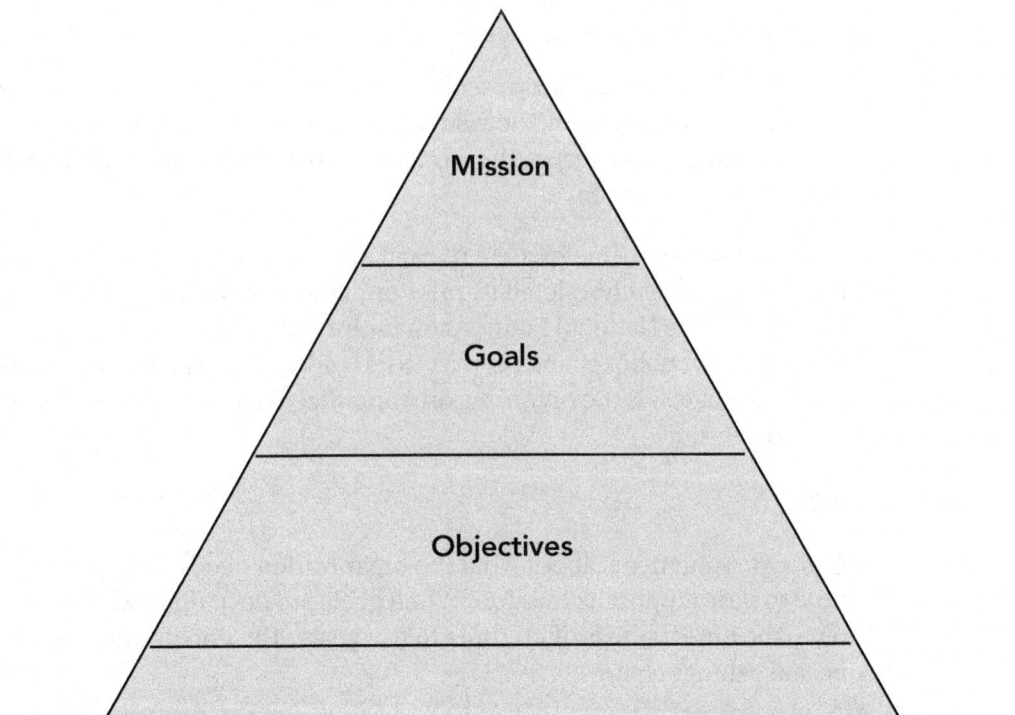

- Mission
- Goals
- Objectives
- Work Plans

Mission

An organization's *mission* is usually broad and inspirational. It is the essential reason your organization exists and provides a long-term vision for the organization. It should be consistent with the charitable purpose outlined in the organization's key documents such as articles of incorporation, by-laws, and similar documents.

Missions are often unattainable because they encompass work that may not end. Here are some examples:

- Girl Scouting builds girls of courage, confidence, and character, who make the world a better place.

- Our mission is to feed America's hungry through a nationwide network of member food banks and engage our country in the fight to end hunger (Feeding America).

- The J. Paul Getty Museum seeks to inspire curiosity about, and enjoyment and understanding of, the visual arts by collecting, conserving, exhibiting, and interpreting works of art of outstanding quality and historical importance.

There is a sense of timelessness in each of these mission statements. Has an organization ever completed its mission? One example is the March of Dimes. Founded as the National Foundation for Infantile Paralysis, its mission was to find a cure for polio. Thanks in part to its work a polio vaccine was invented and in the late '50s the organization announced a new mission: prevention of birth defects.

Goals

Goals are statements about what the organization needs to do over a period of time to best support its mission. When goals are developed within a strategic plan, the time frame is often three to five years. The time frame is important because things change.

When the board and staff periodically review goals and objectives, the process helps an organization answer two key questions: "If we achieved these goals over the next several years, would we make progress toward our mission?" and "Are we doing the best things we could to work toward our mission?"

Being able to explain an organization's goals helps a grantwriter show funders why a particular grant request is important for its community.

Objectives

Objectives outline the steps you need to take to reach a goal. Each goal will probably have several objectives. And occasionally an objective may support more than one goal. Objectives combine the practical with the aspirational. An organization's mission and goals are aspirational. Good objectives articulate time frames and numbers. They are measurable and practical.

Later in the chapter, we cover SMART objectives. SMART stands for Specific, Measurable, Attainable, Reasonable, and Time based. All of these factors are important because they provide a way to connect an organization's work to community needs. These measures are similar to the outputs in a logic model.

Work Plans

A *work plan* describes what an organization needs to do in a given year to accomplish an objective. It provides the day-to-day marching orders for activities during a given year. Work plans can be flexible, and they can change.

Let's look at how that framework may have fit the work of the March of Dimes in the years before it achieved its original mission. That mission was to find a cure for polio. One goal in support of its mission was to find a vaccine to protect children from the polio virus. Doctors knew that the virus was highly contagious, so reducing the number of people who contracted the virus would have had a big impact on reducing the total number of infections.

That goal, developing a vaccine, had a number of objectives. For example, one objective may have been to make grants to support promising research. Another objective might have been work the March of Dimes did itself on vaccine research. Since it usually takes more than a year to achieve an objective, each objective needs a work plan for the day-to-day and week-to-week work that needs to be done toward that objective during a year.

Often the work plan is a way to tie your work to the goals and objectives you outline in your grant request.

Asking for Tools

Funders want to understand how your project will affect community needs. They want to understand your plan to reduce homelessness or to help at-risk youth. But people in your organization often come to you with requests for

> **Perspiration**
>
> ### Keep Asking "Why?"
>
> One skill a grantwriter has to develop is asking questions of other staff, or even oneself, about the reasons behind a particular project. As a result, you may have to ask, "Why?" several times before you can write good objectives that will be at the heart of your grant request.
>
> Let's take a building project as an example. When asked to start looking for grants to construct a new building, a grantwriter should ask, "Why do we need a new building?"
>
> The answer might be something like "We need more room for services." Again, a good grantwriter will ask, "Why do we need room for more services?"
>
> At this point the conversation either becomes easier or more challenging. It becomes easier if the people you're asking are willing to be expansive about their answers. They may answer with informative descriptions of how the organization has to turn away people asking for help, why they think so many more clients are asking for services, and how new a larger facility will help to deal with those issues.
>
> Terse answers such as, "We need more room for services because we're turning too many people away" are harder to deal with. When that happens the grantwriter needs to continue gracefully asking, "Why?" until the full story emerges. It may take four or five "whys" before the basic reasons are uncovered.
>
> A grantwriter has to uncover all of those assumptions in order to make a request about what a project will accomplish for its community. A request to help provide more food for low-income families is much stronger than a request to buy a freezer.

tools, i.e., the actual items that grant monies will buy. So let's begin with an example to show how you might ask questions of others in your organization to create goals and objectives for a specific request.

If you're not already familiar with the model LOI in **Appendix A**, please read it before moving on in this chapter. What follows refers to its content.

Let's say you're the development director or grantwriter for North Counties Food Resources, and one morning the executive director approaches you about getting a grant to purchase a new walk-in freezer. As uncomfortable as it might seem, you need to ask the question, "Why do we need this new freezer?"

This can be a tough question to ask. But grantwriters need to truly understand what they are writing about. One response might be that the organization needs more room to increase the amount of food it can supply to local programs. Another might be that more and more frozen foods are available, but North Counties Food can't accept and distribute them without more freezer space.

A few more questions can provide more details about the motivation for getting this new freezer. Questions about the capacity of the equipment and how much food it might make available can put numbers to the project. When you understand the motivations behind the request to "Find a grant for…" you can make your best case based upon solid goals and objectives. That framework also becomes a tool to check your assumptions by sharing them with the staff and volunteers who were your original sources for information.

SMART Objectives

To make an effective case, objectives need to be concrete and measurable. They describe how you'll make progress toward your goal. That is why many websites and grantwriting books talk about SMART objectives. SMART is an acronym for Specific, Measurable, Attainable, Realistic (relevant), and Time-bound.

SMART objectives include both process and result objectives, similar to outputs and outcomes. A *process objective* sets measures for the work you do. For example, a process objective sets targets for how many clients you'll serve and the time frame. It might be monitored by attendance sheets or check-ins with staff.

A *result objective* measures the impact of your work. For example, setting a target that 90 percent of the people who attend classes will show an increase in their knowledge of the subject information as recorded by pre- and post-test scores.

Specific

When you write an objective, it has to be about something you can observe. An objective describes who and what will be impacted by the project activities. The verb you use to describe the "what" of the project is at the heart of what that objective will achieve.

Measurable

The measure addresses the amount of change you expect to achieve. You can put it into terms such as a number change or percentage change over time.

Attainable

When you write an objective, it should be attainable within the context of the proposal. That would include both the time available and the amount of resources you've planned for.

Reasonable

Reasonable means that the objective must seem relevant to the goal that the objective supports. It must also seem like something the project can actually accomplish.

Time Based

The time frame for your objectives should relate to your project plans. This time frame also guides you in writing your budget.

A Grant Proposal from 1776

Around the time of the American bicentennial, a grantwriter imagined what it would have been like if the Declaration of Independence had been submitted to the administration of King George III as a grant proposal. He claimed that the following letter came to him in a nightmare.

The Court of King George III
London, England

September 10, 1776

Mr. Thomas Jefferson
Continental Congress
Independence Hall.
Philadelphia, Pennsylvania

Dear Mr. Jefferson:

We have read your "Declaration of Independence" with great interest. Certainly, it represents a considerable undertaking, and many of your statements do merit serious consideration. Unfortunately, the Declaration as a whole fails to meet recently adopted specifications for proposals to the Crown, so we must return the document to you for further refinement. The questions which follow might assist you in your process of revision.

1. In your opening paragraph you use the phrase "the Laws of Nature and Nature's God." What are these laws? In what way are they the criteria on which you base your central arguments? Please document with citations from the recent literature.

2. In the same paragraph you refer to the "opinions of Mankind." Whose polling data are you using? Without specific evidence, it seems to us, the "opinions of mankind" are a matter of opinion.

3. You hold certain truths to be "self-evident." Could you please elaborate. If they are as evident as you claim, then it should not be difficult for you to locate the appropriate supporting statistics.

4. "Life, liberty, and the pursuit of happiness" seem to be the goals of your proposal. These are not measurable goals. If you were to say that "among these is the ability to sustain an average life expectancy in six of the 13 colonies of at least 55 years, and to enable all newspapers in the colonies to print without outside interference, and to raise the average income of the colonies by 10 percent in the next 10 years" these would be measurable goals. Please clarify.

5. You state that "whenever any Form of Government becomes destructive of these ends, it is the Right of the People to alter or to abolish it and to Institute a new

Government . . ." Have you weighed this assertion against all the alternatives? Or is it predicated solely on the baser instincts?

6. Your description of the existing situation is quite extensive. Such a long list of grievances should precede the statement of goals, not follow it.

7. Your strategy for achieving your goal is not developed at all. You state that the colonies "ought to be Free and Independent States," and that they are "Absolved from All Allegiance to the British Crown." Who or what must change to achieve this objective? In what way must they change? What specific steps will you take to overcome the resistance? How long will it take? We have found that a little foresight in these areas helps to prevent careless errors later on.

8. Who among the list of signatories will be responsible for implementing your strategy? Who conceived it? Who provided the theoretical research? Who will constitute the advisory committee? Please submit an organizational chart and vitae of the principal investigators.

9. You must include an evaluation design. We have been requiring this since Queen Anne's War.

10. What impact will your program have? Your failure to include any assessment of this inspires little confidence in the long-range prospects of your undertaking.

11. Please submit a PERT diagram, an activity chart, an itemized budget and a continuation plan.

We hope that these comments prove useful in revising your "Declaration of Independence." We welcome the submission of your revised proposal. Our due date for revisions is December 31, 1776. Ten copies with original signatures will be required.

Best wishes,

Lord North
Prime Minister of Great Britain

(Edward Schwartz. 1974. "Dear Mr. Jefferson." Social Policy, 5:10-11)
Reprinted by permission of *Social Policy Magazine*.

Chapter 19—Goals and Objectives

In-House versus Public Goals

When the leaders of a nonprofit create a strategic plan, it is common to come up with some goals aimed at winning a virtual competition with other organizations. They may say something like, "In five years, Spring Green University will be turning out more highly qualified environmental science graduates than any other school in the state."

These are internal goals, not goals to promote outside your organizational family. Funders not already close to your institution don't care whether your organization is better than another.

When creating your long-term plan, highlight goals that the community will care about. For instance you might say: "Spring Green University will work to ensure that there are enough highly qualified environmental scientists to help preserve our wild spaces for the next generation."

Goals like these will persuade funders that your organization cares about making your community and the world a better place, not just about staying in business.

Example

Lord North's critique seems focused on the lack of clarity and specificity found in the Declaration of Independence, issues modern grantwriters would do well to consider. Do his suggestions for measurable goals in #4 meet the requirements of SMART objectives?

Let's say your mission involves improving K–12 education in your community. In support of that mission, one of your goals is to improve the scores of incoming kindergarten students on readiness to learn assessments. One SMART objective might be "to provide early learning activities for four hundred children aged two to four over the next two years."

That SMART objective cites a specific process accomplishment, a measurable amount of work, and the time period. It provides critical information for you to build your program. A new program might need start-up time, so the number of people served in the first six months would be far smaller than the number served in the last six months of the project.

A SMART objective that sets concrete measures encourages work plans that set similar measures with monthly or quarterly targets. Those targets can provide important feedback for your program.

What If You Aren't Meeting Your Targets?

When a process objective shows you've fallen behind your expected measures, it can lead to one of three decisions:

- The next year's work plan could include higher targets to meet the objective.

- You could decide that you won't meet the target due to certain factors and share that information with your funders.

- You could look at why the program fell short and make changes in the program.

SMART objectives show funders that an organization takes its work seriously and is willing to evaluate its methods and results.

Do SMART Objectives Overcomplicate Things?

Grantwriters have shared with us a frustration that objectives overcomplicate their organization's work. An example is a small housing agency that says it will serve as many people as it can over the next year. It claims it can't set measurable objectives because it doesn't know how long families will need to stay in the housing it provides.

First, goals and objectives don't have to be complicated. The point is that an organization writes down what it hopes to accomplish and how it plans to do it. Every organization hopes to do more. Goals and objectives provide a format for thinking about how an organization can do more.

In this example, the housing agency can look at its work over the past several years and estimate what an average length of stay has been. Looking at that information may even reveal emerging trends or other questions. Perhaps the length of stay seems to be getting longer. Why is that? Is it harder to find affordable housing for the families to move to? Are employment issues holding families back? The answers to each of those questions might be critical to your current grant requests or new projects the agency wants to launch.

Second, you don't need goals and objectives for every funder. There are funders that will make grants to a small housing agency just because they want to make grants to organizations working with the homeless.

But when you write a proposal to a funder that wants to help organizations grow, expand, or reach new groups, you'll need goals and objectives. Readers of those proposals want to understand how you plan to move beyond your regular operating budget or the day-to-day needs of your organization.

It can be as easy as stating a goal and the objectives you need to meet to reach that goal, and then showing how a piece of new equipment will help you meet those objectives. That approach makes your grant request about your community rather than an organizational need, which is less appealing.

Measuring Process and Results

Organizations find measures challenging for several reasons. One is a fear of failure. If you cite a specific number as a target, then it's possible you could fall short of that number. Yet if you set a target too low it may not seem large enough to justify the grant request.

Another challenge is that there are two types of objectives: process and result. As we mentioned earlier, process objectives measure the work that an organization carries out. Some examples are numbers of people served, units of service, and pounds of food distributed. While recording that information isn't always easy, an organization can design ways to accomplish that task.

Result objectives are more difficult. The purpose of a result objective is to describe the impact of your work. But measuring those results can be complicated. Usually, you'll want result objectives to be closely related to the needs data you share. If your needs statement says that "60 percent of young people aged eighteen to twenty-five are unemployed in our community," then a funder will expect that one of your objectives will be a result objective about unemployment.

Here's an example of how this works. An organization runs antibullying programs in local elementary schools. A process objective would be that five hundred fifth grade students see your presentations during October and November of the next school year.

One result objective might be that 95 percent of students will improve their knowledge of bullying behavior. You could show this by giving tests before and after the presentations. This is a result objective that you can easily measure.

Your rationale (theory of change) for your antibullying program is that if students really understand bullying, then they will be less likely to engage in it and more likely to discourage bullying by other students. While you've set a measure to see if the presentations increase knowledge of bullying, you'll need a different measure to determine whether that knowledge had any impact.

What kind of result objective would you create to measure that? Think back to the original concerns about bullying. Were certain schools chosen for the program because they were worried about bullying? Perhaps the schools identified bullying as an issue because of incident reports being filed or anecdotal information from the staff.

If the school tracks bullying incidents, you could set a result object such as "bullying incidents will go down by 60 percent within three months after the training." A results objective like this tells you whether your if/then idea is true or not. If students meet the testing score objective but bullying continues, you may need to question your rationale for the project.

This approach gives your organization a lot of power over setting the agenda for evaluating its own work. When a funder asks, as many do, "How will you know if the project was successful?" you have a clear answer. And since that answer connects to impact on the community, it can help build your relationship with that funder.

To Summarize...

- Your organization's goals should support your mission statement. Your objectives in support of those goals guide your work plans.

- The best objectives are specific, measurable, and attainable within the resources and time available, relevant to the goal, and time based.

- Objectives are a way to monitor the implementation of your project.

- It is critical to understand the difference between process objectives and result objectives, and the role of each.

Chapter 20

Project Plans

In This Chapter...
- How do you describe your program or project?
- Who will your clients be?
- Where and when will your project take place?
- Who will lead the project?

The first question funders ask of a proposal is whether the need or opportunity you outline is important to their giving priorities. The next questions they ask are, "How does this organization plan to achieve its goals, and can it carry out that plan?" The way you answer those questions is your project plan.

Many of the Common Grant Application forms from around the country ask grantwriters to "describe the program or project." But what does a funder really mean by that? When you are faced with such a general question, the funder usually wants you to cover four basic questions: who, how, where, and when?

There will be times when you'll need to provide more details about each of those questions, such as when you respond to a Request for Proposal (RFP). In an RFP a funder has already decided what it thinks the needs are and what should be done about those needs. What a funder wants to know from your application is whether your organization is the best one to carry out that work. Thankfully, RFPs usually guide you through the who, how, where, and when questions and spell out the level of detail you should provide.

Whether you need to provide an overview or a detailed description, the outline for describing your plan is still the same. And while the focus of this chapter is about outlining your organization's plan within a grant application, you may find that making sure your organization has at least a draft plan early on can help your grantwriting. A draft plan will help you write a better LOI or respond to the questions on an online form.

Think of it this way: Would you write a better description of a unicorn just sitting at your desk thinking about unicorns or by looking at a picture of a unicorn? For most writers, a picture usually works better. It's the difference between writing about an idea for a project and writing about the project itself.

Whom Will Your Project Serve?

The description of the clients your project will serve says a lot about how your organization views community needs. It can also help funders understand how your program or project will impact the community. For example, Red River Youth Services (RRYS) wants to start offering parenting classes. It already works with the state's Family Services Office on foster care and over the past few months the two groups have discussed the high rate of child abuse and neglect in the community.

While the parenting classes will be generally available to the public, RRYS plans to work with Family Services to recruit parents it believes are at most risk for child neglect problems. That approach makes sense. When an organization wants to reduce the incidence of a problem in a community, it will have the best chance of making a difference if it can focus on those who are most affected.

If you worked for Red River Youth Services and were handed the job of finding grants for this parenting program, you might propose three reasons why RRYS is working on this issue. First, "We know that our area has a higher rate of child abuse and neglect cases than any other area in our county." Second, "We know that parenting classes can help reduce child abuse and neglect, especially for parents at high risk for such behavior." And finally, "The state officer for children's services is eager to help us recruit and work with those parents."

While those reasons would be a good start, you need to put this in a larger context. That description can include the communities you expect to serve as well as any number of demographic factors such as age, income level, ethnic background, and more. Anything relevant you can share about the people or communities you plan to serve adds depth to your proposal.

Uninspired

Are You Reaching the Right People?

Organizations can feel compelled to build a program to serve a lot of people, and sometimes that feeling is encouraged by funders. Big numbers may seem to equate to big impact. But often making sure you impact the right people can be more important than serving large numbers of people.

A group of concerned women started a project in the early '90s with the hope of reducing the number of teen pregnancies in their state. Their strategy was to raise money for professionally produced public service announcements (PSAs). The PSAs would be broadcast by the local affiliates of major networks as a part of the regular rotation of PSAs.

This approach allowed the group to claim that hundreds of thousands of people would see the PSAs. But funders asked, will the right people see it? This group's approach missed key questions such as, "Who are the people who truly affect teen pregnancy rates? What do they need to hear? And are they watching the afternoon broadcast of *As the World Turns* on a major broadcast or MTV on cable after school?" (Remember, it was the '90s.)

The reality was that the high rates of teen pregnancy could be traced to a handful of census tracts, and that for the most part, teenage boys and girls were the ones who needed to hear the message. That approach may not have required PSAs at all. But to the extent the project used media it was important to place ads on the right television shows and radio stations that teens listened to.

A focused approach to a much smaller group could have created a compelling project that had the chance for real impact. Instead, a concern about numbers—hundreds of thousands of people potentially seeing the PSA—produced a diluted approach having little, if any, impact.

Showing Impact

Organizations often feel that the number of people they plan to serve seems small, and thus not that important, in relationship to the whole population of the community. What organizations need to do, and what grantseekers need to share in the proposals they write, is show how a community need is not always spread equally among all people and all areas.

An example might be homeownership rates reported in census data or food insecurity reported in the Household Food Security reports by the USDA. If you only cite county-wide or even city-wide data as evidence of a need, you invite funders to compare the number of people you will serve with those county or city-wide numbers. But if you look more closely at the statistics you may find that the need is more apparent in certain areas, which you might be able to identify by census tract or zip code.

For example, since food insecurity correlates highly with income levels, you can identify food insecurity down to the neighborhoods and quantify the number of people who are most affected by food insecurity. The number of people in those communities and the number of people who are food insecure will be smaller than those numbers for the county or city as a whole. For example, your proposal can outline this by saying, "While our county has one of the highest rates of food insecurity in the state, the people most impacted by hunger live in…" As long as the areas you cite are the ones you plan to serve you've created a context where funders and your organization can compare the numbers of people you plan to serve to the people in need in those communities. That makes what may seem to be a small number look more impactful because indeed it is.

How do You Plan to Help?

You should be prepared to describe how your program will work on a number of levels. While the initial contact with a funder, such as an LOI, only needs a summary of how your program will work, a full application requires more detail. How much detail? Usually a funder's application form provides clues. Those instructions might include:

- Provide titles and job descriptions for each member of the project staff.
- Describe staff qualifications.

- Include résumés for key staff.

- Describe any models used by the program such as evidence-based practices.

- Describe how you will evaluate the program.

Levels of Summarization

Writing summaries is a skill in itself. Even a simple project can have several levels, and when it comes to summarizing a project it can be hard to decide what to put in, what to stress, and what you can leave out. Over time, it's a skill you will build. That skill begins with understanding that your project can be broken down into three levels: the overall strategy, innovative or new aspects of the project, and an outline of the specific program elements.

Sharing the Overall Strategy

Sharing the overall strategy is the most basic level of summary. You might begin with your theory of change such as "If we provide more food through food banks, then we'll reduce hunger in our community." You might also include an overview of the level of service that you'll provide and insight about key factors relating to the needs you've cited.

Innovative or New Aspects of Your Project

When a funder wants to know more than your overall strategy your next level of summary is highlighting any innovative or new aspects of your project. An innovative aspect is one that is just emerging in the field and not widely used. A new aspect is one that is new to your organization but is well known and used around the country such as an evidence-based practice.

Can you submit a grant proposal without an innovative or new element? Generally, not. When you write a grant for a new project, it will have elements that are new to your organization, even if that simply means serving more people.

On the surface, it may seem that a request for a continuing program wouldn't have any new elements. But every organization changes year to year. There may be changes in the demography of the people you serve, the needs they present, the increasing amount of people coming for services, or other changes. If you have a vital and important program, you'll find some new aspect every year, but only if you look for it.

Outline Specific Program Elements

Outlining specific elements of a program includes providing more details about how you plan to carry out your overall strategy. For example, providing more food through food banks might mean opening more food banks to serve areas that are currently underserved, or it might mean changing the way that you offer services. For instance, many food banks have adopted a "shopping" model for service. Rather than giving people a prepacked box of food, this approach allows people to select many items. Many food banks using this approach report that people tell them that their food goes further because they can use every item they bring home.

This level of description can also include information about the staff and/or volunteers who are a part of the project. For example, a neighborhood clinic might describe how it recruits volunteer doctors and nurses for its program. Or another program might outline the experience of key staff members in providing similar services during their careers. A funder that asks you to provide résumés of key staff might be interested in this level of detail in your program description.

Where Services Are Located

Explaining where your services are located covers two questions. One is simply describing the site(s) where the services will take place. This might include your present building, remote sites around your community, in-home services, or some combination. The key is to explain why you chose those sites. One factor, of course, would be convenience to where your clients live.

Describing the geographic area where your clients live can lead into describing the areas your organization typically serves. Don't assume that funders know where your organization is located or where it operates. And you can't assume that they know key details about those areas, even if they have made grants there before. This is especially true for funders that are located far away from some of the regions they serve.

Also, think about the relationship between the geographic area represented on your letterhead and the area you plan to serve with this particular project. Say your offices are located in Adams County. Your letterhead would reflect

Showing Impact for a Regional Organization

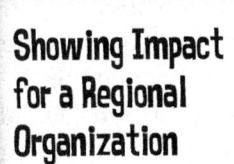

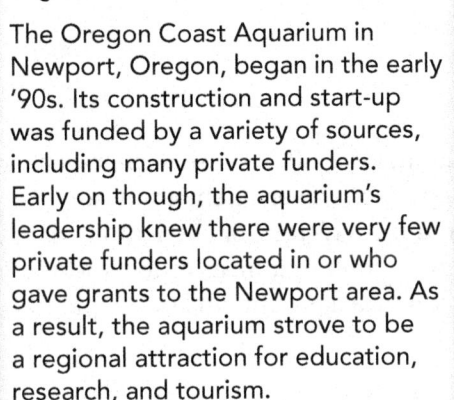

The Oregon Coast Aquarium in Newport, Oregon, began in the early '90s. Its construction and start-up was funded by a variety of sources, including many private funders. Early on though, the aquarium's leadership knew there were very few private funders located in or who gave grants to the Newport area. As a result, the aquarium strove to be a regional attraction for education, research, and tourism.

It made the case to funders in the Portland area, some 130 miles to the northeast of Newport, that the aquarium would be an important regional resource. It was a unique facility that no one expected to be replicated in Portland. As a result, private funders supported the aquarium because it was going to have an impact on the communities they supported.

That fidelity to mission was one reason that the Oregon Coast Aquarium was chosen as the site for rehabilitating Keiko of *Free Willy* fame so that he could be released back into the Atlantic Ocean near Iceland.

Pure Genius!

---

this and perhaps through past history your organization is known as an Adams County nonprofit. But your grant request is about opening a new site in nearby Brown County. When you discuss both the geography your organization serves and communities the new project will serve, stress your work in Brown County.

Finally, a funder will want you to share your history of serving people from an area it cares about before it will consider funding your organization. If your organization serves a region, a funder will look at your request in light of how it affects the areas the funder focuses on. The key is that you provide a significant amount of service, not just impact a few people from the funder's preferred area.

When Will This Happen?

Your project may have a definite start date, or it may depend on when you get the funding. But you can't say in your proposal, "The project will start as soon as we get the grant." If your start date is flexible, look at the funder's timeline for notifying successful grantseekers, and adjust your schedule accordingly. If you're seeking funding from several sources, you'll have to estimate the date by when you expect to have enough resources to begin. Even if the start date is not certain when you apply, you may be able to create a schedule showing what will be accomplished after the first three months, six months, and so on. And of course, state how long it will take to complete the grant-funded portion of the project.

A good example is a building project, which may take several years. If you provide dates for key steps such as groundbreaking, construction, completion, and opening it helps funders understand the flow of your project. You should also share the impact of the services the new building will make possible. Since building projects are often motivated by a desire to serve more people, funders will be interested in what that means. While that benefit begins when the doors open to your new building, it goes on for years and years. If you share the increased number of people the new building will serve over the next five years, you strengthen the case for your project.

Another Who: Project Leadership

Some funders will ask for information about key staff because it can reveal your organization's ability to carry out a project. Government grants are a prime example. Federal grants usually require a résumé or curriculum vitae for project leads. While private grants generally don't require as much information on personnel, many funders do ask for some background on key people, especially your executive director.

Sometimes the qualifications of the person directing the project are a key part of its appeal. If your leader is highly qualified and/or well known, make sure to highlight his or her background, experience, and vision.

In other cases, you may be creating new positions, so you won't have a person in place as you write your proposal. The job description for the new position can help a funder understand the qualifications of the people you plan to hire.

Even when funders don't ask for specifics on staff, a few general statements can assure them that the people in your organization are qualified to carry out the organization's planned work.

> **Keeping Résumés on File**
>
> One resource that grantwriters should keep on hand is copies of the résumés or curricula vitae of key organizational staff. Grant applications often ask for that information as a part of the application packets. As projects are developed, check to see that you have current information on staff in key positions.
>
> *Observation*

To Summarize...

- Funders want to understand the steps your organization will take to accomplish the project.

- Describing the people and geographic areas the project will serve can help make the case for your project and your organization.

- The timeline for a project can include both when the work will be done and the time period over which the community will benefit from the project.

- Information about your organization's staff can help to build your case.

Chapter 21

Evaluation Plans

In This Chapter...

- How do objectives and evaluation relate to each other?
- How can you tell funders what success will look like?
- How do you use your evaluation plan to outline what will happen in the future?
- What are quantitative and qualitative evaluation methods?

When you write a grant proposal the core of your request is an activity your organization wants to carry out. It might be a situation in your community that you want to remedy, such as a lack of affordable housing. Or you might see the chance to improve the quality of life in your community by creating a cultural center. The reasoning behind your idea is, "If we do this, then this good will result." An evaluation plan provides detail for this idea. It asks you to put your "If we do this..." statement in terms of who, what, and when with numbers and dates.

Your evaluation plan for the "then this will happen" portion of your idea outlines what impact you expect to see from your work. Again, these expectations should be put in terms of numbers and dates. Often you will design your evaluation plan based upon what works for the project you're outlining, but funders that require logic models, as we discussed in **Chapter 17**, will guide the design of your evaluation through the logic model.

Even those that don't use the word "evaluation" in their application guidelines still care about what your organization will accomplish with their grants. As you write about the needs that your project will address, you need to keep in mind that the way you outline those needs has a big influence on how you will evaluate your project. That is one reason you want to know how and what you can evaluate as you write your grant requests, from the initial LOI to a full grant application.

Did You Spend the Money for the Stated Purpose?

Funders such as private foundations often specify that grant monies must be spent for the intended purpose as outlined in your grant application. One reason for this is to be sure that grant money isn't spent for purposes that would void a private foundation's ability to count the grant as a qualifying distribution. For example, direct electioneering is a prohibited purpose for grant funding.

So while this specification may seem automatic, it plays an important role in the funder's due diligence.

Observation

Funders and Evaluation

There are three reasons that funders ask questions about evaluation, whether formally or informally:

- To ensure that grant dollars were spent properly
- To see if the work outlined in the grant was performed
- To see what impact that work had on the community

Each of these questions has its own purpose, and they build upon one another to move from simple to complex evaluation.

Spending Grant Dollars

Let's begin with assuring funders that grant dollars were spent as intended. The answer to a question such as, "Did the building get built?" may seem simple. You may even wonder why a funder would ask that question. Yet over the years funders have received grant reports where grantees struggle to complete the basic purpose of the grant, such as constructing a building. One example is when an organization might struggle to raise all the funds it needs to carry out a project. In that case, even though the organization hasn't given up on the project, it will be delayed. Sometimes the idea of telling a funder that a project is delayed causes a grantee a lot of stress. But in a twist on the old saying, "No news is bad news," it's best to keep funders apprised of what is going on with your project, even if that means reporting that it's been delayed.

A report that a project has been delayed is not always bad. There are times when a project is delayed because an organization has learned that its initial assumptions were off. If you have to make a report about that, be sure to share with the funder what your organization has learned from that bump in the road.

One reason funders ask directly about whether grant money was spent as intended is that there are times when it hasn't been spent as outlined in a grant application. The most egregious examples are when money granted for one program is spent on a different program. For example, a small organization is raising money for a capital project, but suddenly it finds that it's running out of operating support. Faced with the choice of closing its doors or dipping into the capital funds, it chooses to keep its doors open.

It's possible that capital funders might allow their grants to be used for operating

> **Keep in Touch When Things Go Wrong**
>
> An organization raised several million dollars for an ornamental garden that would be an amenity to the entire community. It began raising money before the landscaping plans were complete, and partway through, it discovered that part of the land it owned could not be developed because it was designated by the state as a wetland. The organization had to completely redo its plans, and in the process, the money that was supposed to be used for construction and landscaping disappeared into staff salaries.
>
> Because the organization kept its donors apprised of the progress (or lack thereof) on the garden, the donors did not demand the return of their funds. But in the end, the garden and its structures had to be much more modest than the original plans.
>
> **Example**

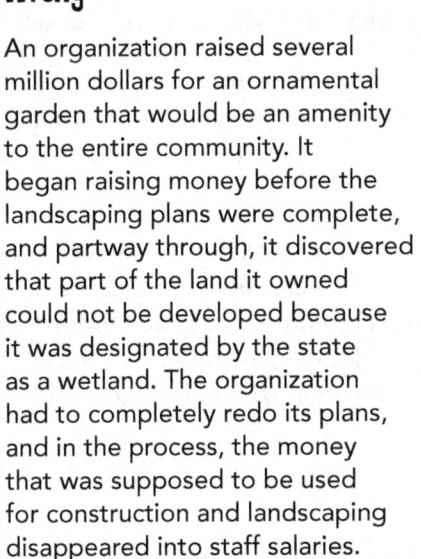

in such a case, but only after being asked. Just going ahead and spending capital funds for another purpose violates your trust with the funder.

Did the Work Get Done?

The question, "Did you do the work outlined in the grant application?" might seem redundant to the first question, but it isn't. For example, an organization can spend its grant money on the project outlined in its application, but the project may fall short of or exceed the work that was outlined in the grant proposal. By work we mean number of people served, the number of units of service provided, or some other measure.

An organization may find that its original estimates of how many people a program will serve might have been too high. In that case, the grantee can look at why it is falling short of its targets and share what it's learned with funders.

Or there may be many more people asking for services than expected and the organization is exceeding its target for the number of people to be served. In that case, a grantee might use that information to make the case for another, and perhaps larger, grant.

Another example is a capital campaign. An organization may raise all the money its budget called for, but unforeseen cost increases or construction problems may arise. As a result, a portion of a building may be left unfinished or planned equipment might be deferred. Or if the organization has the good fortune of getting more than it planned for, the organization may get to add features or equipment.

Reporting on Impact

Finally, reporting on the impact of your project tests your theory of change. Remember, your theory of change says that, "If we do this, then that will happen." Evaluation is about saying, "We did this, and this happened." Your report on how grant money was spent and what work got done addresses the first part of that statement. Reporting on the impact of your work addresses the second part of that statement.

One challenge about reporting on impact is that grant reports are often due well before you'll be able to see the long-term impact. The answer is finding and reporting on short-term results that indicate your project is on track to achieve its long-term results.

For example, a child care agency wants to expand to provide care for children from low-income families headed by women. Its hope for the long term is that access to child care will allow more single mothers to find and hold jobs, and thus improve conditions for families and the community. While that long-term impact may take years to observe, the organization can report on key short-term accomplishments. First, it can report on the enrollment growth in the center. Are most of the new enrollees from low-income, single-parent families? After all, if most of the new families using the center don't fit that profile, how can you expect to meet the long-term goal?

Second, the organization can report on its short-term financial health and ability to sustain its services to low-income families. Assuring a funder that the organization can continue to serve a large number of families that cannot pay the full cost of child care is essential if the organization is going to produce long-term outcomes.

It's important to keep tracking these indicators after the final required grant report has been made. There are always opportunities to share this information with a funder years after a final grant report is made. It can be an informal report to a funder, or part of a new grant proposal. A short update on a past grant can be part of a new LOI for a new grant. In a sentence or two, you can show a funder how a past grant is still serving the community.

Objectives and Evaluation

In **Chapter 19**, we discussed the need for creating specific objectives that will lead to your goals. Ideally, these objectives will be measurable—they will contain some aspect that can be counted—e.g., serving more people. Even if your objectives are not directly about numbers, there are ways to measure them. For example, pre- and post-tests or surveys can measure a change in knowledge and attitudes on a subject.

The key point to remember is that your evaluations should mirror your objectives because they show how you will measure your success in reaching your objectives. And many grant applications ask you to outline your evaluation plans as a part of the project narrative. A good example is the New York/New Jersey Common Application Form. The instructions for the proposal narrative include the following paragraph:

> ***Evaluation***—*Please explain how you will measure the effectiveness of your activities. Describe your criteria for a successful program and the results you expect to have achieved by the end of the funding period.*

There are two key words here: criteria and results. When you describe the criteria for a successful program (what a successful program would look like), you talk about the work that will be done. You describe that work with your objectives. How many people will be served? What will those services look like? And what people or communities should be targeted?

In describing the results, you expect to achieve you talk about the impact that your organization hopes its work will have. Will mothers and fathers learn how to be better parents in a parenting class? Will that knowledge impact how they care for their children?

Funders that stress evaluation, like the W.K. Kellogg Foundation, often use the information they get from evaluations to help set funding priorities, goals, and objectives for their own work. These funders are usually larger than most and have specific programmatic interests. Since they use information from evaluations for mission-related purposes, they usually provide outlines for what they expect from grantees.

When you're creating objectives for an evaluation plan, remember to write SMART objectives as we outlined in **Chapter 19**. Evaluation depends on having something to measure and agreeing on what should be measured. SMART objectives give your organization the power to shape the discussion about what is important, what it looks like now, how it will change, and how you will measure that change.

Matching Objectives to Needs

Let's look at the model proposal letter in **Appendix A**. Every key assertion and plan shared in that letter can be the basis for an objective and thus a part of an evaluation. Let's go through the letter and illustrate how you might create objectives in a full

> ### It's Not Just about the Numbers
>
> Evaluation is about more than meeting or missing targets. It is also about learning.
>
> A report that simply cites numbers and states that the grantee met or exceeded its target may fail to engage the funder. Yet a grantee that falls short of an objective can engage a funder by sharing what it learned and how it is using that learning to improve its services.
>
> Of course, the best option is a grantee that makes its objectives, reports about what it learned, and uses that learning to further improve its services for clients.
>
> **Observation**

grant application based upon this letter. We'll also show how each objective might be measured.

Needs and Objectives

The letter begins by asking the funder to join an effort to increase the amount of food available to low-income families in northern Minnesota. The letter says that if the funder makes the grant, then North Counties Food Resources will increase the amount of food available to low-income families.

If you read further in the model letter, you see that there is one key idea behind the project: increasing the ability to access fresh and frozen food donations will increase the amount of food available for families in need. Your initial contact with a funder provides a general outline of your idea. A grant application will call for more detail, the level of which will vary by funder. Supplying those details requires creating objectives for the project at the heart of the request.

> ### A Leap of Faith
>
> The level of evaluation that a particular funder will want depends upon its attitude toward its grantmaking. Take scholarship grants for example. Scholarship funders could ask many questions about the impact of their scholarship grants: Would these students get to college without the award? Would they do as well in college without the scholarships? Will awardees graduate any faster with the added assistance?
>
> No matter how detailed an answer you provide to these questions, the final decision about making a grant comes down to making a leap of faith that a funder's scholarship grants are important and accomplish something good.
>
> Funders make grants when they gain a level of comfort with a proposal that allows them to make that leap of faith. When you understand each funder's level of comfort, you can design your evaluation to fit the funder's comfort level.
>
> **Observation**

No matter how general or detailed a funder's expectations for evaluation, grantwriters need to realize that they can shape a funder's expectations for a specific grant. You can begin shaping a funder's expectations with the commitments you outline in your LOI and application. Here are sample objectives based on the model LOI in **Appendix A:**

- Put cooler/freezer into service by October 15, 2016.
- Deliver first shipments of fresh/frozen product to partners by December 1, 2016.
- Complete deliveries of first one thousand pounds of fresh/frozen products to partners by December 31, 2016.
- Deliver 150,000 pounds of food to partners during 2017.

You may wonder why that last measure falls short of the 200,000 pounds of food mentioned in the letter. The reality is that it may take time to use the equipment fully. But showing that you can achieve the short-term increase in food provided will show that you are on track for producing, and perhaps exceeding, the 200,000 pounds of food objective over a couple of years.

Each of these is a measure of work, a process objective. They are all fairly easy for an organization to measure if it puts the right procedures in place. This level of evaluation shows funders their grant monies were spent as intended, to install the cooler/freezer and put it into service. The other measures, starting deliveries by December 1 and delivering 150,000 pounds of food during 2016, show that you are using the equipment to produce the impact you outlined in the letter, increasing the supply of food for low-income families in your area.

What if a funder asks, "Does distributing more food really make any difference?" That is a deeper level of evaluation than process objectives show. Objectives that show the effect of distributing more food are impact objectives. Later in the chapter, we'll outline possible impact objectives suggested by the letter.

Not all funders will expect you to evaluate impact. For many funders, providing more food for low-income families, offering more counseling for troubled youth, or similar measures are enough.

Process Objectives

As we touched on in **Chapter 19**, process objectives are important for two reasons. First, they provide a way to monitor a program's implementation. Second, they provide indicators regarding your result objectives because the impact of your work can depend on how much work the project does. For example, will a program serving one hundred people have the same impact as a program serving five hundred? If the impact of your project is predicated

Chapter 21—Evaluation Plans 243

on serving five hundred people, what will happen if your project falls far short of that number? If your project is falling far short of its targets for services, then you can't expect to have the impact you promised.

Monitoring the implementation of a plan is critical. No matter how well a plan is written, things can and will change along the way. Process objectives can help the implementation of a project. For example, a process objective for a counseling organization's expansion project may say it will serve 120 youths a year beyond its present work. If you don't measure that target until the end of the project, all you might learn is a little bit about why the project fell short, met, or exceeded the goal. But what if you break that annual target down into quarterly targets? Your quarterly targets for new clients might be twenty, thirty, thirty-five and thirty-five for the four quarters.

Looking at those quarterly targets gives an organization the chance to adapt while a project is still being implemented. Meeting, exceeding, or falling short of targets is important, but more critical is that looking at those targets is a way to learn about what an organization is doing right or what it may need to change. Some funders encourage this kind of monitoring, by asking for periodic reports during the term of the grant.

Tools for Evaluating Process Objectives

Process objectives usually involve counting. So the tools for evaluating

---

Observation: Learning from Objectives

In his 2010 blog post on the ill-fated business Iridium, Steve Blank coined the phrase "no business plan survives first contact with the customer." While your projects won't involve the billions of dollars that Iridium raised and spent, the lesson is the same. The environment can change in the time between the initial idea and when you have the resources to implement it.

In the nonprofit sector our plans generally depend upon what we think clients need or want. Even if you've included client input in your plans, things can change dramatically when families start showing up at the food pantry or teenagers show up at an after-school program.

Process objectives can be viewed as both targets to help you keep on course and a way to begin conversations about adapting the project when needed. Objectives can be as much about learning as they are about being targets to achieve. And any organization that is paying attention to clients as it does its work will see opportunities to merge the two.

process objectives are all offshoots of counting tools. The major types of these tools are:

- *Client counts*—You might determine that a client is an individual, a family, a couple, or some other unit. Once you determine that, stay consistent. In a client count, once a client is served in a time period, such as a fiscal year, it is counted only once, no matter how many times it returns in that year.

- *Units of service*—Units of service are the individual services that your organization provides. It might be bags of groceries, medical appointments, counseling sessions, or some other unit. Units of service represent your organization's workload for a time period such as a fiscal year. The same unit of service cannot be given out twice. On the other hand, a client can receive multiple units of service. For example, a family could visit a food pantry each week for a month and receive a bag of groceries at each visit. It's still only one client, that family, but four units of service (bags of groceries).

- *Time sheets*—Time sheets can help when the time that a unit of service takes changes significantly from one encounter to another. For example, advocacy services can vary depending on the complexity of a client's issues. One fifteen-minute phone call might resolve one client's issue, whereas it takes four hours of telephone work to assist another client. Simply counting units of service makes those two encounters seem like an equal amount of work. Using a measure such as client hours clarifies that variation.

Result Objectives

Result objectives provide another level of information beyond process objectives. They measure the impact of your work. How do you tell the difference? Sometimes it isn't easy, especially when funders might use different language from one another. For example, you might see a question on a funder's grant application form that asks, "What are the goals of your project?"

Usually, that means, "What are the result objectives?" Look back at the initial objectives that we generated from the needs outlined in the model proposal letter. Those were process objectives. They outlined the work that your organization was committed to doing if the funder made a grant to the project.

What if you were meeting with a funder who asked, "Will it make a difference to the low-income families in your area if you distribute this additional food?"

And since you know the question could be asked, you can anticipate it by having a couple of result objectives as a part of your evaluation plan.

Here are a couple of ideas:

- By December 31, 2017, our supported programs will serve three hundred families never served before.

- We will survey key human service organizations in the counties we serve at the beginning of 2017 and at the end of the year for their perspectives on the food and hunger needs of their clients. We plan for this survey to show a decrease in food insecurity and hunger during the year and to use the feedback to improve our services in 2018.

Serving a large number of new families can be an indicator that your program is having an impact on hunger in general. The survey of community agencies is another way to see the impact of services in the community. In both cases, they help you show that your organization is making the commitment both to doing a certain level of work (increasing the supply of food) and to making sure that work has an impact on the community (reducing hunger).

Results aren't easy to gather and report. You have to decide what it is you want to observe and then how to measure it. There is usually a balance between those two factors. What you might ideally want to know probably won't be easily observable or measurable. On the other hand, what is easy to observe and measure may not be very meaningful.

Why Collect Data?

When I worked on agency allocations with a United Way I looked at a lot of service data reports from the member agencies. Several times when I followed up on those reports I heard agencies say that "the only reason we collect this data is because funders make us do it."

It's understandable that organizations see data collection as secondary. A nonprofit opens its door to provide services. And often more people ask for help than the organization can serve. In such an environment nonprofits see time and money spent on collecting data as money diverted from helping people. Yet that information can be key to better understanding the impact of your work and changes that may be taking place in the community.

Organizations that fail to look at service data to inform their work are missing a key resource for both their own work and building a case for funding.

—Ken

Uninspired

Tools for Evaluating Result Objectives

There are a number of tools for evaluating result objectives. Which ones you use depends on what you are hoping to measure. Here are the major types of evaluation tools for looking at results.

- *Testing*—Presession and postsession testing is one way to show changes in knowledge and/or skills.

- *Surveys*—Surveys are related to testing but would be used to gain knowledge that is more subjective and may vary between individuals. A response such as, "I feel more positive about my life," might be captured in a survey but not by a test.

- *Skills demonstration*—Skills demonstration is also related to testing but is usually used for more complex skills assessment.

- *Tracking*—Tracking is often linked to key factors in your needs statement. A school has an established level of reports of bullying behavior, which may be one reason that school is included in an antibullying program. For a period of time after the program concludes the level of such reports is monitored to see what impact the program may have had.

- *Interviews*—Interviews can be looked at as a method of carrying out any of the approaches we've already noted. Language skills or cultural sensitivities can interfere with the traditional ways of carrying out surveys or skills demonstrations.

All of these measures look primarily at how services affect clients. Much of this can be measured during or shortly after services. What is more difficult to measure is the long-term impact. For example, do the skills or knowledge gained by a client change behavior? Looking for impact like that means measuring the outcomes of your work, which can be another type of result objectives.

Quantitative and Qualitative Evaluation

Whether you are evaluating a process objective or a result objective, there are two types of measures that your organization can use. Each has its own role and, when used correctly, can produce valuable information for your organization and for funders.

Quantitative measures focus on items that can be counted. As you might expect, they are often used for process objectives that count totals for a project and for segments of those totals. Client tallies, units of service tallies, and similar counts are basic quantitative measures. Quantitative measures are objective and verifiable.

Qualitative measures are aimed at measuring the subjective quality of what a program does. A qualitative measure can help you understand how people feel about services and how they are affected by services. For example, a precourse test and postcourse test might tell you that the parents who took your parenting course gained knowledge. A qualitative evaluation could tell you how they felt about the sessions. That information may tell you if they will use that information to become better parents. Qualitative measures can be turned into quantitative measures by using a rating system—for instance, asking clients to rate the value of a program on a scale of one to five.

Quantitative evaluations can be used for large numbers of people such as counting all clients and all units of service. Qualitative evaluations usually focus on a select group. Methods include things such as interviews, focus groups, in-depth surveys, and other approaches that seek in-depth information. That kind of information can help you understand how your program might be improved. It can also look at issues such as cultural competency.

No matter what method of evaluation you use to measure process objectives or result objectives, evaluation can be a key to better understanding how your program works and why it is important to your community. Both of those are key pieces of information that funders want to understand as they review your requests.

To Summarize...

- Funders use evaluation to document the use of funds, the work you do, and the impact of your activities.
- Evaluation plans are the mirror image of objectives.
- Evaluation can help your organization monitor both the implementation of a project and its impact on clients.
- Even funders that don't ask you about evaluation still care about the impact of their grants. The evaluation you do for funders with formal evaluations can provide information to share with those that don't make the request.

Chapter 22

Project Budgets

In This Chapter...
- What is the real purpose of budgets?
- What's the best way to chart expenditures and income?
- How do you handle indirect expenses?
- What goes into the budget narrative?

When we teach workshops and classes on grantwriting, we get more questions about budgets than any other single topic. There is one main reason for this: Budget development within your organization is one thing; the budgets that funders want to see are something else.

Many people find budgets scary because you have to deal with all those numbers and commit to specifics you can't predict. One novice executive director, when asked for budget figures by a consultant, replied, "How do I know what it's going to cost? I won't know that till I get there." While that's understandable, it also reflects a level of planning that may fall short of a funder's expectations.

When you write a grant proposal, you hope that the funder will find it compelling. But even if that happens, the funder will wonder what it's going to cost to carry out the project. That's the purpose of the expense portion of a budget. The line items in the expense portion of the budget tell a funder how you arrive at the total cost.

Once a funder understands what a project will cost the next question is, "Where will those resources come from?" That's the purpose of the income portion of the budget. If you keep these simple ideas in mind, you'll find budgets to be much less of a challenge.

Whether you work with a small organization that manages its finances from a checkbook or a large one with accounting staff, there are basic principles of nonprofit budgeting you need to understand. In this chapter, we'll provide background that will help you understand the various budget formats that funders require.

A Budget Is Only a Plan

We've met many grantwriters who were anxious about budgets. What can reduce that anxiety is remembering that a budget is a plan, not a prediction made with the help of an omniscient crystal ball.

The numbers on each line are estimates. They are based on your organization's experience and planning. Most funders understand this idea and expect that a final accounting for a project may differ from the original budget.

That doesn't mean your planning can be haphazard—any large variations from your budget will later need to be explained to the funder. But as a plan, your budget conveys how you expect to spend grant monies and how those grants work with other sources of support.

Expenditures

Typically, the expenditure portion of a budget is the easiest part to complete. When an organization creates a budget, it sets targets for staffing, space, office supplies, and all the other tools to carry out a project. Turning those items into dollars for a budget is simple math. For example, let's say a new project means adding two part-time positions. Your present salary structure gives you a good estimate of what that will cost.

Yet even with that information at hand, a common question we hear is, "What goes into a budget and what should we leave out?" While the answer to that question varies by the type of budget, a general guideline still applies.

The Time Dimension of a Budget

Every budget needs to be based on some period of time. That's easiest to understand for program budgets. A request "for $25,000 to support expanded counseling services..." is incomplete. A request "for $25,000 to support expanded counseling services during 2017..." provides a context that funders want to see.

Even capital campaigns have a time reference. But rather than committing to a fiscal or calendar year, a capital budget uses benchmarks with target dates. For example:

- Break ground at the new site by September 30, 2017.
- Construct new building from November 1, 2017 to December 31, 2018.
- Open new building for services by February 1, 2019.

These are major benchmarks with dozens of smaller steps in between. They give a funder an idea about your plans and the time it will take to complete them. Some organizations assign costs to specific steps as a way of phasing a project. Every project should have a dimension of time to make the expenditures meaningful.

The time dimension you use helps you answer the question about what needs to be included a budget. A budget shows what it will cost to go from where you are now to where you hope to be in the designated period of time.

> **Salaries Are Not All Overhead**
>
> Board members from smaller organizations sometimes insist that all salaries are overhead. But nonprofit accounting differs from general business accounting. Whether you call salaries overhead or not, they must be allocated by purpose just like any other expense.
>
> For example, some programs require paid staff. Those salaries are integral to running those programs. As a result, they are considered program costs. Staff who spend their time working on more than one program should have their salary and benefits allocated to those areas based upon that work.
>
> *Example*

Types of Budgets

You'll run across three main types of budgets in grantwriting: program, equipment, and capital.

Program Budgets

A program budget is similar to your organization's regular operating budget. But it will break out the direct costs for only one program. Some funders ask for your current operating budget as a part of your application even if your proposal requests funding for a project or a capital campaign. That budget would be in the same format as a program budget.

There are many models for program budgets that show the basic line items that funders will expect. One model can be the budget forms provided (if any) in your region's common grant application. Another example of the line items in a program budget is shown in the Statement of Functional Expenses on page 10 of the IRS Form 990.

Shown here is a simple model for the expenditure portion of a program budget. Notice on this form and the other examples that follow that there is a place to enter a time period for the budget.

Simple Program Budget

Line Item	Amount
Individual contributions	
Special events (net)	
Government grants	
Foundation/corporate grants	
Earned income	
Other	
Total	
Salaries	
Benefits/taxes	
Rent/mortgage	
Utilities	
Office supplies	

Line Item	Amount
Printing/postage	
Telecommunications/web	
Equipment maintenance	
Travel and meetings	
Miscellaneous	
Total	

From __/__/____ to __/__/____

Equipment and Project Budgets

The expenditure portion of an equipment budget can take many forms. This type of budget works for a one-time effort that involves equipment or other items. It also applies to projects involving small remodeling projects on facilities.

The budget for such projects often doesn't fit standard budget forms. As a result, many funders have special forms or allow you to insert your own line-item descriptions. Typical line items are the pieces of equipment you plan to purchase and any special costs for putting them into service. For example, the purchase price would be one line item; installation costs, if any, would be another; and finally, staff training to use the equipment would be another line item. Also, in this context, equipment could mean computer software. Purchasing, installing, and training staff on a new fundraising database would be a typical example.

Capital Budgets

Finally, there are capital budgets. In the nonprofit world, capital campaigns are synonymous with building projects. They include purchasing a building, constructing a new facility, or renovating your existing space.

The expenditure portions of capital budgets include unique line items such as site development, design fees, and construction. It's very common for line items to be listed in the same order in which the expenses come up. Costs such as buying land, acquiring a building, and design fees come up early in a capital project, so those line items come first. Items such as furnishings are usually purchased near the end of the project, so the line for that comes near the bottom of the list. Also, capital budgets usually include a significant contingency—an allowance for unanticipated costs. An entry for a 10 percent contingency is common because the costs of a building project can change due to the time a project takes and its complexity.

Here is an example of a simple capital budget. Notice how the expense line items roughly parallel the stages of a building project.

Simple Capital Project Budget

Line Item	Amount
Individual contributions	
Special events (net)	
Government grants	
Foundation/corporate grants	
Long-term debt	
Other	
Total	
Land acquisition	
Architect/engineering	
Site improvements	
Construction	
Equipment/furnishings	
Landscaping	
Bridge loan/interest	
Contingency	
Permits	
Taxes and fees	
Miscellaneous	
Total	

Fundraising campaign: __/__/____ to __/__/____
Construction: __/__/____ to __/__/____
Occupancy: __/__/____

Mixed Types of Cost

Sometimes you will want to display a budget in terms of one-time costs and ongoing costs. Take a project to expand program services. One part of the budget may be one-time expenses such as purchasing office furniture or moving into new space. Once those items are purchased the organization will continue using them for many years to come. Another part of the budget will be the salaries for staff. Those staff costs will continue each year as long as you operate at that level of service.

As you do your grant research, you'll find that some funders prefer one-time costs while others are more open to funding ongoing costs. If you segment costs this way, you may be able to get grant support from both types of funders.

A similar approach is becoming common with major building projects. Many campaigns for new or renovated buildings now add a component to the campaign that supports transition costs for the new building. For example, when a new building opens the demand for services can grow faster than the revenues to support them. Raising money to help meet those costs means that an organization can serve those clients as soon as the new facilities open.

Also, by defining those costs as either one-time or ongoing, you can be clear as to how each component of the campaign contributes to the whole project. This way, you can appeal to a wide range of funders—even ones that don't usually contribute to capital campaigns.

Income

The income side of a budget is very similar whether attached to a program budget, an equipment project budget, or a capital budget. Many funders will require only

---

Submit the Whole Project Budget

Your budget should correspond to the needs you want to address and your planned approach. Usually, a funder will want to see a full budget for the programs, project, or buildings you plan, even if it isn't the sole funder.

Even though you may approach a funder for a particular piece of a budget, it's a good idea to submit an entire budget. Seeing the whole budget helps a funder see how its grant will contribute to the success of the project.

Observation

a few of the line items you see in the graphic here and some will ask that you insert your own line-item descriptions.

Income Budget Example

	Program Income
Contributions	$22,970
Special events (net)	4,881
Government grants	30,000
Foundation and corporate grants	25,000
Program fees	1,200
Total	84,051
Budget period: 01/01/xxxx to 12/31/xxxx	

Here are a couple of examples of how the income budget shown here would change when being used with a program versus a capital request: In a program budget, it would be unlikely that you would see a line item for long-term debt. In a capital budget, it is unlikely you would see a line item for program fees. Keep in mind that, just like the expense portion of the budget, this is a plan, not a prediction.

Indirect Expenses

What are *indirect expenses*? Sometimes they are called overhead. Sometimes they are called operating costs. They might include costs such as rent, utilities, and insurance. But in nonprofit accounting, some are the direct costs of running a program. For example, rent for space that is exclusively used for a program is a program cost. The idea is that, if the organization weren't running the program, then it wouldn't have to pay that cost.

The True Costs of a Program

It's easy to recognize the direct costs of a program—that's what a program budget is all about. Programs are why people and funders support organizations. Yet their costs are not as obvious as they may seem. You need to look at the true total cost of a program as being a combination of both the direct costs and a share of your organization's indirect costs. You can't have programs without the administrative work to support them. When you recognize the true total cost of a program, it can help you set better goals for grants and other fundraising activities.

Observation

But what about costs such as bookkeeping, the staff time, and materials to hold board meetings, and other costs that help a nonprofit organization exist as an entity year after year? Those are indirect costs. They are essential to an organization's ability to attract grants and other support that pays for program costs. Usually, these indirect costs are supported by an organization's unrestricted income. There has been growing concern and discussion about this approach because project income can grow much faster than unrestricted income. This means organizations find it a challenge to cover their indirect costs. We don't have any quick answers to this dilemma, but you may find times when you want to show a funder the impact of indirect costs on a budget.

When an organization does a good job of meeting an important need, it can attract grant support faster than it can grow its unrestricted resources. As a result, more and more organizations are looking at ways to show indirect costs as a part of their grant requests. Here are two examples of the same project budget, one showing no indirect costs and another showing those costs.

Incorporating Indirect Expenses

Without Direct Expenses		With Direct Expenses	
Income			
New Program		New Program	
Contributions	$22,970	Contributions	$46,202
Special events (net)	4,881	Special events (net)	4,881
Corporation A	25,000	Corporation A	25,000
Corporation B	1,500	Corporation B	1,500
Foundation A	13,000	Foundation A	13,000
Program fees	1,200	Program fees	1,200
Total	68,551	Total	91,783
Expenses			
Salary: executive director	7,200	Salary: executive director	7,200
Salary: program staff	40,000	Salary: program staff	40,000
Employee benefits	12,921	Employee benefits	12,921
Occupancy	7,500	Occupancy	7,500
Utilities	930	Utilities	930
Total	68,551	Indirect expense	23,232
		Total	91,783
Budget period: 01/01/xxxx to 12/31/xxxx Budget period: 01/01/xxxx to 12/31/xxxx			

Look at the income portion of each budget. See how the amount of contributions allocated to the project changes when indirect costs are calculated. This contribution income is often gifts from individuals. This may include your annual campaign, special events, and other donations. It shows how unrestricted gifts help leverage grants and other support for programs.

Another advantage of this budget format is that it shows funders the true level of financial support that the organization is contributing to the project. The budget showing the indirect costs shows that the organization is dedicating twice as much in contributed income to the project as the budget without indirect costs. This approach can help you tell the story about how indirect costs support your organization's mission. It also reveals the true cost of delivering a program. Both are important stories to share with funders when the opportunity arises.

This example shows an organization that can currently fund its indirect costs out of unrestricted contributions and special events. What do you do when your unrestricted contributions aren't enough to support your indirect costs? That's one reason it's important to articulate your indirect costs to funders and to let them know how important it is that grant income cover some of those costs.

Also, understanding this true total cost of a program helps you set better goals for fundraising because you have a better sense of what you need. For example, many arts groups that seek sponsorships for productions set the sponsorship amounts by looking at the budget for the production. Generally, that budget only shows the direct cost of the production. Instead, sponsorship levels should be set looking at a budget that includes the indirect cost. By doing that, you take pressure off of your unrestricted income and build a healthier organization.

Budget Narratives

A *budget narrative* is a document that explains the details of each line item. You should develop a draft narrative for every budget. While not all funders will ask you for a narrative, writing one can be a good exercise in budget building. When grantwriters create budget narratives, they learn more about why a project costs what it costs. Sometimes that knowledge helps answer funders' questions. And there will be times that writing a budget narrative shows that there is a gap. The staff member who develops the budget may not be fully aware of all the aspects of the program. Grantwriters have a role centralizing information from a variety of sources and making sure that it all works together. That role plays itself out when writing budget narratives.

Federal grants usually require budget narratives and provide an outline for them. Private funders that ask for budget narratives will often leave it up to you to design your own form. As you write more grants and deal with budget narratives, you'll be able to refine your format.

For some items, the narrative will be complicated; for others, it can be very simple. The line items for salaries and benefits are often complicated when they cover several staff positions. Your narrative should share the position title, the amount of time dedicated to the program, and the cost of that time, as well as a short description of what tasks those positions are responsible for.

Other items can be very straightforward and need only a short explanation. One example would be the line item for contingency, which might be explained as easily as "being equal to 10 percent of construction costs."

Example

Sample Budget Narrative Example

Salaries:

Mental Health Counselor I: 1 FTE @ $45,000/year (provides counseling services for families; salary is consistent with similar positions in the county)

Mental Health Assistant II: 2 FTE @ $30,000/year/each (provides support to families that helps them follow through on counseling recommendations; salary is consistent with similar positions in the county)

Benefits:

18.75 percent of $105,000 salaries; covers FICA, health insurance, and retirement contribution (health insurance and retirement contribution consistent with other positions in the organization)

Travel:

$3,600 for 750 miles per month (estimate 250 miles per month for each staff person due to commitment to meet families in homes and other sites throughout the rural portions of the county)

The narrative for the income portion of the budget usually looks a little different. It will focus on the key segments for income: fees, government grants, individual giving, corporate and foundation grants, and other.

It's easy to fall into the trap of being very direct and dry in your line-item descriptions. But a program narrative can be an opportunity to educate funders about the importance of each line item toward accomplishing your objectives.

While you need to be succinct, a well-written narrative does more than simply explain a budget—it makes the case for a budget.

To Summarize...

- Budgets estimate what it will cost to fulfill the promises made in your grant request.

- Your budgets need to be defined by a period of time.

- The total cost of a program is the sum of its direct costs and a share of the indirect cost needed to keep the organization running in order to offer that program.

- Budget narratives explain the detailed budget line items.

Chapter 23

Organizational Information

In This Chapter...
- How do you establish your credibility?
- How much history should your proposal include?
- What should you say about your clientele?
- What attachments should you include?

In the section on organizational information, you explain who your nonprofit is, and establish its credibility. This is where you tell funders about your mission, history, and whom you serve. Most importantly, you describe your track record and give evidence of expertise in your field. In some grant proposals, this section will come near the beginning, right after the summary. It does seem logical to explain who you are before describing what you plan to do.

But other funders want you to proceed directly to your project, telling them about your nonprofit's background and history only after you have convinced them that your project is important and feasible. Sometimes, when grantwriters start with the background section, they find they have written the substance of the proposal before they've ever gotten to the needs and goals sections. So it's best to lay out the rationale for your project first, and only later fill in your nonprofit's biography.

The best thing about the background section is that you can usually reuse it for almost every grant you write—in other words, it is "boilerplate." You do need to update it regularly, and you may need to emphasize different aspects of your organization's activities for different funders and projects. But for the most part, this is a section that you'll be able to cut and paste into many proposals. What a relief!

Mission Statement

The first part of the organizational information section will be your mission statement. (We covered mission statements in **Chapters 8** and **19**.) Every nonprofit should have a well-written, concise mission statement approved by the board that explains its purpose and why it exists. If yours doesn't, encourage your board to update its mission statement in a form that will be clear, informative, and inspiring to funders and other potential donors.

> **Formatting Your Mission Statement**
>
> In grant proposals, the mission statement is often put in italics and/or indented, showing that it is a stand-alone statement that serves as a guidepost for everything your organization does.
>
> **Perspiration**

Brief History of Your Organization

You can often cover your nonprofit's history very briefly—sometimes just the dates when it was founded and when it became a 501(c)(3). But it can also be helpful to explain what inspired your founders to create the organization. Was it something from their personal experience—something that led them to realize there was a need for services in their community that was not being supplied by existing agencies? Did they see something that worked well in another place and want to recreate it in their own city? An inspiring personal story about your organization's founding can help readers understand the motivation behind your work.

If your organization has undergone a major name change or merged with another nonprofit in the recent past, include this in the history section.

You'll want to make sure your readers connect your previous name with your current one.

Your Main Programs and Activities

If your grant proposal is concerned with only one of many programs normally carried out by your organization, you'll want to give the funder an overview of the scope of your activities as a whole. Don't go into too much detail, but briefly summarize each of the programs that are part of your ongoing work. This is a place where bullet points work very well. Write a short paragraph on each of your programs, set off by bullets for easy reading. Specify how many people are served by each program.

Clientele

Your clientele—the people you serve—are the most important part of your organization's activities, the reason for its existence. These may be the people served by a social services organization, the patients of a health care institution, the students of an educational institution, or the audience of an arts organization. You need to know how many you serve over a given period of time (such as one year) and explain who they are in terms of demographics—their age range, where they live, racial and ethnic background, education levels, income levels, and so on.

Some organizations collect these statistics every day as part of their ongoing work. For others, such as arts organizations, this information may be a lot harder to come by. You may want to do a marketing survey in which you ask your audience for feedback on your programs, and then include a short demographics section at the end. If asking about income levels seems too personal and might alienate your clientele, you can depend more on information derived from census data about the areas where your clients live. But funders do want to know something about the people you serve, so brainstorm with your staff about ways to obtain this information.

Who Is the Clientele of an Environmental Organization?

Environmental organizations may not always appear to serve people directly. If their mission is to preserve wilderness or save endangered species, it may seem that human beings are the problem, not the clients being served.

Of course, when an organization preserves the environment, it is also serving people. Human beings benefit both physically and spiritually from having places on the planet relatively untouched by human development, having clean water and air, preserving other species, and being able to have contact with nature. But it may be tricky to come up with a specific "number of people served."

When Goodwin posed this question to grantwriters specializing in environmental issues, she received some excellent answers. One person wrote:

> *When I worked with environmental organizations, we would estimate the number of people served by showing the number of people in the region (or the state) who would be benefiting from the water trust, the land trust, the citizen science program, etc. I would then explain the rationale behind that number either in the inquiry letter or in some appropriate section of the grant application. There's always the cover letter if there's no place to explain it in the grant.*

Another respondent pointed out that there are still difficulties in defining numbers served:

> *It's got to pass the laugh test, especially if the funder is doing the math (i.e., grant dollars per person served)... that is, if your grant is for ocean conservation, you can't say "seven billion people"... you have to define some sort of boundaries that make sense and scale to the project and the grant request. It's definitely a challenge! I once tongue-in-cheekily responded to the question "number served" by providing the number of orcas in Puget Sound (hey, the question didn't specify number of people* served*).*

This is an issue to discuss with the leadership of your nonprofit. However you decide to define and count your clientele, it should be an organizational decision, not something that you as a grantwriter need to come up with on the spot.

Achievements, Awards, and Recognition

The best way to establish your credibility as a leader in your field is to describe your achievements. What is your track record? What have you done that shows you are good at what you do? Have you won any awards, or received public recognition? These can apply both to your organization as a whole and to individual staff members. You or someone else should keep a file listing awards, compliments from public figures or leaders in your field, and links to articles describing your achievements. If a public figure says something nice about you in private correspondence or conversation, ask permission to quote the individual in marketing and fundraising materials. You can also describe your nonprofit's outstanding achievements in your own words, citing statistics if possible.

Another way to establish your credibility is through testimonials from the people you serve. Ask your program directors to collect statements about how your organization has changed your clients' lives for the better. These might come from evaluations, exit interviews, or spontaneous notes of appreciation. You don't have to give the clients' names if confidentiality is important, but you might include descriptions of who they are and what their relationship is to your organization. Do use people's own words, and make sure that each quotation really sounds like something a person of that age and background would say. If you make a sixth-grader sound like a college professor, no one will believe the testimonial.

Track Record of Previous Grant-Funded Projects

Some of the questions funders ask when reviewing your proposal are, "Can this organization follow through on its plans? Does it manage money well? Does it have a track record of success with previous grants?" The organizational information section is a good place to demonstrate positive answers to these questions. Refer to previous grant-funded projects and describe their

---

Leveraging Media Exposure

An organization that presents classical guitar concerts once received an excellent review in the local paper. It began like this:

The Seattle Classic Guitar Society's series of recitals at Benaroya Hall is one of the great, relatively undiscovered delights of Seattle's classical-music season. The performers are top-notch, and the venue, Benaroya's Nordstrom Recital Hall, has acoustics that are matched perfectly to the intimate demands of the guitar.

This review was pure gold, because it gave credit to the Guitar Society for presenting the concerts, praised the entire series (not just one concert), and noted that the venue, which was new at the time, was perfect for this type of music. The Guitar Society used this quotation in grants for years to establish its credibility and demonstrate its excellence.

Pure Genius!

successful outcomes. Mention where the funding came from, so the funder to whom you're submitting the current grant proposal can get references from your past supporters. (The guidelines may ask you to list other supporters in the attachments for this very reason.)

If your nonprofit is new, you may not have a track record of accomplishments. So how do you establish your credibility in that case? You can point to the achievements of the founders and leaders of your organization, who probably do have substantial résumés proving their capability. If your leadership is young and longer on enthusiasm than expertise, you should at least have board members and advisers with achievements you can point to. And you will be hiring staff members with skill and experience. One way or another, you have to convince funders that you know what you're doing.

Expertise in the Field of the Project

Even if you have a good track record in general, you'll also need to show that you have particular expertise in the field of the project. For instance, a hospital may be a leader in the field of health care, but if you're writing a grant proposal to fund its work in preventing child abuse and neglect, you'll need to show that it has experience in that field specifically. Discuss the accomplishments of the hospital's department of social work, and show how it works with families to care for children with special health needs. Provide statistics to show it has succeeded in decreasing the numbers of emergency room visits. You'll also need to show that your organization is the right one to launch this project, rather than another agency that specializes in this field.

Be Careful When Soliciting Quotes

Sometimes organizations seeking support from public figures will put words in their mouths. If you call the office of the mayor or your city council representative with a request to say something nice about your organization, the staff person may say, "Sure, the mayor would be glad to support you. Just write out what you want him to say, and he'll sign it."

The trouble is, these statements rarely sound sincere, and usually the reader can tell they were really written by the nonprofit's marketing department. It's a lot better to collect spontaneous compliments as they arise than to ask for praise on demand.

Observation

Attachments

The grant guidelines will almost always ask you to attach a number of documents that provide further information about your nonprofit. It's a good idea to make sure they're in order and ready to go early on in the grantwriting process.

Since these items are standard for every grant, keep them in a file folder and make sure they are up to date. Then when you need them, you can upload or attach them to any proposal you're writing. What you don't want to do is wait until the last minute, when you're all done with the hard part of the grant, and then suddenly scramble to collect these routine but essential components of the proposal. The items below are among the most commonly requested attachments.

> **"Lack of Planning on Your Part Does Not Constitute an Emergency on My Part"**
>
> This is a sign you may see hung above the desks of administrative assistants in some offices. Don't forget, these hard-working and often underpaid employees have many responsibilities and sometimes several bosses. If you wait till the day before a grant is due and then come to them demanding that they produce a board list or an operating budget *right this minute*, they won't be very happy about it, and they may not be able to accommodate you. It's much better to ask them politely to help you collect these documents early in the process so they have plenty of time to produce what you need.
>
> **WATCH OUT!**

IRS Determination Letter or Employer Identification Number

The IRS determination letter, or letter certifying your organization's tax-exempt status, is something you should always have ready. Keep a hard copy in your drawer and a scanned version on your computer. It doesn't matter how old it is or how often it was reproduced on a bad copy machine before the days of digitization—so long as your status is current, the letter is still valid. (Some funders may ask you to write a separate note, signed by your CEO or executive director, stating that the IRS letter is indeed still current.) These days, however, many funders simply ask you to enter your EIN.

Board List

You will usually be asked to provide a list of board members "with affiliations." For most board members, this simply means where they work in their day jobs. Those who do not have paid employment may be listed as community volunteers. Don't provide board members' work or home addresses or other contact information. Some organizations give thumbnail résumés for each, but it's really not necessary and just makes the list too long. You may want to include the dates of their current board terms.

Project Budget

We've discussed this in the previous chapter. It's a standard attachment and should be included with the other documents requested by the funder. It may include a budget narrative with cost justifications.

Current Operating Budget

The current operating budget is the one for this fiscal year, which was approved by your board before the year began. Your actuals may already be quite different from the approved budget, but you shouldn't change anything on the document you attach to the proposal unless the funder's guidelines specifically request a budget with year-to-date actuals. Otherwise, just send in whatever your board approved at the end of the last fiscal year.

Financial Statements

It's important that your financial statements be in order. These come in two parts: a revenue

---

Do You Need an Audit?

Audit in this context doesn't mean a scary interrogation by the IRS—it's short for financial audit. It is a careful review of your organization's finances, performed by a licensed, independent accounting firm. It can take a long time and be expensive. Whether you need one depends on several factors, including the size of your budget and the requirements of funders. The federal and state governments require audits of nonprofits receiving funding above specific levels. If you aren't sure, check with an attorney or accountant to see if you need an audit. Smaller organizations often do not.

Perspiration

and expense statement, and a balance sheet. The *revenue and expense (or profit and loss) statement* shows your cash flow throughout the previous fiscal year; the *balance sheet* is a snapshot of your organization's assets and liabilities on the last day of the previous fiscal year. The IRS has specific rules for how these financial items should be reported by nonprofit organizations, and it's important that you follow them. Your organization needs to have someone available who understands the rules and knows how to produce a proper financial statement according to standard accounting practices. If you don't have a CPA in your office or on your board, you may need to seek outside help from a qualified accounting firm. Some firms will provide help pro bono or at a discount to small nonprofits.

List of Donors

Many funders ask you to include a list of prior donors. Usually, they don't want to see pages and pages of everyone who's given you $25 and up. They're more interested in your institutional donors: foundations, corporations, and government agencies. If you're not sure what they want to have included in the list, call or send an email.

Letters of Support or Commitment

If you're working with other organizations and have letters of support or commitment from them, these should be included in the attachments. A letter of support is just a general endorsement of your organization; it's like a character reference. A letter of commitment expresses a commitment to follow through on some action outlined in the grant. For example, it could be a letter from the state office of children's services outlining the commitment to refer parents to your parenting program.

Different funders may request other attachments—an annual report, your IRS 990 form, a sample of your work if you're applying for an arts grant. Some funders may invite you to include newsletters, brochures, or videos that provide a fuller picture of your organization and its work. But don't send them more than they ask for, and don't load them down with piles of extraneous information. Remember, they're reading dozens or hundreds of proposals. More information isn't always better—what they'll appreciate is a concise and appealing proposal with enough information to help them make a good decision.

To Summarize...

- The organizational information section is where you establish your credibility.
- Establish your track record in terms of achievements, awards, and testimonials.
- Make sure you include all the required attachments.
- Don't send additional information unless the funder invites you to do so. More isn't better; more is often clutter.

Chapter 24

Sustainability

In This Chapter...

- What is sustainability?
- How does sustainability relate to business models?
- What do capital projects mean for ongoing operating costs?
- What is transition funding?

Whether asking for a capital grant, a program grant, or general operating support, grantseekers should expect funders to ask about their organization's plans for sustainability. Not every funder will ask about it, but when one does, it's important to have good answers to the questions. Because what the funder is really asking is, "How do we know that this grant will have an impact over the long term?"

Funder concerns about sustainability have grown over the past twenty years. In the '90s and before, funders usually limited their evaluations to the specifics of the funded projects. For example, does the project budget balance? Is it likely the organization can raise all the funding it needs to build the new building? If a funder asked an organization about the new building's impact on operating expenses, the answers were limited to looking at heat, lights, and building maintenance.

But in the '90s, the stock market growth powered by Internet stocks meant that grantmaking grew, and this growth prompted many organizations to look at constructing long-wished-for buildings. And the buildings got built.

Yet all was not well. To paraphrase the movie *Field of Dreams*, "If you build it, they will come… and then you'll go broke." Organizations put up new buildings and tried to serve many more people with those new facilities. But many organizations had failed to plan for the stress that put on the annual operating budget. And in some cases that stress was ultimately fatal to the organization.

Convincing a funder that your organization, or a particular program you want to start or expand, can be sustained in the future relies on two ideas. First, you must show the funder that your organization understands how it gathers resources to support its current work. Secondly, you need to show that the organization understands the impact this project will have on future operating budgets and that it has planned for those continuing costs.

For example, a particular program that you want to expand is currently supported by a combination of sliding-fee scale payments and donation income. Your plan to expand the number of people served by that program raises a number of questions. Two key questions would be, "Will the new clients be able to pay at the same rate the current sliding-fee scale clients pay?" and "Do you have the capacity to increase your donation income to meet the greater need for donation income?"

You may think these are simple questions, but many organizations don't have a

> **Look before You Leap**
>
> An art museum built a new building to dramatically increase the amount of art it could display. This also made room for many more people to visit exhibits and for special arts events.
>
> Unfortunately, the board of directors failed to consider what that growth would mean to the museum's budget. The museum traditionally supported the vast majority of its budget from fundraising. And while the new gift shop promised some increased revenues, fundraising needed to grow substantially to support the new annual budget.
>
> Though the museum suffered from a variety of budget issues, the key problem was that it was unable to meet those ambitious fundraising targets. It had to close for an extended period until the board could work out a plan for meeting the budget that the new site required.
>
> **Uninspired**

good grasp of where their support comes from or the implications of growing programs. Being able to answer these questions builds the credibility of your organization and your specific request.

What Is Sustainability?

When a grantseeking organization first hears a question about sustainability it might feel that the funder is really asking, "Do you have plans to run this organization, down the road, without having to ask for outside support?" That misunderstanding is one reason that the term sustainability raises negative feelings. The truth is that *sustainability* is about how your organization brings in the resources it turns into mission and how it builds the capacity to secure those resources.

Grantwriters need to be prepared for funders to ask about sustainability, whether grant requests are for building projects, starting new programs, or supporting regular operating costs. Each kind of grant request will require a different type of sustainability plan. This plan outlines how a program or project is supported by various types of income such as contributions, grants, and/or earned income. Also, it outlines how the organization is prepared to do the work needed to obtain that income.

For example, a YMCA plans to open a new branch. Typically, it supports most of its operating costs through memberships. If it wants that new branch to operate successfully, it has to plan to sign up hundreds of new members and add the capacity to handle all those new membership billings. Also, to offer subsidized memberships for people from low-income families, it will need to plan to raise more money from its annual campaign, special events, and/or grants to meet those new costs. Funders want to know that their grantees have thought through these kinds of issues before they invest in an organization.

Three Reasons Sustainability Comes Up

There are three situations that funders have seen over the years that prompt them to ask about sustainability:

- One reason is that funders get many requests from new organizations. Often these requests look only at the short term. That approach leaves the funder to wonder if the project really has a chance to continue after its grant funds have been spent. If you fail to address sustainability, the funder will make its own determination.

- The second situation involves organizations running major capital campaigns for new or expanded buildings. If the case for the building is serving more people, what are the implications for the organization's operating budget?

- Finally, mature nonprofits sometimes find that a source of income goes away, such as major government funding. That loss of income may require the organization to learn different resource development skills to increase private grant funding or individual giving.

In all three of these situations, organizations that have planned for sustainability have the best chance of gaining funder support.

Elements of Sustainability

The best way to answer funder questions about sustainability is to anticipate them. Elements of your sustainability plan can be woven into an LOI or the narrative of a grant application.

What are the key elements of such a plan?

Sustainability and Business Models

The best answer to a question about sustainability includes three parts:

- An outline of how your organization gathers the resources to do its work at current levels, i.e., its revenue profile (see **Chapter 7** for more about revenue profiles)

- If proposing program expansion, your estimates of what it will take to operate at the new level (i.e., pro forma budget)

- An outline of your plan for moving from where you are now to what the new budget requires

Let's use a child care organization with a sliding-fee scale as an example. The organization wants to double the number of children in the program with its new building. The organization estimates that doubling the number of children it serves will increase the overall budget by 60 percent.

Since it expects to serve primarily low-income families with these expanded services, the fee income portion of the budget will increase only slightly. Because of that, the new budget requires the organization to increase its fundraising by 120 percent to serve these families.

This increase in fundraising raises several questions: Has the organization identified how it will increase fundraising? Does it plan some combination of current supporters giving more and new donors? Does it plan to start or expand special events? Are there grants available to help the organization serve more children, including those from lower income families?

Whatever the plan for meeting the increased operating budget, a funder will want to know that the organization recognizes the issues involved. Further, funders will want to see that the nonprofit is making efforts to adapt to the changes the building expansion will cause. An organization can't guarantee that it will hit all the targets in its plan. But a plan increases a funder's confidence that the nonprofit will realize its income goal. It also means that as the program gets underway, the organization has targets to monitor its work.

A sustainability plan tells the funder that there are targets in place for the various sources of support, and having a target is the first step in monitoring how an organization is doing toward meeting that target. For example, what if fee income is falling short of projections? There are several reasons this could happen. But if an organization didn't have a target for fee income, no one would know whether fee income was falling short or not.

No Fee Too Small

A new hire in a cultural institution was getting oriented to the job, part of which was working with school tours. Digging into the files, the new staff person found invoices for past tours that had never been sent to the schools. These fees helped to pay for arts education tours. When the staff person raised the issue with a supervisor the response was, "Those invoices aren't a priority because they don't bring in that much money."

Unfortunately, this is not a unique example. Too often, nonprofit staff fail to understand how budgets are built and the real work it takes to bring in resources. Even if fee income only covers 10 percent of a program's cost, that's 10 percent less that fundraising and grants need to meet.

Uninspired

Your fee income could be falling short of its target because your original plan for sliding-fee scale enrollment was off. Perhaps billings aren't being sent out on time or payments aren't being processed promptly. But whatever the cause, no one would be asking questions and looking for answers if there weren't a target in the first place. And there wouldn't be a target if there weren't a sustainability plan.

Finding Sustainability Models

There are two reasons for grantwriters to understand how each of their organization's programs is supported. First, this information can help you show a funder how its grant fits into the organization's overall budget. If you're asking for support of the operating budget, the funder will want to know how its grant helps.

If you're asking for capital, equipment, or projects to expand or start new programs, your *sustainability plan* is critical. Being able to explain how a program is supported can be the first step to showing how it will adapt to changes. When a project involves a significant investment, such as a building, your sustainability plan assures funders that the investment will continue to be used as intended for years to come.

The second reason you need to understand your organization's business model is that funders will compare it to generally accepted models for similar types of services. Here's an example.

A common model for private, nonparochial, K–12 schools is for about 85 to 90 percent of operating revenues to come from tuition, with the remainder from fundraising, primarily individual giving and special events. Many schools direct that fundraising income to scholarships and other assistance as a way to build a diverse student body.

It can be hard to fundraise year after year for much more than 15 percent of a school's operating budget. The reality is that for most private schools, the fundraising audience is limited. Generally, people who care about private education have a tie to a particular school. As such, a school's annual fundraising is generally directed to parents, relatives of students, and alumni.

A few schools can reach beyond this model, especially those with a focus on specific populations. A school serving inner-city minority youth from low-income families might be one example. That school can make a case to individual donors and funders for annual operating support because the families they serve can't afford tuition rates to make that 85 percent level.

> ### Breaking the Rules Well
>
> You don't have to follow a model, but you should understand the models so you can explain why it's a good idea for you to do something different. In the words of Pablo Picasso, "Learn the rules like a pro, so you can break them like an artist."
>
> When you understand the rules, you can explain why you are breaking them. Funders may not always agree or support your plans to take a different tack. But if you understand the conventional approach, you'll have a more convincing argument about why you need to do things differently.
>
> **Inspiration**

If you know an organization that provides services similar to yours, you can look at its IRS 990 forms through sites such as GuideStar. The 990 allows you to see an organization's general revenue profile, such as earned income by category and donations. You can gain more information by talking with those groups. For example, if they raise a lot of money from donations, where does it come from? This information can help you develop your plan for the initial support of a project as well as the plan for sustaining it. If your plan relies heavily upon ideas you got from another organization, share that in your grant application. It can assure funders that you're following a proven approach rather than a brand new idea that is untested.

Capital Campaigns and Operating Costs

We touched on the idea that funders often ask about sustainability when they look at capital campaigns. Convincing funders and other donors that your organization will be able to fill a new building with programming for years to come helps justify their investments. But there are other facets of sustainability that you should consider.

Government-Funded Organizations

The sources of support for a building project often mirror the sources that support an organization's operating budget. Organizations that rely on government support for operating, whether through fees for service or a steady stream of grants, often don't have much experience raising private funds. That lack of experience means it can be difficult to leverage a lot of private funding for a capital campaign.

Organizations that rely on government funding usually need significant government support for capital projects. This often means grants. But there is another way to leverage government support for a capital project. Many government contracts and grants allow those funds to pay rent for facilities. When an organization has a solid history of providing government-supported services, it may be able to turn rent payments into mortgage payments.

Bridge Loans

Many smaller nonprofits can't afford to carry a mortgage as part of the regular operating budget, and they shouldn't try to. The goal should be to raise all the needed money for a capital campaign from donations and grants. When an organization can do that, it limits the amount of money it will pay for facilities in the future to heat, lights, and minor maintenance.

But you might still see a loan in the construction budget. There is a common type of loan used as a part of a capital campaign for a building called a bridge loan.

Bridge loans, also called construction financing, are short-term loans that provide cash flow. They are underwritten by pledges that have already been raised during the campaign. For example, many building projects will allow donors to pay off large pledges over three to five years. But the building can't

---

Government Contracts Can Help Pay the Mortgage

Early in the campaign for a new building, a staff person called a number of local funders to ask how to apply for grants. Since this organization was primarily funded by government contracts, few funders knew the organization.

When asked about the fundraising plan for the campaign the answer was, "We hope to raise it all from grants and donations." But "We hope..." isn't a plan. The organization eventually found that it needed a mortgage paid by the ongoing state support.

In the end, private fundraising, primarily foundation and corporate gifts, provided about a third of the campaign funds. A mortgage, paid by rent being converted to mortgage payments, provided the other two-thirds of the project cost.

Example

wait that long. So you get a bridge loan against those pledges. You get cash today to build, and the loan gets paid back as the pledges get paid.

The main point is that these loans are paid by the pledges you already have in hand when you get the loan. Unlike a mortgage, a bridge loan isn't a long-term drain on your operating budget.

More Ideas on Sustainability

If an organization has been renting its space and now plans to build its own facilities, the amount it previously paid in rent can now be applied to a mortgage payment. Another source of sustainability may be efficiency cost savings. A new building may cost less to heat and air condition than the old one it's replacing. If the organization was previously having to make frequent repairs to aging facilities, there would also be a savings in maintenance costs.

What Sustainability Means for Grants

The overall message of sustainability is that growing an organization or a program means paying attention to some things that aren't service delivery. Starting a program and providing great services doesn't mean that donations and grants will suddenly show up at your door. But providing great services and working to build a donor base and a grant writing program can help create the support to continue those services.

To Summarize...

- Sustainability is about knowing what it takes to garner resources for your work and build the capacity to do so.
- Understanding your organization's business model is a key to understanding sustainability.
- Capital projects often entail increases in ongoing operating costs that can challenge an organization's ability to support its work.
- Transition funds can help an organization cover the costs of moving to a higher level of services.

REPORTS
disbursals
opportunity
stewards
REQUIREMENTS
PROGRAM
success
development
INFORMATION
PROVIDE
application
celebrate
COMMUNITY
grantwriters
acknowledgment
guidelines
relationships
THANK
HELP
BOARD
VISIT
SHARE
staff
future
date
member
REQUESTS
loi
next
chance
events
hope
DIRECTOR
call
means
done
work
promised
meet
ensure
learn
key
areas
result
discuss
create
reason
decision
conference
LETTER
committee
ORGANIZATIONS
tour
BEGINNING
building
receive
CONTACTS
501c3
read
people
BUDGETS
aspects
money
cost
critical
conditions
news
wants
volunteers
address
UNDERSTAND
advance
GRANT
progress
ideas
steps
materials
REVIEW
PROJECT
prepare
apply
give
foundation
FUNDER

Part 6

What Comes Next?

Your work isn't over after you click "Submit" and send the proposal. If funders like what they read, they may want to conduct a site visit. If you get a grant, there are important follow-up actions you need to take that will show you're a responsible and grateful grant recipient. And even if you don't succeed this time, there are ways to increase your chances in the future. Either way, your goal is to develop a long-term relationship with funders so that both your organization and theirs can continue to benefit your community in the years to come.

Chapter 25

Meeting with Funders: Site Visits

In This Chapter...

- What does a visit looks like?
- What does the funder want to learn?
- Who should attend, and how can you prepare?
- How can you make sure the site visit goes well?

One of the most exciting things for a grantwriter to hear is that a funder wants to make a site visit or has invited the organization to a meeting at its office. When a funder takes the time for a face-to-face visit, you know it means it is interested in your request.

Immediately following that elation, however, there can be a rising wave of anxiety. What does the funder want to see or know? Who needs to attend from your organization? What materials should you prepare?

Fortunately, all the steps you've taken to carefully orchestrate your initial contact, whether through a letter or an online interface, will help to make the funder visit easier. Think of the visit as an opportunity to expand upon the information you've already provided. Your initial contact is succinct because you only have so much room, whether in an LOI or an online form. Even a full grant proposal will have space limitations. But a visit with a funder allows you to exchange much more information about your organization and your grant request. That's why you should look forward to a visit as a major opportunity for your organization.

Why Funders Meet with Grantees

When you hear that a funder wants to meet with you or your colleagues, it's good news. It means your request has passed the first hurdle. If a funder uses a screening process, such as an LOI or an online form, the request for a visit means that the funder is interested in getting to know more about your organization. (Initial contacts that clearly don't fit the funder's grantmaking won't go any further.)

Not every funder will visit with applicants. But those that do want to get to know more about an organization and the project outlined in the initial grant request. This is important for larger funders where the visitor will be a staff person from the funder's office, rather than members of the board or grant committee that makes the final decision about grants. The people you visit with, such as foundation program officers, will make a report that carries weight with the decision makers.

There are other cases where the funder has a policy of visiting all applicants who at least meet basic requirements. These grantmakers can include quasipublic groups such as United Ways, community foundations, and service-club grant committees. Also, review committees that are a part of a local government grant

---

If a Funder Calls, Someone Should Be Able to Answer

Sometimes organizations get compartmentalized. That's why good grantwriters build a rapport with everyone on staff and key volunteers. They also let people know what is going on with their grant applications.

There is nothing worse than having a funder call an organization to follow up on a request and find that no one seems to know anything about it. Even if the people cited as follow-up contacts know what to do, there may be times when those contacts are not available. If the funder calls about the proposal, it's not good if the people answering the phones sound like they have no idea about your grant requests.

WATCH OUT!

process might have a similar policy of meeting with all applicants. For example, some localities have citizen committees that review and make funding recommendations on Community Development Block Grant applications.

Whether the funder's visit is a result of your passing a screening or not, what you need to do for the visit is the same in both cases. In fact, it's a good practice to treat the volunteers from the local Rotary Club Foundation just as well as you would treat the senior program officer from a major family foundation.

Site Visit or Office Visit

A visit with a funder can take place at your site of operations, or in the funder's office. The funder's workload, its location in relation to your site, your history with the funder, and the nature of the grant may influence whether the funder comes to you or you are asked to come and visit the funder. We'll spend the rest of the chapter on site visits because they can be the most challenging. Yet many of the same general ideas apply to meetings when you've been invited to a funder's office to discuss a pending request.

What a Site Visit Looks Like

Each funder will have its own approach to a visit, so it's a good idea to ask a few questions when you schedule the visit. First, be clear about the date, time, and place. Second, confirm whom you will be meeting with from the funder's office, making sure to get names and titles correct. Third, ask how long the funder expects to meet with you. Finally, ask if there is any special information or handouts the funder might want.

There are essentially three aspects to a good visit. Each of those parts parallels the major parts of your LOI or a proposal. Funders want to learn about:

- Your organization
- Your community
- The specific request you're making

You should make sure that you have any materials you want to share with the funder assembled in advance. These should include updates on your project, additional information that expands upon your initial letter, and general background information about your organization.

Who Needs to Be There

When you get the call from a funder about a visit, ask if the funder has a preference for which of your stakeholders should attend. If the funder doesn't specify, there are three people who matter most: a key board member, the executive director, and a development staffer or grantwriter.

While many organizations feel that the board chair is the go-to person to attend these visits, that isn't always true. What's critical is that the board member who attends can speak intelligently about the project at the heart of your request. A board member who is the campaign chair for the new building campaign or who oversees the new program expansion can be much more valuable than a board chair who can't speak meaningfully about your project.

From time to time, it can be appropriate for people who have used your services to be included. This goes beyond just people that funders might see while touring your facility during working hours. If you invite a client, make sure you plan that individual's role in advance. Think of the reason you have that person there. Is this person supposed to typify the people you serve? If so, what do you mean by typical? What attributes do you want that person to share that represent the typical client?

While you don't want to put words into your clients' mouths, work with them in advance so they understand what aspects of their stories are important for the site visit. That way their participation can be succinct and informative, and can reinforce the message of your request.

More Is Not Always Better

While people involved in the project should attend a site visit, overwhelming the funder is never a good idea. One organization brought eight people to visit a funder, none of whom was a volunteer. The group included nearly all the office staff, yet only the executive director spoke. It gave the impression that the director didn't trust the rest of the staff to stay in the office without him.

At another site visit, the tour of the organization ended in a conference room. Soon the conference table had fifteen people from the organization seated together. Most of the fifteen said little more than a sentence.

If you really want to involve several key program people, introduce them to the funder as you tour your facility and let them talk about their work. Bringing everyone into a room at once can overwhelm your funder and gets in the way of sharing important information.

Uninspired

How to Ensure the Visit Goes Well

The best way to make sure that a visit goes well is good planning. As you begin applying for grants, you should meet with the key people you will need at site visits, especially your volunteers. This will allow you to be responsive to a funder's needs and have key volunteers and staff available, even if the funder wants to visit on short notice. Walk the whole team through the visit and make sure they know their parts.

Another key step in getting ready for site visits is doing a walk-through of your organization. Pay special attention to the areas that you plan to tour. Keep an eye out for unsafe conditions or things that need to be repaired. Also, make sure those areas are consistently cleaned. If areas look unkempt or unsafe, it can reflect poorly on your ability to carry out your project.

Meeting with the Funder

At a site visit, it's a good idea to greet the funder and allow a few moments to settle in. Let your visitor know the location of restrooms and offer coffee, tea, or water. When the funder is ready, outline your basic plan for the visit. Those plans should include both a tour of your site and time to sit and talk in more detail about the specifics of the request.

Either before or after you do the tour, you and your colleagues will sit down with the funder, usually in a conference room, to make a presentation about your project and answer questions.

To the extent possible, it's best if a board member can be the key spokesperson. The executive director should have the next biggest role with program staff available to answer questions if needed. And while development staff or a grantwriter should attend, the key role is to listen. Hearing the funder's reactions can help in the next stage of the process such as completing a full grant application.

Keep in mind that you'll have a time limit. A good guideline for a visit is to expect that the funder will give you about an hour. It's important to allow time for questions, so you'll want to keep the presentation to no more than forty to forty-five minutes. And for a site visit, that includes the walking time during the tour.

A visit ought to be crafted much like a letter or grant application. While funders want to understand your whole organization, the main reason they want to meet face-to-face is to gain a greater understanding of the project for which you're requesting funding. You'll want to spend most of your time on aspects specific to your grant proposal.

The Tour

The tour is a chance to show the funder your site. Remember, even if you're showing the funder the entire organization, put everything in the context of your proposal. Spend more time on the areas directly related to the request. When you visit other areas, discuss how they contribute to or work alongside the programs at the heart of your project.

Let program staff know ahead of time about the tour, and make sure they're clear on who the funder is and what the grant proposal is about. Introduce them to the funder as you tour their area; ask them to explain what's going on in that particular room, and give the funder a chance to ask questions.

Finally, take good notes during the visit. The funder may share ideas about your projects and community needs.

> **Confidentiality**
>
> Some organizations have special concerns with client confidentiality. Nonprofits that provide services subject to HIPAA regulations have special considerations, as do domestic violence shelters and organizations working with children. Sometimes there may be limitations on what you can share with funders, such as client testimonies or visiting a portion of your facility while clients are present. Other times organizations can conduct a tour, but they ask visitors to sign a confidentiality agreement.
>
> Funders understand these limitations, so don't hesitate to share them. In fact, it's important to let funders know that you respect your clients' dignity.
>
> **IMPORTANT!**

What Follows the Visit

As the visit concludes, it's a good idea to ask the funder about next steps. You may be asked to provide more detail about some aspect of your request, such as adding more data or fleshing out a fundraising plan. Since the point of the visit is to learn more about the project outlined in your letter, screening, or application, it's fair to expect some resolution to come out of the visit.

If you are fortunate enough to move to the next step in the grant process, make sure that you review your notes from the visit. If the funder's ideas were pertinent to your request, address any action items as soon as possible.

What If You Don't Get the Grant?

Sometimes a funder visit doesn't result in a grant. This may happen when it's an obligatory visit or when the funder finds that the visit failed to confirm what it thought it read in your letter. Or the grantmaker may be visiting several organizations on its short list for funding, knowing that not all of them will make the final cut.

If you don't get the grant, your first reaction may be that you blew it. While that's possible, you can still make the most out of the experience. If you think you committed a major faux pas, such as a board member providing misinformation, write an email or make a phone call. The fact that the funder took the time to visit means there is a seed of interest.

Also, this is a time when you can ask the funder if there is anything else you can do to improve your request next time. Check the guidelines to see how often you can apply, and ask if it will be all right to try again the next time you are eligible.

To Summarize...

- Funders use visits to learn more about an organization and its request.
- Your organization should include key people who can knowledgably discuss your organization and the request.
- Make sure to prepare yourself and colleagues well for the visit.
- Even a visit that doesn't go well can still serve to create a bridge to a relationship with a funder.

Chapter 26

Acknowledgment and Stewardship

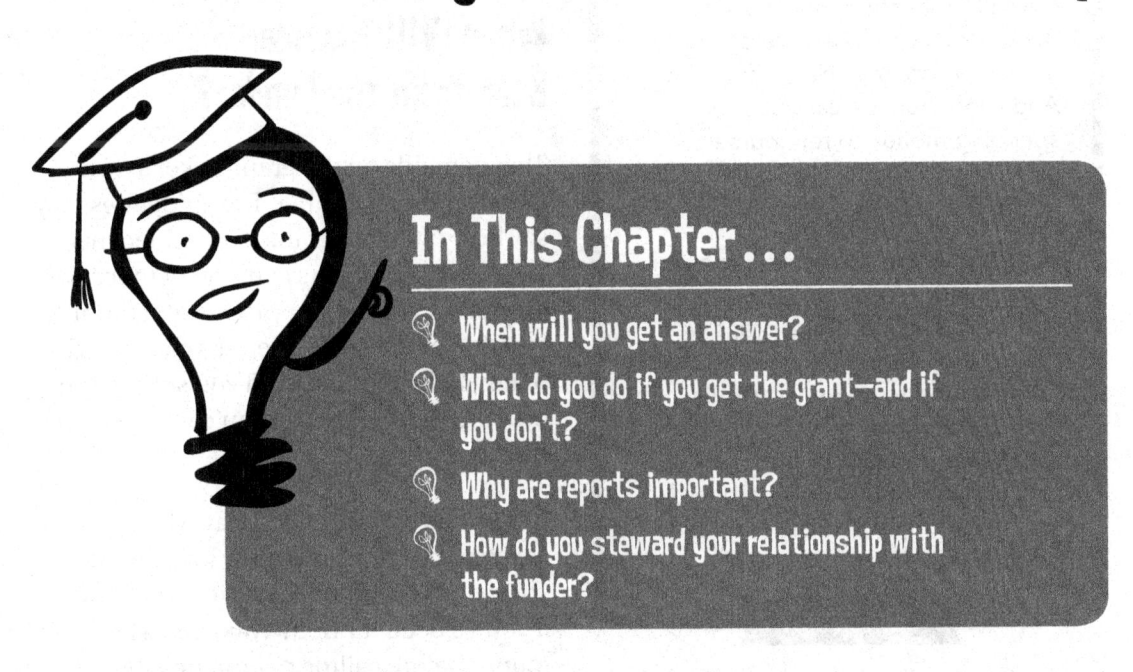

In This Chapter...

- When will you get an answer?
- What do you do if you get the grant—and if you don't?
- Why are reports important?
- How do you steward your relationship with the funder?

So you've submitted your proposal, and maybe even had a site visit. What happens next? When can you expect to hear back from the funder? And when you do hear, what do you do next? In this chapter, we'll discuss issues such as whether it's okay to call a funder if you haven't heard back within a reasonable time, what to do if you get good news, what to do if it's bad news, and how to follow up with the funder either way. It's essential to see a successful grant proposal as the beginning of a long-term relationship with a funder. A grantee organization that is a responsible steward of that relationship can look forward to more grants in the years to come.

One of the key parts of stewardship is turning in timely reports on your grant activities and outcomes, as agreed upon with the funder. Reports give you the opportunity to cite both the successes and challenges of your grant-funded projects and to discuss what you've learned. Funders appreciate thoughtful and informative reports. This is a great way to develop a rapport with a funder.

When Will You Hear Back from the Funder?

That depends on the grantmaker's own review cycle, of course. The guidelines may say how often the grants committee meets and when applicants can expect to receive an answer about their proposal. If nothing is stated in the guidelines, it's okay to call or email the funder when you submit the proposal and ask when you can expect to hear back.

If the grantmaker doesn't say when you can expect a response, how long should you wait before contacting it to find out if you've been funded? Wait at least a month before calling or emailing, but it's not unusual for funders to take three to six months to make a decision, or even longer. The review process can take a long time, especially for large foundations that receive hundreds of proposals.

> **Don't Count Your Chickens before They Hatch!**
>
> Just because you've submitted an application and feel good about your interactions with a funder, that doesn't mean the grant is a sure thing. Don't spend a dime of grant money before the check shows up. And even then, be careful about spending money to reimburse expenses you incur before the date of the grant.
>
> Though it's rare, funders have been sued because applicants felt they had been assured that a grant was going to be approved. As a result, funders tend to be very careful when they explain their processes. They usually warn that a decision isn't final until it's approved by a board or other group that makes the final funding decisions.
>
> **WATCH OUT!**

What If You Get the Grant?

When a funder makes a grant, it will usually send a grant transmittal letter with the check. The letter usually outlines conditions of the grant, primarily that the money will be used for the purpose outlined in the grant application. Most transmittal letters also ask that the recipient sign and return a document that shows agreement to the grant conditions.

Whether you get a grant transmittal letter or not, it's important to send a thank-you letter. The letter should both thank the funder for the grant and provide updates on any relevant news. Make it your responsibility to ensure that this response goes out within a day of receiving the award notice.

But the official acknowledgment shouldn't be the only one. There's an adage in fundraising that every donor should be thanked seven times for each gift. This may seem a little over the top, but several people can thank the funder in a variety of ways:

- Call the program director (or the person you've worked with most closely at the funder's office) and thank that individual personally. Try to reach the person by phone as soon as you can, when your excitement over the grant will be evident in your voice.

- Write a handwritten note as well.

- If it's appropriate, your executive director should personally call or write the top official at the funder's office.

- The director of the program at your nonprofit who will actually be administering the grant can write a note, too.

Some of these communications can be done through email, but a handwritten note will be especially appreciated. Your organization should have some notepaper with your logo on hand for this purpose.

What If You Get More Money Than You Need?

This question almost always comes up in grantwriting classes. Since it is highly unlikely that 100 percent of your grants will be funded at the full amount requested, you will, of course, submit proposals that exceed the total budget for your project. This leads to the concern that you might actually get more money than you need.

Fear not—this hardly ever happens. For one thing, most grant-related projects do not have a hard and fast cost. While you will submit a budget, projected costs can easily change, and they tend to increase rather than decrease. For another, a large project will probably plan for revenue from a variety of sources, including individual donations. If your grant revenue comes in higher than expected, you can allocate individual donations (which are usually not tightly restricted) to other needs.

The only time you might actually get more than you need is if you are writing grants to fund a piece of equipment, which really does have a fixed cost. If this should happen, call the funder whose grant puts you over the top with the good news. Tell the funder how successful you've been, and ask if you may use the grant for a related need. As long as you are honest and open with funders, it's unlikely that they'll ask you to return their checks. But if they do, be gracious about it, and you'll probably receive more funding from them in the future.

What If You Get Less than You Asked For?

Grantmakers' resources are often stretched thin, and they may choose to fund some proposals partially rather than fund just a few in full. This may be somewhat disappointing, but whatever you do, don't let the funder know that you're not pleased. Some grantmakers have called to inform an applicant of a partial award, only to receive a response that sounds crestfallen or even rude. This will not help your future grantseeking efforts. Simply thank the grantmaker, and if asked how you will manage with a lesser

---

> ### Throw Yourself a Party!
>
> Don't forget to celebrate your own success, and make sure others in your office (especially your boss) acknowledge it too. Grantwriters tend to be introverts, and much of their work is done alone. While a successful special event such as a gala auction may be celebrated by the whole office with a party involving cake and balloons, a large grant may elicit no more than a smile and a verbal pat on the back from your boss. Some grantwriters silently resent this treatment, and eventually lose their enthusiasm for their job.
>
> Don't let this happen to you. If you've won a big grant, suggest that the whole office celebrate. This isn't all about you—many people contributed to developing the proposal, and many will benefit from the grant. Everybody should celebrate this success. You'll feel better about your job in the long run if you make sure your work is properly appreciated.
>
> **Inspiration**

amount than requested, say you'll get back in touch after you've met with your colleagues to determine your next steps.

What If You Don't Get the Grant?

This can be depressing, especially if you submitted a big proposal that you worked on for weeks. But the world of grants is highly competitive—especially for large ones—and not every proposal will be successful. Don't take it personally, so long as you know you did the best you could, and don't look for others to blame. Most likely, there were other applications that were a closer fit to the funder's interests, or organizations that had a longer history with the funder. Like the old song says, "Pick yourself up, dust yourself off, and start all over again."

But there are things you can do to create a better chance next time. Some organizations actually write a "thank you for considering our proposal" note, even if they weren't funded. This will impress funders as a polite gesture, and they'll think well of you for it. (Remember, grantmakers don't like saying "no" any more than applicants like hearing it.)

Wait a week or so, and then call the program officer and ask if there's a specific reason why your proposal was rejected and what you might do to have a better chance of success next time. Sometimes you'll get some excellent advice with this tactic, and you may have your wounded feelings salved if the staffer tells you the grants committee really liked your proposal and was sorry it was unable to fund it. (But don't make this call if the rejection letter specifically says, "We are unable to provide information about why any particular proposal was declined.")

Make Sure Evaluation Procedures Get Done!

In your proposal, you probably stated that your organization would carry out particular activities to evaluate the success of your project. Make sure these evaluation procedures are actually completed, and that those entrusted with this responsibility understand what was promised. You may need to work with your boss or another executive in your organization to ensure that this gets done. Don't just assume that everybody knows about it and will produce the necessary report in six months or a year. You could have an unpleasant surprise when it's time to do the report if your colleagues don't know what the grant proposal promised.

Turn in Reports on Time!

The grant transmittal letter or other information in the application materials should outline the formal reporting requirements. Submitting reports on time is a critical step in building a good relationship with a funder.

Another reason that grant reports help you deepen your relationship with funders is that they pay attention to those documents. While funders try to read everything sent to them, many like to look at reports from current grantees before anything else. Reports that educate funders in addition to fulfilling the reporting requirements are another way to build your relationship with them.

Formal reporting requirements generally ask you to report on your progress toward the program goals and the budget. Yet you still have choices in how you compose those reports.

A one-page report that provides a simple, terse update on your progress may meet the formal requirements. But the report is an opportunity to say much more. It is a chance to talk about what you've learned so far, how you may have adjusted your plans, and anything else that might enliven your basic report.

What kinds of information can you add to your reports? Since no plan ever works exactly as written, there will always be variances. Falling a little short or exceeding the targets for your program can be a way to begin a conversation about the project. What is critical is that you report something that you've learned and how you are using that information. A report that says, "We're not recruiting as many low-income families as we had planned, but we hope this will change in the next few months," doesn't provide enough information. The first part of that statement

> ### The Funder Wants You to Succeed
>
> Once funders have awarded your organization a grant, they want the project to succeed as much as you do. Ask the funder for advice as you proceed in your project, if you think it might be able to help. And if something major goes wrong, let the funder know immediately. It may be able to help you find a solution, or make adjustments.
>
> The worst thing you can do is to try to cover up a fiasco, only to have the funder hear about it from a third party months later. As many politicians have learned, it's not the initial misstep that brings you down so much as the cover-up.
>
> **Inspiration**

is fine, but the second part should be proactive, describing an action you're going to take to address that shortfall.

On the other hand, if your recruitment of low-income families is exceeding expectations, you can use that information to lay the groundwork for expanding your program. While you may not have an expansion fully planned, you can at least address the importance of thinking about expanding your efforts.

Stewarding the Relationship with the Funder

After the grant period is over and you've turned in your final report, stay in touch with the funder, but don't be a pest. Ask if it's all right to put the grantmaker on your organization's mailing list so it receives regular newsletters and annual reports. (Since most organizations now send these materials electronically, they won't clutter up the funder's desk the way they did in the old days of paper mailings.)

If there's an update or an article specifically on the project funded by the grant, send a personal email to the funder with the relevant article as an attachment. Thank the funder again for the grant, and let the funder know what the project is accomplishing. Photos of happy, grateful clients—especially children—are a welcome addition.

Invitations to Events

If there's a follow-up event specifically honoring donors to the project, send funders a personal invitation and let them know how much you hope they will be able to join you. If your organization hosts other events not specifically related to the grant, you can include funders on your mailing list, but don't necessarily expect them to come. They are invited to hundreds of such events every year, and they can't go to all of them, but they may appreciate the invitation.

Beginning the Next Phase

We end this book with this chapter on Acknowledgment and Stewardship for two reasons. The most obvious is that acknowledgment and stewardship are the last phases of the grant process when you look at a single grant in a linear fashion. Thanking a funder and reporting on the grant follow all the other key steps from the LOI, the full application, and the site visit.

While a single grant can be outlined like that, an organization's strong grantseeking program doesn't fit that model. Funders often say that reporting on your current grant is the first step to your next grant. We hope we've conveyed that idea throughout the book. Relationships are a key part of grantsmanship. And the most important relationship is the one you create between your organization and its various funders by saying thank you when a grant is awarded and reporting on the progress of your project as work is done.

Even a "thank you for your consideration" note when you've been turned down can help to create a relationship that will put the next request in a better light.

As such, while this chapter is at the end of the book, in many ways it is also a part of the beginning of the process. Acknowledgment and stewardship are the keys to building good relationships with funders. And the more good relationships with funders you have, the greater your grantwriting success.

To Summarize...

- How you acknowledge and follow up on your current grant can help you get a foot in the door for your next one.

- Thank-you letters are important!

- Turning reports in on time and making them informative are essential elements in building good long-term relationships with funders.

- After the grant period ends, steward your relationships by keeping funders updated on the progress of the program they funded.

Appendix A

Model LOI

North County Food Resources
310 Wells Avenue
Virginia, MN 55792
(218) 555-1212

> All letters should go on letterhead, even if it is only a page header you produce on your word processor. This tells a funder where the organization is located and how to contact the organization.

February 25, 2015

Ms. Philomena Dollar
Executive Director
The John P. Jones Memorial Trust
300 Great Lakes Blvd
Duluth, MN 55802

> Address your letter to a specific individual when you can. Most funders provide that information on a website or a 990-PF. Letters addressed "Dear Trustees" or "Dear Director" are less effective.

Dear Ms. Dollar:

    We're writing to ask The John P. Jones Memorial Trust to help North Counties Food Resources increase the amount of food available to low-income families in the rural areas of northern Minnesota. North Counties Food Resources began as the St. Ann's Food Bank in 1982. The food bank was founded by volunteers from three local churches to serve the town of St. Ann's and nearby rural areas. Our mission was to provide food to families experiencing unemployment or underemployment due to the declining mining industry.

> This first sentence tells the funder what the letter is about: "increase the amount of food...." That accomplishment should align with the funder's interests. Note that the letter does not begin: "We are writing for a $10,000 grant."

    In 2000 the St. Ann's Food Bank became North Counties Food Resources to focus on collecting and distributing food to 30 food programs throughout three rural counties in northern Minnesota. These programs range from food pantries in small churches to community food banks and congregate meal sites. Last year they served 100,000 people, including low-income families and seniors. These program provided just over 800,000 meals. North Counties Food Resources supported these local programs by distributing approximately one million pounds of food to them. Our program runs on a cash budget of $200,000 and in-kind donations, primarily the food we distribute that would cost well over one million dollars a year to purchase.

> The second line of the first paragraph and the next paragraph share the organization's history, mission, and current operations.

> Now you share more about an aspect of your work that is key to your grant request, "...increasing the amount of food...."

    The network of food programs we support grew out of the success of the St. Ann's Food Bank. Communities throughout northern Minnesota reached out to St. Ann's for assistance. At first people would drive to St. Ann's from these areas. Over the years St. Ann's helped volunteers set up programs in their own communities. By 2003 these groups had formed a network serving thousands of square miles of rural and isolated communities. North Counties supports this network by collecting and distributing large donations of food. We also make bulk purchases of key items at highly favorable prices in order to supply needed foods that are not regularly donated.

> This paragraph provides background about the community needs. In some cases you might have statistics or other information to bolster your case. In the end, however, make sure to share the information in a way that shows how your observations come from your organization's day to day work.

    The needs of our communities continue to grow. In the 1980s many hoped that the economic downturn in mining would be short-lived. While mining and timber still provide some jobs, our local economy has changed. The tourist industry is now the main employer throughout northern Minnesota. As a result, many people transition between two or three different jobs during the year. Often there are gaps in those transitions and a family needs its local food pantry to help fill that gap.

    To keep pace with these needs we must keep pace with the change in the overall food system. Traditionally food banks collected and distributed large amounts of rice, beans, flour,

> This paragraph begins to create the link between the community needs and your project.

© Ken Ristine 2014

cereals, and canned goods. These were typical of every family's weekly groceries, whether they purchased those groceries from a store or were given a box of food at a food bank. In recent years the American food system has dramatically increased the amount of fresh and frozen foods available due to concerns about health and a desire for healthier foods. For example, a serving of canned peas contains 310 milligrams of sodium where a serving of frozen peas contains only 145 mg of sodium. You have probably seen the result of this change. In recent years both of our local supermarkets have more than doubled their frozen food and fresh foods sections. This change in the commercial sector has a big impact on donations we receive from the food system.

These lines show that the desire to provide more fresh and frozen produce reflects a societal trend and the shift in the donations available. In addition, it provides examples that most readers have seen for themselves.

We are a key conduit between Feeding America and large food brokers and the local programs we serve. Our ability to handle this donated food has a direct impact on what local food programs can distribute. Ten years ago the ratio of fresh and frozen food to canned and dry food was 1:5. Now that ratio is 1:3; that means 25% of our distributions are now fresh and frozen foods. Since our distributions also grew during that time it means we are now handling 300 % more fresh and frozen foods than we did ten years ago.

You can increase your credibility by sharing a concrete example of ideas you're sharing. This example both reinforces the impact of the trend on your organization and its place serving the community.

This shift presents a challenge for local food programs. Many have only limited space to store fresh and frozen foods. That is where North County Food Resources plays a critical role. We coordinate deliveries so that fresh and frozen food can leave our warehouse in the morning and be distributed by local food programs that afternoon, some of which are over 100 miles from our warehouse.

This paragraph links the impact of the trend to a practical solution at the heart of your grant request. This approach shows how the request has grown out of your work.

This work requires cooler/freezer space for the fresh and frozen food donations we receive. By adding 4,000 cubic feet of cooler/freezer space we can continue our present level of service and distribute another 100,000 pounds of food each year. That will translate into approximately 80,000 more meals through local programs each year.

Here you share the tool(s) need to respond to the needs you've outlined. Also, you set an outcome (200,000 lbs. more food and 250,000+ meals), by stating what you plan to accomplish with the tool(s).

We've gotten some very good help on this project from our volunteer Roger Crittenden. Roger recently retired from a refrigeration wholesaler and has worked with several refrigeration equipment vendors. Our budget for purchase and installation is $53,460. In addition we have some minor work that needs to be done on our facility to make the installation workable. With the cost of that work the total budget is $60,000.

This paragraph outlines the budget. Citing your volunteer's qualification bolsters the credibility of the budget. Remember, a budget is a plan.

We began fund raising for this project last fall. Our funding plan has three aspects: government grants, individual donors, and foundation and corporate gifts. As of last week we've raised just over one-half of the $60,000. St. Clare County has committed $15,000. Two past board members have committed a total of $5,000 while other individuals have added another $10,000 to date. Finally, we have a commitment to donate a part of the bid cost of the equipment, motor, and condenser from the bidder we've chosen. That in-kind donation is worth $3,200.

These amounts total $33,200. The remaining $26,800 will come from $5,000 we are confirming with the City of St. Ann's, another $5,000 from past individual supporters, and grants. We've sent requests to seven foundations and businesses to raise the remaining $16,800 from that sector.

These two paragraphs outline the plan for raising the needed resources, report on the progress towards that goal, and the work planned to garner the remaining resources needed.

We request that the John P. Jones Memorial Trust consider a grant for $10,000 towards the project. Some funds are already designated to specific portions of the project due to both the

Here you make a specific request to the funder, including how the grant would be used. That use can be as general as support of the entire project or as specific as a budget line item, depending upon the funder

© Ken Ristine 2014

nature of the in-kind gift and government restrictions. If the grant is made we would use it to meet costs as they arise towards completing the entire project.

While we haven't raised all the funds yet, we believe that we are on a timeline that will allow us to commit to the vendor by August 1st. The equipment would be onsite for installation by mid-September and put into service in early October.

This project is a priority for our board because it promises to increase our distributions of food to rural communities throughout our area. Since fresh and frozen foods are such a key component of the donated and bulk purchase foods available to feeding programs, we feel that this project is an investment in our work for many years to come.

Please contact me if I can provide any further to evaluate this request. My direct phone line is (555) 555-5555 and my email is JWBonaparte@northcountyfood.org. I hope we have the opportunity to speak with you more about this project.

Sincerely,

John W. Bonaparte

John W. Bonaparte
Chairman

© Ken Ristine 2014

Appendix B

Sample Grant Proposal for SCUM

The following "grant proposal" was originally written as a group project for a course that Goodwin took with the Grantsmanship Training Center. While it is a parody, it is also an excellent example of a grant proposal written according to the standard model. We have updated and revised it to make it better fit the template and recommendations we provide in this book. We hope you will find it both educational and entertaining.

Note that the goal of the project is focused on outcome—decreasing the number of slugs in danger of extinction—not just on outputs. Outputs (identifying and relocating a certain percentage of slugs) are among the objectives. One objective, psychological well-being, is more difficult to measure, but established means of measurement are identified in the evaluation section. The capital portion of the project—remodeling a building—is a tool listed in the methods section, and is not an end (or goal) in itself.

> **IMPORTANT!**
>
> ## Satire Alert!
>
> The contents of this proposal are not meant to be taken seriously. For those of you from drier climes who may not be familiar with slugs, they are nasty little garden pests that leave a trail of slime behind them wherever they go. Salt is lethal to them. However, they are very fond of beer, and will readily drown themselves in shallow bowls of beer left at ground level—a form of organic pest control. (Hence the reference to slugs with substance-abuse problems.) They are by no means endangered.

Save Our Slugs

A Proposal submitted to
The American Endowment for Invertebrate
Organization Underwriting
by
SCUM

March 17, 2016

SCUM: A.E.I.O.U.
Sample Proposal

SCUM
The Society for the Care & Understanding of Mollusks

3169 Humus Way, Suite 4 info@scum.org (206) 754-SCUM [754-7286]
Seattle, Washington 98104

March 17, 2016

Dr. Phylum Chordata:
American Endowment for Invertebrate Organization Underwriting
910 Bugg Street
Los Angeles, CA 90015

Dear Dr. Chordata:

We are writing to A.E.I.O.U. because we share your concern for the preservation of mollusk species, those marvelous but misunderstood members of the animal kingdom. We admire your work in preserving the *Plaxiphora caelata* or Hairy Chiton of New Zealand.

The Board of Directors of the Society for the Care and Understanding of Mollusks (SCUM) has reviewed the enclosed project proposal and expressed its complete support. This project, with A.E.I.O.U.'s assistance, will allow for the survival of 35,000 *Slimus alongus*, a slug endemic to east Seattle, through the creation of a Wild Slug Preserve.

The preserve, 49 square miles of prime natural habitat, will provide a safe living environment for the slugs, who are being forced out of their present habitat by the rapid expansion of the greater Seattle metropolitan area. Without the preserve, the last remaining population of *Slimus alongus* would become extinct within the next three years.

The creation of the Wild Slug Preserve has long been at the top of SCUM's priority list. As a result, we have been able to organize extensive support from the local community for the establishment of the preserve. The budget for developing the preserve and the associated visitor and research center is $1,285,700. To date we've raised $480,000, 37% of the project cost

Because A.E.I.O.U. is such a leader in this field we would like to name the Slug Visitor Center after your foundation. The thousands of visitors we expect each year will be keenly aware of A.E.I.O.U.'s generosity.

If you have questions or need further information, please contact our Executive Director, Dr. Aimee Vermicelli, at aimee@scum.org or (206) 754-4982.

Sincerely,

Dr. John Doolittle, President
SCUM Board of Directors

SCUM: A.E.I.O.U.
Sample Proposal

SCUM PROPOSAL

SUMMARY

The Society for the Care and Understanding of Mollusks (SCUM), the foremost organization for the advancement of mollusk species in the Western hemisphere, is dedicated to preventing the extinction of the last remaining population of *Slimus alongus*. In the course of our work we have observed that unchecked urban development has resulted in the loss of the species' natural habitat, threatening its survival. To remedy this situation, SCUM is proposing the establishment of a 49-square-mile Wild Slug Preserve to be located in east Seattle, Washington. Our goal is to decrease the number of *Slimus alongus* in danger of extinction by 90 percent over a 12-month period. Our objectives are to identify and relocate at least 88% of the existing population, and to provide a new environment that will allow them to thrive and develop their potential.

Our plan for raising funds is for approximately 56% of the funding to be raised from foundation and corporate, 17% from our community campaign, 15% from major donors (including significant support from our board of directors), and 12% from state and local government grants. Our request of A.E.I.O.U. is for a grant of $350,000 to be used for the year-long project to create the preserve and open it to the public.

I. NEEDS STATEMENT

"In east Seattle, the last 35,000 *Slimus alongus* are currently in peril of dying, thus resulting in the complete extinction of the species." So stated Dr. Engrith "Slugo" Olsen, doctor of zoology, at the annual Conference of Worm Appreciators this Year.

Only five years ago, the *Slimus alongus* species, endemic to Seattle, Washington, included over 100,000 healthy slugs (see 2010 Slug Census Report, attachment 2). Studies conducted by Seattle University show that the current *Slimus alongus* population numbers only 35,000, a drop of 65% over a five-year period (see attachment 3).

Unchecked and poorly planned development of the greater Seattle metropolitan area has destroyed vast expanses of slug habitat, reducing the population to dangerously low levels. At the current rate this species, which has been culturally invaluable to area residents, will be extinct by 2018.

Surviving slugs have been forced into dwindling habitat, resulting in overcrowding, depression, and ill health. King County sheriffs have reported a sharp increase in the number of traffic accidents involving suicidal slugs, and incidences of substance abuse and vagrancy have risen dramatically (King County Health and Welfare Department). Homeless slugs have crowded emergency relief stations which have been set up to aid in the crisis, and local veterinarians are worried by the number of surviving slugs who are suffering from malnutrition (see Letters of Concern, attachment 4).

Dr. Georgia Nospine, a leading invertebrate veterinarian, recently stated: "Conditions are getting worse all the time. I don't know how much longer the little guys will be able to hang in there."

II. GOALS AND OBJECTIVES

The goal of this project is to decrease the number of *Slimus alongus* in danger of extinction by 90% over a twelve-month period. Studies by the St. Louis Institute of Mollusk Ecology (SLIME) indicate that *Slimus alongus* requires one square mile of natural, unspoiled habitat per 1,000 slugs to maintain a healthy population. This project will provide adequate habitat for most of the remaining 35,000 members of the species.

Objective 1: To locate and identify at least 88% of *Slimus alongus* currently living in unsafe areas of east Seattle and environs.

SCUM: A.E.I.O.U.
Sample Proposal

Objective 2: To relocate 97% of the identified slugs to the Preserve with a casualty rate of no more than 5%. (Unfortunately, relocation is stressful for the delicate slugs, and not all individuals are expected to survive the journey.)

Objective 3: To establish a healthy, thriving community where slugs will be free to grow and develop their individual potential.

III. METHODS

In 2012 the world-renowned Escargot Society, in an effort spearheaded by their leader Jacques Escargot, raised $1,000,000 to purchase 49 square miles of prime slug habitat in the east Seattle area. This land was subsequently donated to SCUM in order to establish a wild slug preserve. Such a preserve will not only provide a safe environment for threatened slugs, but will also allow a great number of people to view the magnificent beasts in their native habitat.

A 6,200-square foot building located on the property will be renovated to serve as a visitor center, park headquarters and research center. A ground search will be conducted to locate displaced and needy slugs who will then be transported to the Preserve using a specialized transport sling and helicopter.

In order to prevent newly relocated slugs from accidentally wandering off the Preserve, a trained orangutan from the Woodland Park Zoo will be engaged to lay a three-inch wide barrier of salt around the perimeter of the property. The salt will be treated with red dye powder to increase its visibility and to prevent inadvertent nasal ingestion by slugs with substance abuse problems.

IV. EVALUATION

The criteria on which our evaluation will be based consists of monthly population counts of the preserve's *Slimus alongus* community

Transects and Dobenmeier squares, both established scientific methods of determining accurate population counts, will be used on a monthly basis by graduate students from Seattle Community College to collect population data, which will then be analyzed by the SCUM staff biostatistician. This will allow for timely adjustments to be made to assure the successful execution of the project.

To evaluate the psychological health of the newly relocated population, researchers will use Evidence-based Practices and established instruments such as the Beck Indicator of Mollusk Depression. Tests will be administered on arrival and again one year later.

The results of the project, along with supporting data, will be published in the Journal of the American Mollusk Association (JAMA) and on our website.

V. BUDGET NARRATIVE

While this is a capital project, there are key personnel assigned solely to this project over the next year. They will be liaisons with contractors that are making site improvements, including fencing and berms, irrigation, and building renovations.

Personnel costs include allocations of time by the Executive Director, Preserve Director, Research Director, Zoological Humanist, Biostatistician, three rangers, and one administrative assistant.

SCUM: A.E.I.O.U.
Sample Proposal

Consulting and contract services will be provided by a veterinarian (Dr. G. Nospine), four graduate students, and one trained orangutan.

VI. ORGANIZATIONAL INFORMATION

The Society for the Care and Understanding of Mollusks was established in 1965 by an endowment from the Jed Clampet family. SCUM is a mollusk advocacy group whose mission is to increase the number, protect the habitat, and improve the quality of life of American mollusk species. SCUM is headquartered in Seattle, Washington, and has been responsible for securing over $98.5 million for the research and protection of mollusks throughout Latin America, Mexico, Canada, and the United States.

Previous endeavors include the establishment of the Geoduck Aquatic Research Program and Farm at Evergreen State College in Olympia, Washington. SCUM was also instrumental in arresting and reversing the extinction of the arctic Harp Snail found in Barrow, Alaska, and provided technical assistance in establishing the Avarios Sanctuary for Injured and Orphaned Mud Snails in Costa Rica.

SCUM currently has available the resources and capabilities necessary to establish a wildlife preserve as proposed in this project, including qualified staff (see resumes, attachment 1), and a specialized helicopter transport sling used in mollusk relocation.

Marlin Perkins, a wildlife expert from the University of Omaha, has stated: "SCUM is the foremost authority in recognizing and addressing problems in the mollusk community. They are the only organization currently capable of arresting and reversing the crisis which faces the Seattle slug population."

VI. SUSTAINABILITY

Future funding of the Wild Slug Preserve will be required for slug feeding and health care. Funding will also be needed to maintain preserve headquarters and research facilities. These monies will be raised through an Adopt-a-Slug program which is currently being developed by the King County Latchkey Association and will expand to include other members of the Pacific Northwest Latchkey Cartel. Additional funding will be raised through annual benefit performances of Slug Lake by the Pacific Northwest Ballet. An admission fee will be charged to visitors to the Preserve and profits from the sale of slug gift items and books and will be donated by the Friends of SCUM. We will develop membership options that will allow visitors unlimited admission to the Preserve over a period of one year.

If further funding is required, the King County United Way has indicated a willingness to consider the Preserve's needs when distributing monies over the next five years. SCUM staff is also currently involved in an effort to identify additional sources of long-term funding.

SCUM: A.E.I.O.U.
Sample Proposal

Expenditures

I   Personnel (for start-up)

	Salaries	$ 132,900
	Fringe Benefits	$ 74,000
	Consultants	$ 55,000
		$ **261,900**

II   Capital Costs

	Architect/Engineering	$ 85,000
	Site Improvement	$ 95,000
	Slug Relocation	$ 150,000
	Building Rehab	$ 522,800
	Permits/Taxes	$ 55,000
	Misc.	$ 23,000
	Contingency (10%)	$ 93,000
		$ **1,023,800**

Project total: $ 1,285,700

Income

Project Budget:	$ 1,285,700
Raised to date:	$ 480,000
Amount Remaining:	$ 805,700

Raised to Date:

Gastropod Foundation	$ 100,000
Pneumostome Inc.	$ 75,000
State Wildlife Dept.	$ 75,000
Major Donors	$ 127,500
Community Campaign	$ 102,500
Total:	$ 480,000

Planned or Applied for:

A.E.I.O.U.	$ 350,000
Other Private Grants	$ 200,000
Local Government	$ 75,000
Major Donors	$ 70,000
Community Campaign	$ 110,700
Total:	$ 805,700

SCUM: A.E.I.O.U.
Sample Proposal

ATTACHMENTS

1. Resumes of Project Staff

2. 2010 Slug Census Report, National Science Foundation

3. Seattle University Study of *Slimus oblongus* Population Levels

4. Letters of Concern

5. Letters of Support and Commitment

6. SCUM Board of Directors

7. 501(c)(3) Letter of Federal Tax Exempt Status

8. Audited Financial Statements for Fiscal Year 2015

Appendix C

Code of Ethics

The **Grant Professionals Association** (GPA), a nonprofit membership association, is committed to serving the greater public good by practicing the highest ethical and professional standards. Ethics refer to the rules or standards governing the conduct of a person or members of a profession.

Members have joined forces to be the leading authority and resource for the practice of grantsmanship in all sectors of the field. Membership in this association promotes positive relationships between grant professionals and their stakeholders, provides a vehicle for grant professionals to gain professional growth and development, and enhances the public image and recognition of the profession within the greater philanthropic, public, and private funding communities. Members' foundation is stimulated by the rich diversity within the grant profession.

Members, among others, are to:

- Practice their profession with the highest sense of integrity, honesty, and truthfulness to maintain and broaden public confidence
- Adhere to all applicable laws and regulations in all aspects of grantsmanship
- Continually improve their professional knowledge and skills
- Promote positive relationships between grant professionals and their stakeholders
- Value the privacy, freedom, choice and interests of all those affected by their actions
- Ensure that funds are solicited according to program guidelines
- Adhere to acceptable means of compensation for services performed; pro bono work is encouraged
- Foster cultural diversity and pluralistic values and treat all people with dignity and respect
- Become leaders and role models in the field of grantsmanship
- Encourage colleagues to embrace and practice GPA's Code of Ethics and Standards of Professional Practice.

Standards of Professional Practice

As members respect and honor the above principles and guidelines established by the GPA Code of Ethics, any infringement or breach of standards outlined in the Code are subject to disciplinary sanctions, including expulsion, to be determined by a committee elected by their peers.

Professional Obligations:

1. Members shall act according to the highest ethical standards of their institution, profession, and conscience.
2. Members shall obey all applicable local, state, provincial, and federal civil and criminal laws and regulations.
3. Members shall avoid the appearance of any criminal offense or professional misconduct.
4. Members shall disclose all relationships that might constitute, or appear to constitute, conflicts of interest.
5. Members shall not be associated directly or indirectly with any service, product, individuals, or organizations in a way that they know is misleading.
6. Members shall not abuse any relationship with a donor, prospect, volunteer or employee to the benefit of the member or the member's organization.
7. Members shall recognize their individual boundaries of competence and are forthcoming and truthful about their professional experience, knowledge and expertise.
8. Members shall continually strive to improve their personal competence.

Solicitation and Use of Funds:

9. Members shall take care to ensure that all solicitation materials are accurate and correctly reflect the organization's mission and use of solicited funds.
10. Members shall take care to ensure that grants are used in accordance with the grant's intent.

If Applicable:

11. Members shall take care to ensure proper use of funds, including timely reports on the use and management of such funds.
12. Members shall obtain explicit consent by the grantor before altering the conditions of grant agreements.

Presentation of Information:

13. Members shall not disclose privileged information to unauthorized parties. Information acquired from consumers is confidential. This includes verbal and written disclosures, records, and video or audio recording of an activity or presentation without appropriate releases.
14. Members shall not plagiarize[1] in any professional work, including, but not limited to: grant proposals, journal articles/magazines, scholarly works, advertising/marketing materials, websites, scientific articles, self-plagiarism, etc.
15. Members are responsible for knowing the confidentiality regulations within their jurisdiction.
16. Members shall use accurate and consistent accounting methods that conform to the appropriate guidelines adopted by the American Institute of Certified Public Accountants (AICPA) for the type of organization involved. (In countries outside of the United States, comparable authority should be utilized).

Compensation:

17. Members shall work for a salary or fee.
18. Members may accept performance-based compensation, such as bonuses, provided such bonuses are in accordance with prevailing practices within the members' own organizations and are not based on a percentage of grant monies.
19. Members shall not accept or pay a finder's fee, commission, or percentage compensation based on grants and shall take care to discourage their organizations from making such payments.
20. Compensation should not be written into grants unless allowed by the funder.

Revised: October 2011

"The GPA Code of Ethics reflects only the highest standards in professional behavior and incorporates the standards promulgated by American Fundraising Professionals and other professions dedicated to serving the greater public good."

Appendix D

Chicago Area Grant Application Form

Introduction

Working collaboratively, representatives from Chicago's foundations and corporate giving programs and a broad range of nonprofit organizations designed this form in order to streamline the grant seeking process.

Be strategic. Make sure that the goals, objectives, and amount requested in your proposal match the criteria of the funder you are approaching. A cover letter should be included with each proposal which introduces your organization and your request, and makes a strategic link between your proposal and the funder's mission and grantmaking interests. Information about many individual grant programs is available from each funder in the Forefront Library.

How To Use The Application Form

Type in the gray boxes to fill out the form. Use your mouse or the <Tab> button to move from one field to the next. When finished filling out the form, click File and then Save As...to save the file. You can e-mail the form to co-workers for review or to add additional information to the form.

Please fill out each blank section in the application. To get help at any time, press the F1 key. When you have completed the application, you can print and sign your application for submission.

This form uses macros for calculations; verify macros are enabled in order to get the full benefit of the form.

This application form is compatible with MAC and PC.

Important Notes

1. Please keep in mind that different funders have different guidelines, priorities, deadlines and timetables. In addition, funders who accept this form may require a preliminary concept paper or request additional information at any stage in the proposal process.

   - Know each funder's grantmaking philosophy, program interests, and criteria.
   - It is important to follow specific instructions from the funder.
   - Be aware of each funder's application process, including timetable and preferred method of initial contact.

2. Include a cover letter that outlines the strategic link between your proposal and the funder's mission.
3. This form must be completed in its entirety.
4. Develop your proposal using the format on page iii.

ForefrOnt
Engaging for impact

Chicago Area Grant Application Form
Rev. 10/2015

Resources

- Call or write each funder to obtain a copy of funding guidelines and/or annual report.

- Attend a free Introduction to Prospect Research workshop in the Library. Visit myforefront.org/library to register.

- Visit Forefront's Library to conduct research on private grantmakers. The Library is open to the public and is located at 208 South LaSalle, Suite 1535, Chicago, IL 60604. Regular hours are from noon to 5 p.m. Monday through Friday. The Library's telephone number is (312) 578-0175.

Frequently Asked Questions

I want to type more in the field, but it won't allow me to.

Most fields (the space where you type in the answers to questions) have a limit of characters. They are limited so that users cannot create extremely long proposals. With your cursor in the field press F1 for more information on the character limitations.

Why can't I spell check?

Spell check is not available for fillable forms. To spell check, type the text in another document, spell check that document, then copy and paste the text into the Chicago Area Grant Application form.

Why can't I change the font or use bold, italics and other font formatting?
Forms are preset in this form and cannot be changed.

Who accepts the Chicago Area Grant Application and Report Forms?

The list of foundations and corporate giving programs that accept the form changes periodically. The list of grantmakers that accept the Chicago Area Grant Application is on page 5 of this document.

Need more assistance? Call (312) 578-0175.

Forefront
Engaging for impact

Chicago Area Grant Application
Form
Rev. 10/2015

Chicago Area Grant Application Form

Attachments

Please provide the attachments in the following order.

A. Finances

1. Audited financial statements for the last fiscal year, if available, or Form 990. If neither document is available, include unaudited financial statement.

2. Current year's operating budget to include both projected expenses and revenues. Categorize expenses under program, general and administrative, and fundraising.

3. Program budget (with narrative, if applicable).

4. If request is for a multi-year grant, include multi-year program budget.

5. Capital budget and a list of Campaign Committee members (if applicable).

6. A list of foundations, corporations, or governmental agencies which funded the organization in the last fiscal year, including amounts contributed ($1,000 and above).

7. Itemization of use of requested funds (if requested by funder).

B. Other Supporting Materials

1. Verification of the organization's or fiscal agent's tax-exempt status under Section 501(c) 3 and 509(a) of the IRS code. If using a fiscal agent, please include Letter of Authorization.

2. Grantee report (if previously funded).

3. Latest annual report or a summary of the organization's prior year's activities.

4. Current board list with related employment affiliation.

5. A description of ethnic and minority representation of Board of Directors in percentages (if requested by funder).

6. Qualifications of professional program staff (if applicable).

7. If the project for which funding is sought is a collaboration with other agencies, include letters of agreement from the collaborating agencies.

8. Letters of support and/or reviews (if applicable).

ForefrOnt
Engaging for impact

Chicago Area Grant Application Form
Rev. 10/15

316 Appendix D

Chicago Area Grant Application Form

Grant Request

This request is for: _____ Amount Requested: _____

Specify (if other): _____

Program/Project Title: _____

Organizational Information

Organization Name: _____

Address: _____

City: _____ State: _____ Zip: _____

Telephone: _____ Fax: _____

E-mail: _____

Executive Director: _____ Telephone: _____

Name/Title of Contact Person: _____ Telephone: _____

Total Organization Budget for Current Year: _____

Date of Incorporation: _____

United Way Funded? ☐

FEIN # (or equivalent): _____

Is Your Organization Tax Exempt under Section 501(c)3? ☐ Section 509(a) ☐

If not, do you have a fiscal agent? *(please identify organization, contact person, and telephone number)*

_____

Primary Service Category of Organization

Human Services   Specify (if other): _____

Summarize the Organization's Mission

_____

ForefrOnt
Engaging for impact

Chicago Area Grant Application
Form
Rev. 10/15

Chicago Area Grant Application Form

Geographic Service Area(s)

- City of Chicago
- County (specify)
- Suburbs (specifiy)
- Chicago neighborhood(s) (specify)
- Other (specify)
- Northwest Indiana
- Regional/National

Provide Percentages and/or Descriptions of the Populations Your Organization Serves
Race/Ethnicity (if applicable)

% African American	% Asian American/Pacific Islander	
% Caucasian	% Hispanic/Latino	
% Native American	% Other	Total % (should equal 100%)

% Female	% Male	Total % (should equal 100%)

% Other (ie. disabled, age, gay/lesbian, etc)

Staff Composition in Numbers

	Support	Professional
Paid full-time		
Paid part-time		
Volunteers		
Interns		
Other		
Totals		

Summarize the Purpose of Your Request (5 sentences of fewer)

Forefront
Engaging for impact

Chicago Area Grant Application Form
Rev.10/15

318 Appendix D

Time frame in which the funds will be used: From: _____ To: _____

List other private and public funding sources for this particular request (if this is a request for general operating support, please see Attachment A6 on page iii).

Funding source - to date	Amount	Date Received

Funding sources - pending	Amount	Notification Date

Organizational Budget Expenses $ _____   Revenues $ _____

Program/project budget If applicable _____

Signature of authorized officer

Name/Title: _____   Date: _____

ForefrOnt
Engaging for impact

Chicago Area Grant Application
Form
Rev. 10/15

Chicago Area Grant Application Form

Proposal Narrative *Please provide the following information in this order. Do not use more than 5 single-spaced pages, exclusive of attachments. Please staple; do not bind your application.*

A. Background

1. Organization's mission, history, overall goals and/or objectives.

2. Description of current programs and activities. Please emphasize major achievements of the past two years.

3. Description of formal and informal relationships with other organizations.

B. Purpose of Funding Request

1. If applying for general operating support, briefly state how this grant will be used.

2. If your request is for a specific project or capital campaign, please provide the following information:
   - The community and/or agency needs or problems that this effort will address, including population served.

   - Describe how the project will address these identified needs.

   - Program or Capital Campaign description to include strategies employed to implement the proposed project:
   (1) goals and objectives, (2) timetable for accomplishing stated goals and objectives, (3) program methodology (program only), (4) staffing, (5) collaboration with other agencies.

   - If this is a collaboration, briefly describe the partners.

   - If this is a request for a specific program, explain how it will be supported after termination of the grant.

C. Evaluation

1. Explain how you will measure the effectiveness of your activities.

2. Describe your criteria for success.

3. Describe the results you expect to have achieved by the end of the funding period.

Foundations/Corporate Giving Programs that accept the Chicago Area Grant Application

- Aon Foundation
- The Baxter International Foundation
- BP America, Inc.
- The Bufka Foundation
- Elizabeth F. Cheney Foundation
- Chicago Bar Foundation
- Chicago Tribune Foundation
- Commonwealth Edison Company
- RR Donnelley Foundation
- Exelon Corporation
- Jamee and Marshall Field Foundation
- First United Church of Oak Park
- Lloyd A. Fry Foundation
- GATX Corporation
- Lillian and Larry Goodman Foundations
- IBM Corporation
- ITW Foundation
- Mayer and Morris Kaplan Family Foundation
- John and Editha Kapoor Charitable Foundation
- Kraft Foods, Inc. (accepts Grant Report Form only)
- John D. and Catherine T. MacArthur Foundation
- The McCall Family Foundation
- C. Louis Meyer Family Foundation
- The Elizabeth Morse Charitable Trust
- New Prospect Foundation
- Northern Trust Company
- Peoples Energy Corporation
- Michael Reese Health Trust Relations Foundation
- Retirement Research Foundation
- Hulda B. & Maurice L. Rothschild Foundation
- SBC Foundation
- Sears Holdings
- Albert J. Speh, Jr. and Claire R. Speh Foundation
- Steans Family Foundation
- Irvin Stern Foundation
- VNA Foundation
- Washington Square Health Foundation, Inc.

ForefrOnt
Engaging for impact

Chicago Area Grant Application Form
Rev. 10/15

Index

990 Form, 43, 81–82, 84
990-PF Forms, 43, 102, 104–8, 116

A

acknowledgment, 181, 291, 293, 295, 297–98
agencies, 52–53, 79, 102, 111–12, 129, 222, 245, 262, 266
  federal, 51–52, 110–11
arts, 33–34, 52, 57, 71, 73, 108, 117, 143, 147, 207, 212, 214, 272
  organizations, 69, 74, 117, 207, 209, 263
awards, 42, 46, 51–52, 181, 197, 241, 264–65, 270, 293

B

board, 23–24, 38, 43–44, 46, 48, 57, 73, 77, 91–96, 99, 117, 119–20, 124, 130, 161, 171–72, 185, 200, 203–4, 214, 262, 268–69, 272, 284, 292
  chair, 24, 149, 156, 171, 286
  lists, 138, 267–68
  members, 9, 48, 77, 90, 95, 107, 110, 117, 119, 124–25, 127, 129, 151, 212, 251, 266, 268, 286–87, 289
bridge loan, 167, 254, 278–79
budget, 14, 22–23, 48, 52, 56–57, 71, 73, 80, 83, 92, 138, 162, 166–70, 173, 183, 192–93, 197, 218, 238, 249–53, 255–58, 260, 268, 272, 274–76, 293, 296
  equipment project, 255
  expense portion, 22–23, 166, 250, 256
  formats, 250, 258
  income portion, 23, 166–68, 250, 258, 260
  narratives, 258–60
  new, 274–75
  period, 167, 256–57
  program, 83
    expansion, 23
  summary, 126
building, 13, 50, 66–67, 72, 76, 78, 83, 124–26, 165–67, 181, 193, 201, 230, 236–38, 245, 253, 255, 272, 274, 276, 278, 296, 298
  new, 13, 77, 202, 216, 232, 251, 255, 271–72, 274, 277–79
  projects, 13, 20, 67, 76–77, 216, 232, 253–54, 273, 277–78

C

campaign, 66, 76–77, 91, 167, 191, 201, 255, 278
capacity, 71, 78, 80, 83, 217, 272–73, 279
  building, 65–66, 71–72, 147
capital budgets, 253–56
capital campaigns, 75–77, 104, 167, 201–2, 238, 252–53, 255, 277–78
capital projects, 66, 72, 237, 253, 271, 278–79
Casey Family Programs, 43
CDBG (Community Development Block Grants), 50
CGAs (common grant applications), 11, 13, 156–58

clientele, 69, 202, 209, 261, 263–64
common grant applications. *See* CGAs
Community Development Block Grants, 50
  applications, 285
community foundations, 36, 41, 44–45, 284
  staffs, 44
consultants, 51, 89, 94
contacts, initial, 7, 9, 11, 15, 22, 25, 228, 241, 283–84
Corporation for Public Broadcasting (CPB), 130
corporations, 41–42, 45–49, 53, 67, 70, 95, 106, 109–10, 126, 181–82, 257, 269
  foundations, 46–47, 102–3, 105, 107–9, 112
costs, 21–22, 33, 36, 58, 60, 67, 72, 75, 78, 82, 92, 162, 166–69, 192–93, 197, 207, 238, 249–51, 253–60, 272, 279, 294
  direct, 252, 256, 258, 260
  indirect, 256–58, 260
  one-time, 193, 197, 255
  ongoing, 192, 197, 255
  project, 193, 258, 278
  total, 22, 155, 166, 250, 256, 258, 260
county, 50, 52, 112, 226, 228, 245, 259
coworkers, 114, 135–36, 139–41
CPA, 95, 269
CPB (Corporation for Public Broadcasting), 130
credibility, 21–22, 25, 115, 160, 261, 264–66, 270, 273
crowdfunding, 91, 99

D

databases, 102, 106, 108–10, 112, 169, 179, 208
deadline, 51, 111, 117, 138–39
Declaration of Independence, 218–21
directors of development, 124, 129, 139, 171, 217
donations, in-kind, 73, 92, 197
donor-advised funds, 44
donors, individual, 23, 35, 43–44, 69, 71, 76–77, 168, 182, 277

E

EBPs (evidence-based practice), 61, 162, 196, 229
endowments, 65–66, 73–74, 107
evaluation, 160, 162, 183, 235–36, 238–41, 247, 265, 271
  evaluating result objectives, 246
  level of, 241–42
  plan, 235–37, 239–41, 243, 245, 247
evidence-based practice. *See* EBPs
executive director, 24–26, 70, 114, 118–19, 149, 154, 156, 171, 232, 249, 257, 267, 286–87, 293

F

facilities, 76–77, 82–83, 165, 201–4, 216, 253, 278–79, 286, 288
family foundations, 38, 43–44, 92, 110, 116, 180
FDO (Foundation Directory Online), 79, 103–5, 109, 208
Federal Emergency Management Agency (FEMA), 81
federal grants, 15, 41–42, 49–52, 102, 110–12, 148, 186, 232, 259
  proposals, 51, 53, 149, 177

financial statements, 95, 99, 138, 268-69
fiscal sponsor, 14, 89-91, 99
fiscal year, 23, 81, 107, 244, 268
Foundation Center, 102-3, 106
  funder data tab, 102, 106
Foundation Center, Funding Information Network, 103
Foundation Center, My Foundation Manager, 105
Foundation Directory Online. *See* FDO
foundation grant databases, 102
  Foundation Directory Online, 102
  FoundationSearch, 102, 104-5
foundations, 1, 11-12, 23, 29, 32, 34-35, 38-39, 41-45, 47-48, 53, 56-57, 61, 67, 74, 79, 92, 95, 102-5, 107-8, 110, 112, 115-17, 126-31, 154, 168, 172, 178-79, 182, 252, 254, 256-57, 269, 278
  corporate, 46-47, 102-3, 105, 107-9, 112
  independent, 44
  private operating, 41, 43
  public, 41, 44
FoundationSearch, 102, 104-5
funders, 25, 32, 67, 90, 98, 131, 143, 158, 241, 250, 255
  corporate, 101, 108
  expectations, 241, 249
  government, 118, 179
  grant application form, 244
  guidelines, 39, 108, 123, 127, 135-37, 141, 151, 177, 183, 268
  local, 63, 81, 114, 278
  mission, 15, 18, 63, 125
  office, 125, 128, 139, 155, 173, 179, 181, 185, 284-85, 293
  potential, 105, 114, 119
  priorities, 108, 143, 154, 156, 198
  questions, 11, 14, 139, 160, 194, 211, 265
  website, 61, 115, 128, 154, 179

Funding Information Network, 103
fundraising, 10, 35, 37, 76, 80, 82, 120, 258, 272, 275-76, 293
  plan, 23, 168, 170, 193, 278, 288

G

general operations, 38-39
gifts, 36, 39, 43-44, 46-48, 66-67, 74, 76-77, 106-7, 109, 129, 170, 181, 258, 293
  corporate, 109-10, 168, 278
giving programs, corporate, 11, 23, 33, 36, 109
goals, 3, 13-15, 20-21, 25, 35, 37, 42-43, 45, 56, 60, 68-70, 74, 93, 115, 128, 148, 155, 159, 162, 172-73, 185, 195-96, 200, 202, 206, 211-15, 217-25, 239-40, 243-44, 256, 258, 278, 281
  measurable, 219, 221
  organization's, 60, 212, 215, 224
  programmatic, 13
government, 32, 34, 38, 41-42, 50, 52, 101, 112, 219-20
  contracts, 97, 278
  federal, 49-50, 184
  funders, 118, 179
  government-funded organizations, 277
  grants, 23, 49, 52, 73, 82, 84, 102, 105, 168, 232, 252, 254, 256, 260
  local, 102, 284
  opportunities, 111, 118
  programs, 36, 150
  programs, 97, 193
GPA (Grant Professionals Association), 94, 123
grant announcements, 50, 111

grant applications, 11, 13, 15, 33, 38, 42, 44, 47, 50, 52-53, 72, 75, 79, 84, 92, 104, 110, 113, 116, 122, 136, 138-39, 144, 150, 156, 163, 165-67, 189, 196, 211-12, 226, 232, 236-39, 241, 252, 264, 274, 277, 284, 288, 292, 295
  common, 11, 156, 252
  full, 236, 287
  funder's forms, 12, 135, 228, 244
  process, 10, 12, 36, 52, 114-15, 125-27, 189, 198
grant awards, federal, 51
grant budget, 13, 169
grant consultants, 51, 89, 94
grant funding, 2, 32, 49, 60, 68-70, 74, 80, 90-91, 98, 144, 172, 185, 236-38, 273, 292
grant guidelines, 46, 57, 126, 148, 267
grantmakers, 4, 11, 20, 22, 25, 67, 91, 94-96, 103-4, 114, 122-24, 193, 284, 289, 292, 294-95, 297
grantmaking, 15, 43, 61, 102, 189, 241, 272
grantmaking foundations, 43
grant opportunities, 50, 76, 112
  newsletter listing, 105
grant period, 37, 60, 66, 71, 297-98
grant process, 15, 110, 131, 135, 169, 267, 289, 297
Grant Professionals Association (GPA), 94, 123
grant proposal
  actual, 183-84
  full, 175, 177, 184, 284
grant proposals, 11, 35-36, 38, 42, 59, 63, 94, 111, 116, 125-26, 129, 186, 200, 206-7, 218, 229, 235, 238, 250, 261-63, 266, 288, 295
  successful, 89, 291
  writing, 10, 92

grant reports, 151, 238
grant request, 7, 11, 18, 90, 167-68, 170, 212, 215-16, 223, 231, 260, 264, 273, 284
grant research, 76, 103, 255
grants
  capacity-building, 71
  capital, 65-66, 76-77, 271
  corporate, 110, 112, 252, 254, 256
  operating, 38, 60, 76-77, 79
  program, 65, 67, 71-72, 74, 271
  role of, 75, 81, 83
grants committee, 292, 295
grant searches, 112, 155
grantseekers, 4, 11, 22, 55, 60, 106-7, 115, 121-23, 125, 136, 228, 271
grantseeking, 2, 74, 102
  strong program, 298
grants.gov, 50-51, 110-12
GrantStation, 105, 110
grant transmittal letter, 292-93, 296
grantwriters, 29, 55, 216, 284
  freelance, 94
  new, 1, 76
grantwriting classes, 175, 208, 293
guidelines, 1, 45, 47, 51-52, 58, 65, 108, 115-16, 127-28, 136-37, 139, 141, 150, 169, 179, 183-85, 200, 266, 289, 292

H

history, organization's, 11, 13, 18, 160

I

impact, 79, 83, 115, 117, 159, 189-91, 194, 198, 218, 220, 223-24, 226-27, 231-32, 236, 238, 240-47, 257, 271-72

income, 23, 38, 73-74, 80-82, 95-96, 107, 167, 191, 249, 252, 255, 257, 260, 273-74, 277
   fee, 82, 193, 275-76
   program service, 81
information, organizational, 3, 90, 183, 261, 263, 265, 267, 269
interests, funder's, 14, 94, 108, 115, 127, 173, 198, 295
IRS, 31-33, 35, 39, 42-43, 46, 89-90, 102, 104-5, 212, 267-69, 277

J

jargon, 140, 143-48, 151

K

Kresge Foundation, 61-62

L

leadership, 71, 200-201, 211, 264, 266
   organization's, 171, 213
letter, 1, 3, 7, 9-15, 17-20, 22, 24-25, 39, 105, 114-15, 117, 126, 128, 133, 136, 149, 151, 153-58, 161, 166-68, 170-73, 177-81, 184, 186-87, 218, 240-42, 264, 267, 269, 283, 288-89, 292-93, 298
   draft, 12, 173
   format, 163, 173
   letterhead, 25, 151, 170, 179, 230
      formatting, 178, 184
      organizational, 25, 178
      phone number, 170
   model, 15, 241
Letters of Inquiry, 3, 9-12, 15, 25, 31, 90, 115, 117, 129, 133, 149, 153-55, 157, 159-61, 163, 165-73, 177, 181, 186, 213, 228, 241, 264, 274, 284-85, 297
   first drafts of, 155
   model, 15, 18, 153, 157, 217, 241
Letters of Support, 269
libraries, 101, 103, 105, 204
logic model framework, 197
logic models, 147, 162, 189-98, 215, 236
   simple, 190-91
long-term impact, 162, 238-39, 246
long-term outcomes, 162, 189-90, 195-96, 239

M

matching grants, 73
mission statement, 26, 56, 61, 92-93, 196, 214, 224, 262
   formal, 19
   walking-around, 19
model proposal letter, 158, 240, 244
models, 83-84, 114, 161-63, 190, 197, 229, 252, 276-77, 298
My Foundation Manager, 105

N

naming opportunities, 67, 77, 181
NOZA, 106, 109, 112

O

objectives, 65, 68-69, 93, 162, 183, 185, 200, 211-19, 221-24, 235, 239-43, 247, 260
   framework, 213

officers, foundation program, 284
online screenings, 9, 22, 136-37, 166
operating budgets, 23, 75, 78-80, 83, 267, 272, 274, 276-77, 279
organization
  new, 78, 83-84, 91, 93-94, 273
  small, 94, 162, 237, 250
organization's budget, 37, 75, 77, 79, 81-83, 157, 171
organization's mission, 2, 212, 214-15, 258
outcomes, 37, 60, 65, 74, 118, 183, 189, 191-98, 217, 246, 292
  short-term, 190, 195
outputs, 190-97, 215, 217

P

parameters, 103-4, 106, 208
partners, 56, 95, 98, 128, 242
partnerships, 2, 21, 90, 115
pilot projects, 65, 68
plan, strategic, 71, 92-93, 99, 211-14, 221
private foundations, 31-32, 35-36, 39, 41-44, 46, 102, 105, 107-8, 116, 154, 236
private funders, 15, 82, 150, 178, 231, 259
private grantmaking foundations, 43
private grants, 23, 168, 232
process, grantseeking, 31, 56, 59
process objectives, 224, 242-44, 246
program
  areas, 108, 136-37
  budget, 72, 94, 251-52, 255-56
  costs, 251, 256-57
  director, 24, 69, 169, 265, 293
  elements, 229-30
  expansion, 20, 274
  fees, 256-57
  models, 83
  officer, 58, 126, 128-29, 172, 295
program staff, 72, 139, 257, 287-88
project
  new, 222, 229, 231, 250
  special, 65, 67-69, 76, 95
project budget, 95, 165-66, 169-70, 173, 182, 255, 257, 268, 271
project grants, 60, 77, 78
proposal, organizational information section, 262, 265, 270
PSAs (public service announcements), 227
PSGA (Puget Sound Grantwriters Association), 4, 58, 123
public charities, 14, 31-33, 35-37, 39, 42-44, 80, 98, 106
  public support test, 32
public service announcements. See PSAs
public support test, 32
Puget Sound Grantwriters Association (PSGA), 4, 58, 123

Q

qualitative evaluations, 246-47
Quick-Start Letter, 2, 7, 10-12, 14-15, 17-18, 20, 22, 24, 26, 29, 31, 36, 153, 157-58

R

RAGs (Regional Associations of Grantmakers), 11, 122-23
Regional Associations of Grantmakers. See RAGs

Requests for Proposals. *See* RFPs
result objectives, 217, 223–24, 242, 244–47
  evaluating, 246
revenue models, 75, 83
revenue profiles, 79–80, 83–84, 274
RFPs (Requests for Proposals), 114, 116, 118, 226

S

salaries, 38, 67, 70–71, 192, 251–52, 255, 257, 259
scholarships, 34–35, 80, 108, 241, 276
  grants, 108, 241
  seed money, 65, 68
Simple Capital Project Budget, 254
Simple Program Budget, 252
skills, 12, 47, 94, 113–14, 120, 145, 160, 194, 216, 229, 246, 266
SMART objectives, 211, 215, 217, 221–22, 240
social services organization, 206–7, 263
special events, 23, 71, 82, 84, 124, 252, 254, 256–58, 273, 275–76
sponsorships, 49, 69–70, 80, 258
staff, 4, 20, 24, 38, 44, 48, 61, 70–72, 92–93, 95, 108, 114, 116, 124–25, 139, 150, 161, 166, 190, 193–94, 203–4, 212, 214, 216–17, 224, 230, 232, 251, 255, 263, 284, 286–87
  development, 71, 78, 127, 253, 287
stewardship, 291–93, 295, 297–98
stories, 11–12, 14, 20, 96, 115–17, 130–31, 153, 158–59, 258, 286
summary, 13, 22, 155, 163, 165, 168, 173, 177–78, 183–86, 198, 228–29, 261
summary budget, 126

sustainability, 74, 84, 183, 271, 273–75, 277, 279
  plan, 273–76

T

taxes, 32, 34, 37, 90, 106, 252, 254, 293
theory of change, 189, 196–97, 223, 229, 238

V

vision, 56, 61, 83, 92–93, 97–98, 156, 232
volunteers, 2, 4, 9, 46–48, 72, 92–93, 124, 127, 166, 212, 217, 230, 285–87
  community, 83, 268

W

website, foundation's, 117, 127

For the GENIUS® Press is an imprint that produces books on just about any topic that people want to learn. *You don't have to be a genius to read a GENIUS book, but you'll sure be smarter once you do!*™ Here are some of our recently published titles.

ForTheGENIUS.com/bookstore

for the GENIUS
PRESS

CPSIA information can be obtained
at www.ICGtesting.com
Printed in the USA
FSOW04n0210270716
23105FS

9 781941 050347